The Definitive Christian D. Larson Collection

6 Volumes
30 Titles

Compiled and Edited
by
David Allen

Volume 3 of 6

Copyright © 2014 by David Allen / Shanon Allen
All rights reserved. No part of this publication may be reproduced, distributed, or transmitted in any form or by any means, including photocopying, recording, or other electronic or mechanical methods, without the prior written permission of the publisher, except in the case of brief quotations embodied in critical reviews and certain other noncommercial uses permitted by copyright law.
Printed in the United States of America

Reprint

First Printing November 2014

ISBN: 978-0-9909643-2-2

Visit Us At **NevilleGoddardBooks.com** for a complete listing of all our books and **1000's of Free Books to Read online and download.**

Books include: The Power of I AM 1, 2, 3, The Neville Goddard Collection, Neville Goddard's Interpretation of Scripture, The Money Bible, The Creative Power of Thought, The Secrets, Mysteries & Powers of The Subconscious Mind, Your Inner Conversations are Creating Your World, The World is At Your Command - The Very Best of Neville Goddard, Imagining Creates Reality - 365 Mystical Daily Quotes, Imagination: The Redemptive Power in Man, Assumptions Harden Into Facts: The Book, David Allen - Your Faith Is Your Fortune, Your Unlimited Power

First Printing
Copyright © 2014

Foreword

The Definitive Christian D. Larson Collection is a 6 volume set of 30 titles from one of the most renowned and prolific new thought authors and lecturers of his day. No metaphysical, new thought, law of attraction collection would be complete without Christian D. Larson's books. Before Neville Goddard, before Ernest Holmes, before Joseph Murphy and Napoleon Hill and a host of many of the great authors and teachers of today, there was Christian D. Larson (1874 – 1954) who was credited by Horatio Dresser as being a founder in the New Thought movement.

Christian D. Larson books contain hidden secrets (hidden from the conscious minds of those not prepared to receive them) and treasures that you are unlikely to find anywhere else and if you do it is likely it originated from Christian D. Larson.

David Allen

All Christian D. Larson's books are in the public domain.

* Editors note: Some Christian D. Larson books were originally published without chapter titles. They were later added by other editors of Mr. Larson's works. To my knowledge none of them are copyrighted.

Christian D. Larson Titles
Volume - Original Year Published - Title

Vol.	Year	Title
Vol. 1	1913	Brains and How to Get Them
Vol. 1	1912	Business Psychology
Vol. 1	1907	How Great Men Succeed
Vol. 1	1912	How the Mind Works
Vol. 2	1920	Concentration
Vol. 2	1912	How to Stay Well
Vol. 2	1908	How to Stay Young
Vol. 3	**1908**	**The Great Within**
Vol. 3	**1912**	**The Mind Cure**
Vol. 3	**1912**	**What is Truth**
Vol. 3	**1912**	**Your Forces and How to Use Them**
Vol. 4	1916	The Good Side of Christian Science
Vol. 4	1912	The Ideal Made Real
Vol. 4	1910	Mastery of Fate
Vol. 4	1907	Mastery of Self
Vol. 4	1916	My Ideal of Marriage
Vol. 4	1916	Nothing Succeeds Like Success
Vol. 4	1916	Steps in Human Progress
Vol. 5	1918	Healing Yourself
Vol. 5	1912	Just Be Glad
Vol. 5	1940	Leave it to God
Vol. 5	1908	On the Heights
Vol. 5	1910	Perfect Health
Vol. 5	1922	Practical Self-Help
Vol. 5	1912	Scientific Training of Children
Vol. 5	1912	Thinking for Results
Vol. 6	1912	The Hidden Secret
Vol. 6	1916	In Light of the Spirit
Vol. 6	1912	The Pathway of Roses
Vol. 6	1907	Poise and Power

Volume 3

The Great Within 6
The Mind Cure 75
What is Truth 129
Your Forces and How to Use Them 274

The Great Within

The Great Within

Table of Contents

Chapter 1 - Unlimited Possibilities	8
Chapter 2 - Desire and Faith	10
Chapter 3 - Impressing the Subconscious	14
Chapter 4 - Removing Wrong Impressions	18
Chapter 5 - Think on These Things	22
Chapter 6 - You Can Become What You Desire to Be	25
Chapter 7 - Developing the Genius Within	29
Chapter 8 - You May Become What You Wish to Be	34
Chapter 9 - Use of the Conscious and Subconscious	36
Chapter 10 - Solutions to Problems	42
Chapter 11 - Direct Assistance in Everything	46
Chapter 12 - Make Your Desires Subconscious	50
Chapter 13 - Produce Perfect Health	55
Chapter 14 - Impress the Subconscious Before Sleep	59
Chapter 15 - Sleeping on Difficult Problems	63
Chapter 16 - Sleep on the Superior; The Ideal	66
Chapter 17 - Awaking the Great Within	70

The Great Within

Chapter 1

Unlimited Possibilities

THE mind of man is conscious and subconscious, objective and subjective, external and internal.

The conscious mind acts, the subconscious reacts; the conscious mind produces the impression, the subconscious produces the expression; the conscious mind determines what is to be done, the subconscious supplies the mental material and the necessary power.

The subconscious mind is the great within — an inner mental world from which all things proceed that appear in the being of man.

The conscious mind is the mind of action, the subconscious mind is the mind of reaction, but every subconscious reaction is invariably the direct result of a corresponding conscious action.

Every conscious action produces an impression upon the subconscious and every subconscious reaction produces an expression in the personality.

Everything that is expressed through the personality was first impressed upon the subconscious, and since the conscious mind may impress anything upon the subconscious, any desired expression may be secured, because the subconscious will invariably do what it is directed and impressed to do.

The subconscious mind is a rich mental field; every conscious impression is a seed sown in this field, and will bear fruit after its kind, be the seed good or otherwise.

All thoughts of conviction and all deeply felt desires will impress themselves upon the subconscious and will reproduce their kind, to be later expressed in the personal being of man.

The Great Within

Every desire for power, ability, wisdom, harmony, joy, health, purity, life, greatness, will impress itself upon the subconscious, and will cause the thing desired to be produced in the great within, the quality and the quantity depending upon the depth of the desire and the conscious realization of the true idea conveyed by the desire.

What is produced in the within will invariably come forth into expression in the personality; therefore, by knowing how to impress the subconscious, man may give his personal self any quality desired, and in any quantity desired.

Personal power, physical health, mental brilliancy, remarkable ability, extraordinary talent, rare genius — these are attainments that the subconscious of every mind can readily produce and bring forth when properly directed and impressed.

The subconscious mind obeys absolutely the desires of the conscious mind, and since the subconscious is limitless, it can do for man whatever he may desire to have done.

What man may desire to become, that he can become, and the art of directing and impressing the subconscious is the secret.

Unlimited possibilities do exist in the subconscious of every mind, and since these possibilities can all be developed, there is no end to the attainments and achievements of man.

Nothing is impossible; the great within is limitless — the inexhaustible source of everything that may be required for the highest development and the greatest accomplishments in human life, and whatever we may direct the within to produce, the same will invariably be produced.

Chapter 2

Desire and Faith

TO properly direct and impress the subconscious, the first essential is to realize that the subconscious mind is a finer mentality that permeates every fiber of the entire personality. Though the subconscious can be impressed most directly through the brain-center, the volume of subconscious expression will increase in proportion to our conscious realization of subconscious life in every part of mind and body.

To concentrate attention frequently upon the subconscious side of the entire personality will steadily awaken the great within; this will cause one to feel that a new and superior being is beginning to unfold, and with that feeling comes the conviction that unbounded power does exist in the deeper life of man.

When the awakening of the subconscious is felt in every part of mind and body, one knows that anything may be attained and achieved; doubts disappear absolutely, because to feel the limitless is to believe in the limitless.

While impressing the subconscious, attention should be directed upon the inside of mind, and this is readily done while one *thinks* that the subconscious mentality permeates the personality, as water permeates a sponge.

Think of the interior essence that permeates the exterior substance, and cause all mental actions to move toward the finer mental life that lives and moves and has its being within the interior mind. This will cause the conscious action to impress itself directly upon the subconscious, and a corresponding reaction or expression will invariably follow.

While directing attention upon the subconscious, the idea that is to be impressed should be clearly discerned in mind and an effort should be made to feel the soul of that idea.

The Great Within

To mentally feel the soul of the idea will completely eliminate the mechanical tendency of mental action, and this is extremely important because no mechanical action of mind can impress the subconscious.

Perfect faith in the process is indispensable, and to inwardly know that results will be secured is to cause failure to become impossible.

The deeper and higher the attitude of faith while the subconscious is being impressed, the more deeply will the impression be made, and the deep impression not only enters the richest states of the subconscious, but always produces results.

The attitude of faith takes the mind into the superior, the limitless, the soul of things, and this is precisely what is wanted.

When the mind transcends the objective it enters into the subjective, and to enter into the subjective is to impress one's ideas and desires directly, deeply and completely upon the great within. Such impressions will invariably produce remarkable expressions, not only because they have entered more deeply into the subconscious, but also because every impression that is made in the attitude of faith is given superior quality, greater power and higher worth.

The subconscious should never be approached in the attitude of command or demand, but always in the attitude of faith and desire. Never command the subconscious to do thus or so, but desire with a deep, strong desire, that the subconscious do what you desire to have done, and animate that desire with the faith that it positively will be done.

To combine a high faith with a strong desire while impressing the subconscious is the secret through which results may invariably be secured.

The subconscious should never be forcefully aroused, but should be gradually awakened and developed through such actions of mind as are deep and strong while perfectly serene.

Deep thoughts on all important subjects, lofty aspirations on all occasions, and a constantly expanding consciousness will aid remarkably in awakening the great within.

Whenever attention is directed upon the subconscious, an effort should be made to expand consciousness by picturing upon mind the expanding process while the deeper feeling of thought is placing itself in touch with the universal; a strong, deep desire for greater things should be impressed upon the inner mentality, and a deep stillness should animate every action of mind.

The inner side of mind should always be acted upon peacefully, though not with that peacefulness that has a tendency to produce inaction, but with that peacefulness that produces a high, strong action that continues to act in serenity and poise.

To concentrate a strong, deeply felt, well poised mental action upon the entire subconscious mentality a number of times every day will, in a remarkably short time, develop the great within to such an extent that the mind will inwardly know that unlimited power and innumerable possibilities have been placed at its command, and when this realization comes the mind may go on to any attainment and any achievement; failure will be simply impossible.

When the development of the subconscious has been promoted to a degree the conscious mind will instinctively feel that failure is impossible, and will, consequently, leave results to the law. There will be no anxiety about results because to feel the presence of subconscious action is to know that results must follow when the subconscious is properly directed and impressed.

Perfect faith in the law that the subconscious will invariably do whatever it is impressed to do will eliminate anxiety completely, and this is extremely important, because the subconscious mind cannot proceed to do what it has been impressed to do so long as there is anxiety in the conscious mind.

Provide the proper conditions and the law will positively produce the desired results, and to inwardly know this is the first essential in providing the proper conditions.

The subconscious mind is somewhat similar to the phonograph; under certain conditions it can record anything, and under certain other conditions it can reproduce everything that has been recorded. There is this difference, however: The subconscious not only reproduces exactly what has been recorded, but will also form, create, develop and express what mind may desire when the impression is being made; that is, the subconscious not only reproduces the seed itself, but as many more seeds as the original seed desired to reproduce, and also the exact degree of improvement in quality that was latent in the desire of the original seed or impression.

The subconscious not only reproduces the mental idea contained in the impression, but also every essential that may be required to fulfill the desire of that impression.

Through this law the subconscious can find the answer to any question or work out any problem when properly impressed with an exact idea of what is wanted.

Chapter 3

Impressing the Subconscious

The subconscious provides the essentials, but the conscious mind must apply those essentials before practical results may be secured.

When the subconscious is directed to produce health, those mental actions will be expressed that can produce health in the body when combined with normal physical actions, and it is the conscious mind that must produce the normal physical actions; that is, common sense living.

When the subconscious is directed to produce success, those elements, qualities and powers will be expressed in mind and body that can, if consciously applied, produce success.

That the subconscious can do anything is absolutely true, but it is true in this sense, that it can supply the power, the capacity and the understanding to do anything, but the conscious mind must practically apply what the subconscious has brought forth into expression.

The subconscious supplies the power and the mental elements, but these must be used by the conscious mind if the desired results are to be secured. Nothing comes readymade from the subconscious, but it can give us the material from which we can make anything.

The subconscious can give you the powers and qualities of genius, and if you apply, practically and constantly, those powers and qualities, you will become a genius.

The subconscious can give you the life and the power that is necessary to remarkable talents, and if you use that life and power in the daily cultivation of your talents, those talents will become remarkable.

The Great Within

The law is that the conscious mind must impress its desires upon the subconscious in order to secure the mental essentials that may be required to fulfill those desires, but the conscious mind must *use* those essentials before results can be secured.

It is the conscious mind that does things, but it is the subconscious that supplies the power with which those things are done, and by learning to draw upon the subconscious the conscious mind can do anything, because unbounded power and innumerable possibilities are latent in the great within.

The proper conditions for recording an impression upon the subconscious are deep feeling, strong desires, conscious interest and a living faith. When these are blended harmoniously in the conscious actions of mind the subconscious will be directed and impressed properly and the desired response will invariably appear.

The principal essential, however, is deep feeling; no idea or desire can enter the subconscious unless it is deeply felt, and every idea or desire that is deeply felt will enter the subconscious of itself, whether or not we desire to have it do so.

It is through this law that man is affected by his environments, surroundings and external conditions, because whenever he permits himself to be deeply impressed by that with which he may come in contact those impressions will enter the subconscious.

What enters the subconscious of any mind will become a part of that mind, and will, to a degree, affect the nature, the character, the quality, the thoughts and the actions of that mind.

When the subconscious is impressed by external conditions the impressions will be like those conditions and, as like produces like, conditions will be produced in the subconscious that are exactly like those external conditions from which the impressions came.

The individual, therefore, who permits his subconscious to be indiscriminately impressed by external conditions will think and act, more or less, as his environments may suggest. In many respects his life will be controlled completely by those persons and things with which he may come in contact, while in nearly all other respects his life will be greatly modified by the presence of those persons and things.

The mind that does not control its feelings may be subconsciously impressed by any external action, be that action good or otherwise, while the mind that can give deep feeling to any idea can impress any idea upon the subconscious, and as the whole of the individual life is determined by what the subconscious is directed or impressed to do, the former will become, more or less, like his environment, having control neither of himself nor his destiny; the latter, however, may become what he wants to become and will master both himself and his destiny.

No undesirable feeling should ever be permitted; no wrong idea should ever be given in thought; nor should one ever think seriously, feelingly or sympathetically about wrong or evil in any shape or form.

To think feelingly about wrong is to impress wrong upon the subconscious; it is to sow undesirable seeds in the garden of the mind, and a harvest of weeds — sickness, trouble and want, will be the result.

Good thoughts, deeply felt, will bring health, happiness, harmony, peace, power, ability and character. Wrong thoughts, deeply felt, will bring discord, depression, fear, sickness, weakness and failure.

To properly impress the subconscious at all times, it is therefore necessary to train the mind to think only of those things that one desires to realize and express in tangible life;

The Great Within

and what one does not wish to meet in personal experience should never be given a single moment of thought.

What we mentally feel we invariably impress upon the subconscious, and there is a tendency to mentally feel every thought that is given prolonged or serious attention.

To think about that which we do not want, is to impress upon the subconscious what we do not wish to impress; and as every impression produces a corresponding expression, we will thereby receive the very things we desire to avoid.

It is through this law that what we fear always comes upon us, because what we fear will impress itself upon the subconscious without fail.

To fear disease, failure or trouble is to sow seeds in the subconscious field that will bring forth a harvest of diseased conditions, troubled thoughts, confused mental states and misdirected actions in mind and body.

The more intense the fear the deeper the subconscious impression, and the more we shall receive of that which we feared we should receive.

Through the same law we always receive what we continue to expect in the desire of the deep, strong faith. The more faith we have in the realization and attainment of that which has quality, superiority and worth, the more deeply we impress the subconscious with those mental seeds that can and will bring forth the greater good that we desire.

To have faith in the attainment of peace, harmony, health, power, ability, talent and genius, while directing the subconscious to produce those things, is to cause those very things to be created within us in greater and greater measure.

Chapter 4

Removing Wrong Impressions

THE purpose of consciously and intelligently directing the subconscious is first, to correct every wrong, every flaw, every defect, every perversion, and every imperfect condition that may exist in the personality of man; and, second, to bring out into fuller expression the limitless possibilities that exist in the great within.

Everything that is wrong in the personal life of the individual comes from a corresponding wrong impression in the subconscious; the wrong subconscious impression is the cause, the wrong external condition is the effect; it is therefore evident that to remove all wrong impressions from the subconscious is to establish complete emancipation throughout the entire personal being of man.

To remove any wrong impression from the subconscious, the opposite correct impression must be made in its place. A wrong impression cannot be removed by mental force, resistance or denial; produce the right impression and the wrong impression will cease to exist.

By training the mind to think only of that which is desired in actual realization and experience, and by deeply impressing all those thoughts and desires upon the subconscious, every undesirable impression will be removed; the cause of every flaw, defect or perversion in the personal man will be removed, and in consequence, the flaws, defects, and perversions themselves will cease to exist.

The entire subconscious field can be changed absolutely by constantly causing new and superior impressions to be formed in the great within; and every change that is brought about in the subconscious will produce a corresponding change in mind and body.

There is nothing adverse in the mentality or the personality of man that cannot be corrected by causing the correct impression to be formed in the subconscious. All wrongs, flaws or defects, whether they be hereditary, or personally produced, can be removed completely through the intelligent direction of the subconscious.

Every impression that is properly made in the subconscious mind will produce a corresponding expression in the personality; that is the law, and it cannot fail; but the impression must be properly made.

The subconscious does not respond to mere commands, because it neither reasons nor discriminates; it does not obey what it is told to do, but what it is impressed to do. It is the idea that enters into the subconscious that determines subconscious action; but the idea must not simply be given to the subconscious, it must *enter into* the subconscious.

The idea that predominates in mind while the subconscious is being directed, is the idea that will be impressed; therefore, negative desires will impress the subconscious to do the very opposite to what is desired by the desire.

To direct the subconscious to remove sickness is to impress the idea of sickness, because the mind thinks principally of sickness at the time; in consequence, more sickness will be produced.

It is not what the subconscious is directed to do, but the predominant thought that is conveyed through that direction that determines results; therefore, the predominant thought must be identical with the final results desired.

When health is desired, no thought whatever should be given to sickness; the subconscious should not be directed to remove sickness, but should be directed to *produce* health.

The subconscious should always be directed to produce those qualities and conditions that are desired, but those conditions that are to be removed should never be mentioned in mind. Adverse conditions will disappear of themselves

When true conditions are established; but the mind cannot impress, create and establish the true while attention is being concentrated upon the adverse.

To direct the subconscious not to do thus or so, is to impress the subconscious to do that very thing. When you try to impress the subconscious with the idea that you do not wish to get sick any more you have sickness in mind, and it is the idea that you have in mind that you impress upon the subconscious. To remove sickness forget sickness absolutely, and impress upon the subconscious the idea of health, and that idea alone. Desire health with all the power of mind, and fill both sides of mentality, conscious and subconscious, so completely with that desire that every thought of sickness is forgotten.

A denial will impress upon the subconscious the nature and the power of the very thing that is denied; therefore, to deny evil or resist evil is to produce causes in mind that will, in the coming days, produce more evil.

To try to deny away adverse conditions is to continue in perpetual mental warfare with those very things that mind is trying to destroy. Temporary states of seeming freedom in some parts of the system will be followed regularly with outbreaks of adversity in other parts; while the subconscious cause of undesirable conditions in mind or body will not be removed.

So long as we continue to resist or deny evil, we will think about evil, and so long as we think about evil, evil will be impressed upon the subconscious; and whatever we impress upon the subconscious, that the subconscious will reproduce and bring forth into the personal life. When we have a great undertaking that we wish to promote, and desire to secure as much added power, ability and capacity as possible from the great within, the subconscious should not be directed to prevent failure. To think of failure is to impress the subconscious with the idea of failure, and detrimental conditions — conditions that will confuse the mind and produce failure — will be expressed.

The Great Within

All thought of failure should be eliminated, and the subconscious should be deeply impressed to produce success. The subconscious will respond by bringing forth the power, the capacity, the ability, the understanding and the determination that can and will produce success.

Chapter 5

Think on These Things

WHEN properly directed, the subconscious mind can inspire the conscious mind to do the right thing at the right time, to take advantage of opportunities during the psychological moment, and to so deal with circumstances that all things will work together to promote the object in view. It is, therefore, evident that when the subconscious is trained to work in harmony with the objects and desires of the conscious mind, failure becomes impossible, and success in greater and greater measures may be secured by anyone.

When trying to remove undesirable habits, tendencies or desires, the mind should never think, "I shall not do this anymore," because through such a thought or statement, the habit in mind will be reimpressed upon the subconscious and will gain a deeper foothold in the system than it had before.

The proper course to pursue is to forget completely what you desire to remove; refuse to think of it; when tempted to think of the matter turn attention upon the opposite qualities, desires or tendencies. Should you fail to become sufficiently interested in those opposite desires to forget what you want to forget, look for the most interesting points of view connected with those desires. The mental effort employed in trying to find the most interesting point of view connected with those desires will cause the mind to become thoroughly interested in those desires, and will, consequently, forget those things that should be forgotten.

When the mind is being interested in those desires that you wish to cultivate, they should be impressed upon the subconscious with all the depth of feeling that can possibly be aroused. These impressions should be repeated a number of times every day, and the new desires will soon take root in the subconscious.

The Great Within

Every desire or tendency that takes root in the subconscious will begin to develop and express itself in the personal self, and will be felt throughout the personality. When the new desire is fully expressed, it will be thoroughly felt; and since no two desires of opposite nature can exist in the person at the same time, the old desires will disappear; the old tendencies and the old habits will have vanished completely.

To impress upon the subconscious a strong desire for the better, the purer and the superior, is to cause the system to crave something better; the force of desire will be refined; the entire organism will be purified, and the wants of the personal self will become normal on a higher plane.

All kinds of undesirable habits may be removed by constantly impressing upon the subconscious the idea of pure desire; and all tendencies to anger, hatred and similar states, may be removed by causing the qualities of love, kindness, justice and sympathy to be more fully developed in the great within.

To remove fear and worry, impress the subconscious, as frequently as possible, with the deep feeling of faith, gratitude and mental sunshine.

To have faith is to know that man has the power to perpetually increase the good, and that he may constantly press on to better things and greater things. To have faith is to be guided by superior mental lucidity, and thereby know how to select what is safe and secure; and he who knows that he is on the safe path, the ascending path, the endless path to better things and greater things, has eliminated fear absolutely.

To live constantly in the spirit of gratitude is not only to remove worry, but the cause of worry. To be grateful for the good that is now coming into life is to open the way for the coming of greater good. This is the law; and he who is daily receiving the greater good, has no cause for' worry; he will even forget that worry ever had a place in his mind. To constantly impress the subconscious with mental sunshine, is to establish the tendency to live on the bright side, the sunny side; and to live on the bright side is to increase your own brightness; your mind will become more brilliant, your thinking will have more lucidity and clearness, your nature will have more sweetness, your personality will be in more perfect harmony with everything, your life will be better, your work will be better — everything will be better; therefore, by living on the bright side, all things will steadily become better and brighter for you.

When all is dark, and everything seems to go wrong, arouse all your energies for the purpose of impressing and directing the subconscious to produce the change you desire. Give the deepest possible feeling to those impressions, and have stronger faith than you ever had before.

Continue persistently until the great within begins to respond; you will then feel from within how to act, and you will be given the power to do what you feel you should do. Ere long, things will take a turn; the threatened calamity will be avoided by the coming forth of that power within, that is greater than all adversities, all troubles, all wrongs; and instead, this power, having been awakened, will proceed to create a better future than you ever knew before."

Chapter 6

You Can Become What You Desire to Be...

WHILE the subconscious is being impressed, no thought whatever should be given to limitation, and no comparisons should be made with other persons or previous attainments.

To think that you wish to do better today than you did yesterday, is to give the subconscious two unrelated ideas upon which to act — the idea of the lesser achievement of the past and the idea of the greater achievement of the future. The subconscious will try to reproduce them both, but as they are antagonistic, they will neutralize each other, and there will be no results. The greater and the lesser cannot be produced by the same force at the same tune.

To impress the desire that you may become greater than anyone else, will also present to the subconscious two conflicting ideas; and the results again will be neutralized.

The course to pursue is to forget the lesser achievements of yesterday; think only of the greater achievements that you wish to promote today; then direct the subconscious to do today what you wish to have done today. This will cause the great within to give all its power and attention to the one idea — the greater achievement of today; and the greater achievement will positively follow. Know what you desire to become; resolve to become what you desire to become, whether others have reached those heights or not; forget the lesser heights that others have reached and give your whole mind and soul to the greater heights that you have resolved to reach.

You can become what you desire to become; the great within is limitless, and can give you all the wisdom and all the power that you may require. Knowing this, direct the great within to bring forth what you may need to reach your lofty goal, and the same will be done. The subconscious never fails to do what it is properly directed to do.

The Great Within

While impressing the subconscious, think of the perfect in regard to quality, and the limitless in regard to quantity. Never specify any exact amount, nor any special degree; always desire the limitless and the perfect; desire nothing less; and animate consciousness with a strong desire to expand constantly during the process, so that the highest quality and the greatest quantity possible may be realized.

Desire the fullest possible expression in the great eternal now; realize that your own inherent powers and capabilities are limitless, and impress that idea upon the subconscious.

Give no thought whatever to the lesser attainments in your own life or in the lives of others, but keep your mental eye single upon what you wish to become, knowing that you can become what you wish to become because there are no limitations in the great within.

When the subconscious begins to respond, a distinct sensation is frequently felt of some interior power working through you; this means that greater power from within is being awakened, and the outer mind should give full right of way so that a complete expression may be secured; that is, the conscious mind should become quiet, serene and thoroughly receptive, and should forget the personal self, for the time.

When the personal self is forgotten and the greater interior self is given full possession of both the mentality and the personality — it is then that one's greatest work is done. It is then that real ability, real talent and real genius can appear in tangible life and action.

When the musician forgets herself, there is something in her music that awakens the very depths of the soul, and you are lifted to a faker world than you ever knew before.

When the artist forgets himself, his pictures are given immortal life and every touch reveals a universe of indescribable beauty.

The Great Within

When the orator forgets himself, he speaks as one having authority, and you inwardly feel that every word is true.

When the practical man of affairs forgets himself, he is given a power that is irresistible, and the obstacles that are encountered in the way, disappear as if they never had the slightest existence.

It is such people that do great things in the world; it is such people who live in the human heart after ages have passed away; and their secret is this — the greatness within them was awakened, and was permitted to give full expression to its rare and superior power.

When you feel this higher power mysteriously moving within the greater depths of mind and soul, you know what is taking place; be calm, and give the superior self the right of way.

At first this power may feel as if it were distinct from yourself; but it is not, it is your own superior power; the coming forth of your own limitless power; the very power that you have for some time been directing the subconscious to produce; and when you *feel* that it is your own it is placed in your full conscious possession, and will do whatever you may desire or direct.

To inwardly feel that the entire within is your own is extremely important, because the more completely the conscious mind is united with the power of the subconscious, the more perfectly can the conscious mind impress the subconscious, and the more thoroughly can the greater power of the subconscious express itself in external, tangible action.

When you are about to do something that demands the best that is within you, impress the subconscious for higher power; then wait a few moments for this power to appear; and when it does appear, let the outer self obey. The great within has come forth to do your work, and no power in existence can do it better.

The Great Within

To enter into full conscious possession of the higher power from within, and to give full right of way to this power, is to give your objective talents and faculties the greatest power and the best power at your command.

Chapter 7

Developing the Genius Within

TO impress the subconscious for more power it is necessary to give to that impression all the power that mind is conscious of now; in other words, the seed that is already at hand should be placed in rich soil; the power that is now active in the conscious mind should be caused to act upon the subconscious; there will be increase; and by reimpressing the added power upon the subconscious every time added power is gained, this increase will become perpetual.

To proceed, concentrate attention upon the subconscious side of the entire personality, and desire gently, but with deep feeling, to draw all the present active energies of the system into the subconscious.

The more energy that is drawn into the subconscious during this process, the more power will be impressed upon the subconscious, and the more power that is impressed upon the subconscious the more power will be expressed from the subconscious.

The law is that whatever power is impressed upon the subconscious will return to the outer personality with added power, just as every seed sown in rich soil will reproduce itself, ten, twenty, sixty and even a hundredfold.

Therefore, to daily arouse all the power that we personally possess, and to impress all of that power upon the subconscious, is to increase perpetually the quantity of personal power; and the quality of that power can be steadily improved by transmuting and refining all the present forces of the system before they are impressed upon the subconscious.

Before the conscious mind begins to act upon the subconscious all thought and all feeling should be elevated into the highest states of quality, worth and superiority that can possibly be realized. This will cause the impression to be superior, and a superior impression will produce a superior expression.

That which is common, ordinary or inferior should never be held in mind, nor deeply felt for a moment, because to feel the ordinary is to impress the ordinary upon the subconscious; it is sowing inferior seed, and the harvest will be cheap, common, worthless.

No person should ever think of himself as inferior, or permit himself to recognize the imperfect in his nature. To recognize or feel the imperfect is to sow more seeds of imperfection, and reap another harvest that is not worthwhile.

There is a superior nature within man; this nature alone should be recognized and felt; only those thoughts and ideas that are formed in the exact likeness of the superior should be impressed upon the subconscious, and the subconscious will respond by giving superiority to the entire mentality and the entire personality.

The average person fails to improve because he lives mainly in the consciousness of his imperfections; he feels that he is ordinary and constantly impresses the subconscious with this feeling of the ordinary; the subconscious naturally responds by producing the ordinary, both in mind and body.

That person, however, who lives in the ideal, who thinks constantly of the greater worth that is within him, and who tries to feel and realize his superior nature, will give quality to every impression that may enter the subconscious; and according to the law of action and reaction, will steadily develop greater quality and worth throughout his entire nature.

The quality of the impression that is given to the subconscious always corresponds with the degree of quality of which we are conscious at the tune the impression is made. To refine, elevate and enrich all thought and feeling before the conscious mind begins to act upon the subconscious, is therefore of the highest importance.

The more quality that is given to the power that is being developed, the greater the results that may be secured through the application of that power.

It is quality and quantity combined that produces greatness, and greatness — greater and greater greatness, is the purpose we all have in view.

To constantly feel the greatness of the great within, is to constantly impress upon the subconscious the idea of greatness; this will cause the subconscious to develop greatness and express greatness through every part of the personal man.

As greatness develops, the feeling of greatness will become deeper, stronger and more intense; this will cause larger and finer ideas of greatness to be impressed upon the subconscious; and the result of these later impressions will be larger and greater expressions; a larger measure of greatness will be developed perpetually through the law of much gathering more, or "to him that hath shall be given."

All development comes from the subconscious, and since the possibilities of the great within are limitless, anyone can, through the proper direction of the subconscious, develop remarkable ability, extraordinary talent and rare genius.

All genius is the result of a large subconscious mentality therefore, anyone can become a genius by awakening a larger and a larger measure of the great within.

That a genius is asleep in the subconscious of every mind is literally true, but to awaken this genius is not the only essential; the conscious mind must be cultivated scientifically, so that the superior ability from within may find free and full expression.

The Great Within

The conscious mind should be cultivated, the subconscious should be developed; the conscious mind should be trained to do things, while the subconscious should be directed to give more and more power for the doing of greater and greater things.

The subconscious has the capacity to produce genius in any mind — the greatest genius imaginable, but the conscious mind must be highly cultivated so as to become a fit instrument through which great genius may find expression for its superior work.

When quality and worth are received from the subconscious, the conscious mind should use those things in practical action, so that the outer elements and forces of mind may be trained to appreciate quality and appropriate worth in all their tangible expressions.

The conscious and the subconscious sides of mind should be placed in the most perfect harmonious relations, so that every impression of the conscious mind may enter deeply into the subconscious and every expression from the subconscious may work through the conscious mind without any restriction or interference whatever.

The entire mind develops through the attainment of deeper and higher states of consciousness of the great within; and as this interior realm is boundless, there is no end to the possibilities of mental development.

To gain this ulterior consciousness, objective consciousness should be constantly deepened toward the unfathomable within, and this is accomplished by training all the mental tendencies to move toward the within.

The mental tendencies will move toward those states of being to which we give the greatest amount of attention; therefore, by constantly *thinking with deep feeling* of the great within, all the mental tendencies will move toward, and into, the great within; and will carry into the subconscious

The Great Within

every idea, thought or desire that the conscious mind may wish to realize and fulfill.

When all the mental tendencies move into the subconscious, and all thought is given feeling, worth and quality, the subconscious will constantly be impressed with superior ideas, which means a constant expression of superior life, superior ability and superior power.

The more deeply the tendencies of mind enter the subconscious, the more of the great within will be awakened; and whatever is awakened in the within will invariably come forth into the personal man.

It is therefore evident that when we cease to live on the surface of personal life we shall constantly improve that surface; by mentally living in the within we shall strengthen, enrich and perfect the without; that is, we improve external effects by going more deeply into the subconscious and increasing the quality and the power of internal causes.

The person who actually enters the deeper life to live will not ignore the body; those who simply dream of inner states of life may neglect the body, but those who thoroughly develop the greater, inner life will become able to give the body the best that can be secured; and they will enjoy physical existence infinitely more than those who simply live on the surface.

It is the truth that whatever we awaken and develop in the great within will invariably come forth into tangible, personal expression.

Chapter 8

You May Become What You Wish to Be

EACH person is, no more and no less, than what has been given to him by his subconscious mind; and as the subconscious is prepared to give as much as anyone may desire, the statement that we all may become whatsoever we may wish to become, is therefore absolutely true; but what the subconscious is to give to any person depends largely upon the movement of his mental tendencies. All the creative energies of the system follow the tendencies of the mind; therefore, when all the mental tendencies move toward the subconscious, all the surplus energy that is generated in the system will enter the subconscious; and the more energy that enters the subconscious the more of the subconscious will be awakened and developed.

The larger the field that is placed under cultivation the greater the harvest.

Every mental tendency that is trained to enter the subconscious will cause a corresponding tendency to be permanently expressed; therefore, by causing all the worthy tendencies to move toward the subconscious, the subconscious will respond by expressing through the personality the tendencies to be just, true, honest, virtuous, kind, sympathetic, sweet-tempered, cheerful, fearless, faithful, persevering, industrious — in brief, everything that goes to make a strong and worthy personality.

By a simple system of subconscious training, anyone can build up the strongest and most beautiful character imaginable, and in a reasonable time make it a permanent part of himself.

A lack of character is due wholly to the fact that the subconscious has been improperly impressed; misleading tendencies have been formed, and let it be remembered that nothing can tempt man to go wrong except the perverse tendencies that are expressed from his own subconscious mind.

Every weak place in mind or character is caused by a subconscious tendency that is going wrong; such tendencies may have been inherited — many of them are, but they can all be corrected by daily directing the subconscious to produce the opposite quality.

To think, with conviction, that human, nature is weak, is to impress upon the subconscious the idea of weakness, and the subconscious will respond by producing a tendency to weakness. Therefore, he who thinks he is weak will cause his nature to continue to be weak. We are weak or strong according to what we direct the subconscious to produce in us.

To realize that the great within contains the power to make the personality as strong as we may wish it to be, and to impress upon the subconscious a strong desire for that power, is to direct the subconscious to make us strong; and whatever we direct the subconscious to do, the same will invariably be done.

There is no reason whatever why any person should continue to have a weak body, a weak character or a weak mind; anything in the being of man can be made strong if the subconscious is properly directed to bring forth the greater life and the greater power.

When the great within is awakened we have the powerful personality, the giant mind, the irresistible character and the great soul. The natural result is a great life — a life that is too strong to be tempted, too strong to be swayed or disturbed by adversity, too strong to be turned from the path to its lofty goal. Such a life will not only live a *life* that *is* life, but will be an endless inspiration to the race; and such a life is waiting in the great within of every soul.

Chapter 9

Use of the Conscious and Subconscious

THE great within is the source of inspirations, all real music, all permanent art, all poetry with soul, all rich thought, all ideas of genuine worth, all invention, all discovery, all science, and the truth that is absolute.

Everything that has worth, be it in a small degree, or in a very great degree, comes directly from the richness of the subconscious; therefore, to do the greater, the mind should enter into the closest touch with the great within, and should expect the very best that the limitless within can produce.

When in need of ideas, plans, methods, ways and means, call upon the subconscious; the call will not be in vain; the subconscious can supply every need, and will invariably do so when properly directed.

While directing the subconscious, however, all conscious action must be in absolute poise; it is not only necessary to impress what we desire but to impress that desire in such a way that it will actually produce an impression.

When in the presence of the great fact that the within is limitless, the mind will naturally become enthusiastic; feeling will run high and is very liable to become overwrought; but such a feeling has no depth, it is simply superficial emotionalism; it will waste any amount of energy, but will never produce a single impression upon the subconscious.

To impress the subconscious, the mind must be calm, the entire personality must be in poise, and this feeling of poise must have that great depth that touches the very soul of life itself.

Not the slightest trace of emotional enthusiasm must be permitted, nor must feeling run toward the surface at any time; the actions of mind, especially those of feeling, must

The Great Within

move toward the great within if the subconscious is to be reached.

There must be no anxiety connected with the desire to impress the subconscious, and every form of doubt must be eliminated completely.

To properly impress the subconscious, faithful application is necessary; also constant practice, and a perseverance that will not give up; but the prize is worthy of the effort.

To realize that the subconscious can, and will, do anything when properly impressed, is to persevere until the proper impression has been made; and it is those who work in this realization that secure the marvelous results.

To eliminate the tendency to feel emotional while acting upon the subconscious, cultivate the substantial feeling; train yourself to *feel* substantial at all times, and wild, empty, overwrought feelings will entirely disappear.

It is the proper feeling that determines the proper impression; the attainment of the deep, substantial feeling is therefore extremely important, though it is equally important to be able to feel the vibrations of the finer forces of the system.

It is the finer forces that impress the subconscious and the subconscious is invariably impressed whenever these forces are felt.

To develop the consciousness of the finer forces, attention should be frequently concentrated upon that life that permeates the tangible elements in every part of being; and during this concentration the feeling of consciousness should be deepened and expanded as much as possible.

Every conscious action should be trained to penetrate to the very depth of life, and during this process the mind should act in the realization that the more deeply it penetrates any element in the personality, the finer will be the forces into which consciousness will enter.

To awaken or arouse any force or element, attention should be concentrated upon that state in which the desired force or element is known to exist, and the mind should *think* of the nature of that force or element according to the best possible understanding that can be formed of that nature.

The same method may be employed in the development of the subconscious side of any desired faculty or talent.

The creative energies of the system always build up those qualities of which the mind may be thinking; therefore, to actually and continually think of the real nature of a great talent is to develop that talent into the same degree of greatness that is discerned in mind.

The power of this method in the development of ability, talent and genius is practically unlimited, because the mind is capable of discerning higher and higher degrees of greatness, and the subconscious is capable of providing creative energies of as high a state of fineness and power as may be required.

To secure the best results from any method through which the great within is to be unfolded and expressed, it is extremely important to use properly the conscious and the subconscious factors of mind at the various stages of the process.

While impressing the subconscious, the conscious mind should be strong, firm, positive and highly active, but should become perfectly quiet and receptive while expecting a response from the subconscious.

Harmony, serenity and poise are indispensable states both when the impression is being made and when the expression is expected.

The Great Within

The right use of the will is of extraordinary importance; and neither time nor effort should be spared in establishing this right use, because where the will is misapplied the subconscious expressions are interfered with to such an extent that results are completely neutralized.

While the subconscious is being impressed, the will should act firmly and directly upon that consciousness that is felt in the subconscious, but when the subconscious is expected to respond the will should be relaxed into a state of complete inaction.

It is not the purpose of the will to control the outer person by acting directly upon the outer person; the will controls the outer person by causing the subconscious to produce in the outer person whatever may be desired; but when the subconscious begins to express what the will has desired and directed, the will must, for the time being, cease to act.

The true function of the will is to act upon the finer states of consciousness; that is, the subconscious states, those states that are felt in the deeper life of the personality or the mentality; and while in such action, to impress upon the subconscious those causes that can produce the desired effects.

When these causes have been impressed, and the time has come for the expected results, the will must withdraw so that the personality may become sufficiently receptive to give the subconscious response the fullest and freest possible expression.

The subconscious expression will come of itself, at the tune designated, if the impression has been properly made; but every attempt of the will to help draw forth that expression will interfere with results.

When the desired subconscious expression fails to appear at the time designated, the impression has either not been properly made, or the subconscious response is being prevented by too much active will force, anxiety or objective commotion.

The subconscious cannot express itself, or do what it is directed to do unless the outer mentality and personality are in poise; but perfect poise is not possible so long as will power is applied upon the external side of mind or body.

Train the will to act upon the subconscious, and the subconscious only, and this is readily accomplished by always turning attention upon the subconscious whenever the will is being employed.

When acting upon the objective, the will only interferes with normal functions, and can accomplish absolutely nothing. To move a muscle the will must act upon the subconscious life that permeates that muscle; should it act upon the muscle itself, the muscle would become rigid, and muscular motion be made impossible.

No one can do anything by objectively willing to do it; he can do what he wants to do only by causing the will to act upon that part of the subconscious that can do what he wants to have done.

This law is absolute in all human actions, be they physical or metaphysical, intellectual or emotional, mental or spiritual.

To train the will to act only upon the subconscious, will increase the power of the conscious mind to impress the subconscious; the conscious action will not be divided, acting partly upon the objective and partly upon the subjective, but will give its power and attention absolutely to the idea that is being subconsciously impressed.

When the will acts only upon the subconscious, there will be no will force in the outer mind or body to disturb the normal functions of the systems; and when the entire system is normal the subconscious can readily do whatever it may be directed to do.

The Great Within

The conscious mind should employ the will solely for the purpose of impressing and directing the subconscious, but should give the subconscious unrestricted freedom to take full possession of the personality when expressions from within are expected to appear.

Those who hesitate to give the subconscious expressions full right of way, should remember that to move a muscle, the subconscious must take full possession of that muscle; and to think, the subconscious must exercise complete control of the mental faculty, and also, that the subconscious will only do what it is directed to do.

Though the personality must be controlled completely by the subconscious, the subconscious must be directed, in all its actions, by the conscious mind; therefore, the wide-awake self continues to be the master.

Chapter 10

Solutions to Problems

THE subconscious has the power to work out any problem, and find the exact answer to any question, at the time designated by the conscious mind; in fact, no problem is ever worked out by the conscious mind alone; the subconscious gives the real secret in every instance, though it is the conscious mind that makes the practical application.

To secure the direct and the fullest assistance from the subconscious when there are problems to solve, form a clear, distinct idea of what you wish to know, and impress that idea upon the subconscious with a deep, strong desire for the information required. Have perfect faith in the faith that you will receive the answer, and you will.

When you have something special to do at some near future time, that requires more power and mental brilliancy than you usually possess, direct the subconscious to give you the added power and intelligence at the exact time. The subconscious is exact as to time, and will produce, at the time desired, as much power and intelligence as you felt you needed for the special work when the impression was made.

To simply impress upon the subconscious a desire for more power is not sufficient; the impression must contain a clear idea of how much power is required and what the added power is expected to do.

While the subconscious is being impressed for more power, the mind must try to discern and feel the life of more power; and the amount of power that is discerned while the impression is being made, the subconscious will express at the time fixed for the expression.

Whenever an impression is made upon the subconscious, the conscious mind should try to gain the very highest and the very largest conception possible of the idea that is being impressed; and the more clearly the conscious mind discerns the largeness, the worth and the superiority of that idea, the larger, the worthier and the more superior will be the corresponding expression brought forth from the within.

When the conscious mind can see clearly the amount of power and mental brilliancy required for the special future action, and impresses that idea upon the subconscious with the deepest and the strongest desire for its realization, the impression thus made will call for the exact amount of power and intelligence required; and whatever the impression calls for the subconscious will supply.

The law is this, that the subconscious will respond with the exact quality and the exact quantity that you were conscious of, or that you can mentally discern and feel at the time the impression is being made. It is, therefore, extremely important to elevate the conscious mind into the largest and the most superior states of thought and feeling possible before an effort is made to impress the subconscious. In fact, this is the real secret in directing the subconscious to express a larger quantity and a higher quality than we ever received in tangible life before.

To live constantly in the deep, interior feeling of greater power, greater intelligence, greater personal worth and greater mental brilliancy, is to constantly call upon the subconscious to produce these things in larger and larger measure; and the subconscious will invariably do whatever it is called upon to do.

Though we should not live in the future in the sense that the mind dwells wholly in the thought of the future, nevertheless, we should always plan ahead.

Place your future plans in the hands of the subconscious; impress upon the subconscious what you wish to have done tomorrow, next week, next month, or even next year; then direct the great within to work out the best plans and the best methods possible, and to give your faculties the understanding and the power to carry out those plans to the most successful termination.

When there is something upon which you cannot decide, inform the subconscious that a definite decision is desired at such and such a time; impress clearly and deeply the facts on all sides concerned, and *know* that the great within can give the desired decision at the time stated.

When this time comes you will receive your answer through the feeling of a strong, irresistible desire to take one particular course, and that alone.

While the answer is being expected, no anxiety should be felt, even though the last minute should arrive before anything definite appears; the mind that continues in serenity and faith will receive the right answer before it is too late; but the anxious mind will, through the confusion produced by the anxiety, prevent the subconscious from giving expression to the desired information.

When two antagonistic decisions appear at the time fixed, the subconscious expression has not been given full right of way. One of these decisions will be of the conscious mind who judges according to appearances; the other will be of the subconscious who judges according to facts, but which is which may seem difficult to discern.

The decision of the conscious mind may sometimes be the stronger, but at other times the weaker; one's strongest feelings, therefore, at such times will not prove to be safe guidance.

To reimpress the subconscious for an immediate and a definite decision is the proper course to pursue under such circumstances, and if the conscious mind is kept quiet, in faith, the true answer will shortly appear. You will then feel a strong desire to take but one course, and will lose all desire to even think about the other, because when the subconscious action is given full and free expression, everything that is antagonistic to that expression will cease to exist.

It is therefore evident that we may completely eliminate the wrong by directing the subconscious to express the right, and by giving the subconscious absolute freedom to do what it has been directed to do.

Chapter 11

Direct Assistance in Everything

THE subconscious should be called upon to give direct assistance in everything, even in the most insignificant of everyday affairs; this practice will not only cause all things to be done better and better constantly, but the conscious mind will be more thoroughly trained to impress the subconscious for anything desired, and the subconscious mentality will be perpetually enlarged along all lines.

To enlarge the subconscious mentality in every phase of interior action is to awaken a larger measure of the great within, and the more of the within that is awakened the greater will man become.

For these reasons the subconscious should be called upon for superior aid before anything, even the least, is undertaken. Everything that is worth doing should be done better than before, and the subconscious can provide the power.

Impressions of this nature should be made a few hours in advance, or, when possible, a few days in advance; though the subconscious can respond upon a moment's notice; its superior power should therefore be sought upon every occasion.

In the commercial world no one should ever attempt to decide upon important transactions before directing the subconscious to inspire the mind with the highest insight, the keenest judgment, and the broadest understanding; and no great enterprise should be undertaken before directing the subconscious to work out the best possible plans and methods.

The subconscious can do these things, and when all practical men will go to the greater mind for their plans and ideas, instead of depending upon the limited intelligence of the lesser mind, failures will be reduced to a minimum, while great achievements will steadily increase, both in numbers and in greatness.

Those who are engaged in literary work will find the subconscious indispensable, because any idea desired may be gamed from the great within.

Orators and public speakers should never attempt to prepare or deliver a discourse before going to this great source of ideas for their thought; and the same is true of musical composers, creative artists, inventors, and all others who require ideas that have originality and worth.

Every person who is engaged in study, or in any line of improvement, may increase results from ten to two hundred per cent by securing the direct assistance of the subconscious; and as all advancement and promotion in life comes directly from the improvement of self, the fact that the subconscious can supply any amount of ability, capacity and power, becomes extremely important.

All memory is subconscious, therefore, whatever one desires to remember should be deeply impressed upon the subconscious at the time the fact or idea is received; and the subconscious may be directed to bring back to mind these facts and ideas whenever their recollection is desired.

Through this simple process memory can be developed and cultivated to a remarkable degree, and the power to recall anything at any time will become practically perfect.

The subconscious can be trained to keep the conscious mind clear and active, and all sluggishness or obtuseness can be completely eliminated from every faculty. This will enable the student to learn with far greater rapidity, and every mental effort will be conducive to growth.

To produce these results the subconscious should, several times every day, be directed to express continuous clearness, mental lucidity, and a high, well-poised mental activity. While producing that impression, picture in the conscious mind the same clearness and action that you desire the subconscious to express.

To picture perfect lucidity, and to feel high activity in the conscious mind for a few moments while the subconscious is being impressed, will cause the subconscious to express that same clearness and activity for several hours; and when the impression contains a deep desire for greater clearness and activity than the conscious mind can discern, the greater clearness and activity will be expressed.

It is a well-known fact that nearly all great minds, and also most minds that are trying to develop greatness, have moods when they can do most excellent work, but when they are not in those moods little or nothing of worth can be accomplished. To such minds the ability to create the right moods, or mental states, whenever desired, would be of exceptional value, and by properly directing the subconscious it may readily be accomplished.

Form in the conscious mind a very clear idea of the mood or mental state in which you can do your best work, and impress that idea upon the subconscious with a strong desire for the continuous realization of the desired state. Repeat the impression several times every day, and every evening before going to sleep. Perseverance will produce the most remarkable results.

While engaged in any particular study, impress frequently upon the subconscious the real nature of that study, and direct the subconscious to express all the essentials that may be necessary to thoroughly understand and master that study.

Expect superior intelligence from within, and make the best possible use of that intelligence as it is being received. Thus the conscious mind and the subconscious will work together for the promotion of the highest conceivable attainments.

The Great Within

To promote advancement in one's vocation, better plans and methods will constantly be in demand; and by directing the subconscious to work them out these may be secured as required; in addition, the necessary power and ability to practically apply those methods may also be secured if the subconscious is called upon to supply them.

It is the truth that whatever the subconscious is properly impressed and directed to do, it positively will do.

Chapter 12

Make Your Desires Subconscious

TO promote the highest development of mind and soul, a sunny disposition is indispensable; the brighter, the happier and the sweeter the disposition, the more easily and the more rapidly will any talent develop; and it is a literal truth that a sunny disposition is to the talents of the mind what a sunny day is to the flowers of the field.

Every form of disposition comes from the subconscious, be it sweet or otherwise; but the undesirable may be removed completely, and the sweetest and brightest disposition imaginable be permanently established, by daily impressing upon the subconscious your most perfect idea of a sweet and wholesome nature.

As the sweetness of human nature develops, all undesirable feelings and dispositions will disappear; no thought, therefore, should be given to the elimination of perverse characteristics, but the whole of attention should be concentrated upon the development of the wholesome, the sweet and the beautiful.

When there is a tendency to feel out of sorts, turn attention upon the finer side of your nature — the subconscious — and think deeply, strongly and feelingly of joy, brightness, kindness, amiableness, cheerfulness, sweetness and loveliness; try to enter into the very life of those states and *feel* that your entire nature is being recreated in the image and likeness of all that is sweet and beautiful.

To permit yourself to feel surly whenever there is a tendency to feel that way is to impress the subconscious with such a state of mind, and the subconscious will respond by giving your nature a stronger tendency to feel surly and out of sorts at the least provocation.

The Great Within

The first indication of ill-feeling in any shape or form should be counteracted at once by immediately directing the subconscious to give expression to the sweet, the wholesome and the beautiful.

It is not only the privilege of every mind to attain greatness, but no mind is doing justice to self that is not doing its utmost to develop greatness; and since a sunny disposition is absolutely necessary to the steady development of ability, talent and genius, neither time nor effort should be spared in recreating the subconscious so completely that every part of its vast domain is permeated through and through with the highest order of human sweetness and mental sunshine.

To recreate the subconscious mentality in the likeness of higher ideals, every impression given to the subconscious should have *soul*. It is the conscious realization of soul that gives quality, worth and superiority to everything that appears in human life; the reason being that the soul *is* superiority, and that everything gains superiority that comes in conscious touch with the soul.

To feel *soul* is to feel the life of real worth, and to impress that feeling upon the subconscious will cause the subconscious to give real worth to every part of the personality.

The subconscious should be directed daily to give worth and superiority to the entire being of man; and this is positively can do.

The great within should be directed to work for greater things, and when every impression is impressed in the feeling of soul, every impression will cause the within to unfold, develop and give expression to greater things.

All greatness comes from the awakening of the great within; to awaken the great within is to feel greatness, and to be filled with the power that is greatness — the power that will invariably produce greatness.

The Great Within

Ability, talent and genius of the highest order must inevitably follow the development of the great within; likewise, the strong mind, the invincible character and the beautiful soul.

Every faculty increases in power, capacity and quality as its subconscious side is being developed, and this subconscious side may be developed by concentrating attention upon the interior, finer essence of that faculty while the most perfect idea or conception of that faculty is held in mind.

The development of the subconscious side of the entire personality will increase the drawing power of the personality, the power that attracts both directly and indirectly, whatever the mind may desire.

This power is the result of subconscious action, and therefore increases, both in volume and in natural attraction, as a greater measure of the within is awakened.

There are many personalities that are strong, but that do not attract, while there are many others that lack in power but that are very attractive in proportion to the power they do possess. The cause of the former condition is an awakened subconscious life that does not receive free and orderly expression; the cause of the latter condition is a limited subconscious life that is not disturbed nor hindered in its expression.

To steadily increase subconscious action and give that action a well-poised expression will cause the personality to become practically irresistible in its power of attraction.

The drawing power of the subconscious lies in its ability, not only to give extraordinary power to the personality, but also to produce ideas that draw, plans that draw, methods that draw and systems that draw.

It is not only ideas, but the way those ideas are arranged, that determines results; and it is not only high-class work,

The Great Within

but the way that work is presented, that determines the measure of success. The best ideas may be ignored completely by the world, and the best work may have to be abandoned through the lack of appreciation, and the subconscious life that is expressed through those ideas or efforts is at fault.

Direct the subconscious not only to give you the best ideas, the best plans and the best methods, but also direct the subconscious to give the proper expression to those ideas and methods. When the proper expression is made the attention of the world will be attracted; your ideas will be understood, the real worth of your work will be appreciated, and your efforts will be in constant demand.

The subconscious can work out the best ideas and create the best expression of those ideas; it can give the power and the ability to do greater things, and can give your work that mysterious something that will attract both the attention and the appreciation of the world.

The subconscious in every mind should therefore be directed to do these things, because no person is just to himself who does not make the best use of everything that exists in his nature.

The subconscious, when so directed, will give a natural drawing power to all the finer thought currents; these in turn will convey the same qualities to every part of the mentality and the personality; this will cause everything that man is, and everything that he does, to be stamped with that something that attracts attention and commands appreciation; his desires will consequently become irresistible.

The desires of such a mind will have the power to create their own way to their own goal, no matter how lofty that goal may be. The power of the subconscious is limitless, therefore, nothing becomes impossible when we awaken the great within.

The Great Within

All desires should be made subconscious, and when those desires are constantly expressed with the deepest feeling and the strongest desire that can possibly be aroused, you will positively receive what you want. If it fails to come through one channel it will come through another; but come it will, because the subconscious has the power to do whatever it is directed to do.

To subconsciously desire something is to make yourself strong enough and able enough to command, create or attract that something.

Make your desires subconscious and the subconscious will make you worthy of what you desire; the subconscious desire will awaken the same quality and worth in yourself that already exists in that which you desire, and, as like does attract like, you will invariably get what you desire when you become equal to what you desire.

The subconscious desire for abundance will develop in yourself the power to earn and create abundance; it will increase your earning capacity, and will, both directly and indirectly, change your personality so that you will be naturally drawn into environments and associations where you can make the best possible use of that increase of capacity.

The subconscious, being limitless, can work out ideas and plans that you can use in your present position in furthering your desire for the better position; the subconscious, if directed, will find a way; especially so if the desire is very deep and very strong; and you will also receive the power and the ability to do whatever that way may demand.

It is therefore evident that whatever a person's conditions or circumstances may be today, the subconscious can, and will, open the door to something better, providing there is a strong subconscious desire for something better.

Chapter 13

Produce Perfect Health

TO awaken the great within is to awaken to a universe of higher attainments, greater achievements and more far-reaching possibilities than one has ever dreamed of before; it is to enter that world where every desire will be granted, every aspiration realized and every ideal fulfilled.

To promote this awakening, direct the subconscious to give its best to every thought and every action, and when this best has been received, direct the subconscious to produce something still better. It can; the subconscious can do whatever we may wish to have done.

Every condition that appears in the body, be it favorable or otherwise, comes either directly or indirectly from the subconscious; that is, it may be the direct effect of a corresponding subconscious cause, or it may be the effect of external causes that were permitted to act upon the body because the true subconscious expression was absent.

No external cause can produce disease in the body so long as the subconscious is giving a full expression to perfect health; and no curative agent from the without can restore health in the body so long as the subconscious is giving expression to diseased conditions.

The majority of physical ills can be cured by nature when the subconscious ceases to give expression to weakening and disease producing conditions, and all diseases can be permanently removed by training the subconscious to give a full and constant expression of health.

Personal and physical conditions are effects; they are caused either directly or indirectly by the subconscious; therefore, any condition desired in the personality may be produced through the proper direction of the subconscious.

The Great Within

To direct the subconscious to produce perfect health, the first essential is to gain a clear conscious realization of the state of perfect health, and the second essential is to permeate the subconscious with this realization.

The subconscious mind is a deeper and a finer state of mental life that exists within every atom of the human system; it is another mental world, so to speak, and is so immense that the ordinary conscious mind is mere insignificance in comparison. But it obeys perfectly the directions of the conscious mind, and, having limitless power in every part of the body, can readily banish any disease when properly directed to do so.

To impress the subconscious, attention should be concentrated upon this superior mental world, and all thought should be gradually refined until one can feel that the conscious thought has been completely transformed into the spiritual fineness of the subconscious thought.

The subconscious may be reached most directly by concentrating upon the brain center, though attention must not be fixed upon the physical brain, but upon that finer mental life that permeates the physical brain.

All general directions given to the subconscious should be given through the brain center, but for the curing of physical ailments attention should be concentrated upon the subconscious mentality that permeates the organ, muscle or nerve where the ailment is located.

To impress the conscious realization of health upon the subconscious life of any part of the body will cause the subconscious to bring forth into that part of the body the same condition of health which the conscious mind realized while the impression was being made; it is, therefore, necessary to attain the very highest possible conscious understanding of the real state of perfect health before the subconscious is directed to produce health.

The Great Within

No thought of disease should form in mind while the subconscious is being impressed with perfect health; neither should one think of the body. To think of the body is to form mental conceptions of the way physical conditions now feel, and if these conditions are undesirable, undesirable impressions will enter the subconscious, to be followed by the formation of more undesirable conditions in the near future.

The imperfection of physical conditions should never enter mind at any time, because such conditions are liable to be deeply felt, and whatever is deeply felt will be impressed upon the subconscious, whether we so wish or no; neither should there be any desire to remove or overcome that which may seem undesirable. To desire to remove the wrong is to deeply think about the wrong, because all desires tend to deepen the actions of thought, and to deeply think about the wrong is to impress the wrong upon the subconscious. It is sowing weeds in the fields of the mind, and the harvest will be accordingly.

All thought should be animated with the consciousness of that perfection in health and wholeness that we desire to realize in expression, and all feeling should be trained to feel the health, the life and the harmony that the subconscious is being directed to produce.

To consciously live through and through the finer subconscious mentality for a few moments, several times every day, and deeply impress one's most perfect realization of health upon the entire subconscious mentality will cause the subconscious to give a full and constant expression of health.

The result will be perpetual health, without a moment of any form of sickness at any time, and if the conscious mind will seek to daily impress upon the subconscious a more and more perfect realization of absolute health, the subconscious will steadily improve the quality of the health that is being expressed.

The Great Within

To eliminate a local ailment the subconscious mentality that permeates that part of the body should be impressed with the conscious feeling of the health that is desired.

Concentrate upon the finer mental life in that part of the body where the adverse condition appears and *feel* the reality of perfect health. Do not concentrate upon the physical organ, nor even think of the physical organ, but enter mentally into the interior subconscious life of that organ and, while in that state, *feel* the spirit of perfect health with all the depth of mind and soul.

What you feel, while in that state, you impress upon the subconscious, and the subconscious will cause perfect health to be expressed through every atom of that organ.

To eliminate a chronic ailment, impress perfect health upon the subconscious as a whole, while concentrating upon the subconscious mentality within the brain center. Also concentrate frequently upon the subconscious side of the entire personality, feeling the state of perfect health in the subconscious life of every part of the system.

If certain parts of the body are specially affected, impress those parts in the same way as for a local ailment, though local attention should be given, not so much to those parts of the body that feel the effects of the ailment as to those parts where the adverse condition has its origin.

Before impressing the subconscious the entire system should be made as calm and peaceful as possible, and the principal directions should be given to the subconscious immediately before going to sleep.

The most important of all, however, is to live, think and act in the absolute faith that the subconscious *can* and *will* do whatever it is directed to do.

Chapter 14

Impress the Subconscious Before Sleep

DURING the waking state the conscious ego acts directly upon the conscious, or wide awake mind, while during sleep it acts entirely in the subconscious.

When we go to sleep all the principal thoughts, desires, intentions, tendencies, feelings and ideas that have formed during the day are taken into the subconscious, unless we eliminate the undesirable mental material before we permit sleep to take place.

Every thought, desire, idea that is taken into the subconscious as mind falls asleep will be impressed upon the subconscious, and will cause corresponding expressions to be brought forth into the personality. To eliminate all undesirable thoughts and feelings from mind before going to sleep is therefore extremely important.

Before going to sleep the conscious mind should be thoroughly cleansed from everything that one does not care to reproduce or perpetuate, and the subconscious should be given definite directions as to what should be developed, reproduced and expressed.

The hours of sleep may be employed in the development of anything we may have in view, because whatever we impress upon mind when we go to sleep will enter the subconscious and will cause the within to give expression to those effects that we desire to secure in the without.

Before going to sleep the subconscious should be given full directions as to what is to be done in the near future, and the exact time for each particular action should be specified as far as possible. In the meantime the subconscious will work out the best plans, methods and ideas, and provide the added understanding, insight and power required to apply those plans in the most effective manner.

When the subconscious is properly directed in this way the results from future actions may be increased to a degree that will frequently be remarkable, and, as much produces more, these results will follow the law of perpetual increase.

During the waking state the mind forms a definite conception of everything that is given real, conscious attention; these conceptions individualize themselves into ideas and as mind goes to sleep all those ideas are taken into the subconscious.

Therefore, what the subconscious is given to work out and develop during sleep will depend upon what we think about during the day, and what we give the subconscious to develop and express will determine what character, mentality and personality are to be.

The subconscious makes us what we are, in every respect, but what the subconscious is to make will depend upon what our thoughts, feelings and desires may direct.

The more we think during the day, providing our thought has quality, the more good seeds we shall place in the garden of the mind during sleep, and the greater will be the quality and the quantity of the coming harvest.

The stronger our desires for wisdom, power, attainments and achievements during the waking state, the more thoroughly will the subconscious work for those things during sleep.

The subconscious can provide all the essentials required for the highest attainments and greatest achievements and will do so if directed.

The subconscious works during sleep, and works to develop the ideas and the desires that the conscious mind brought into the subconscious while falling asleep, but the subconscious will give the same attention to ideas and desires that are detrimental, just as rich soil will apply the same productiveness to the weed as to the Sower.

It is therefore wisdom to sow good seeds only; to eliminate all undesirable thought, ideas and feelings before sleep begins.

The habit of going to sleep every night with all sorts of thoughts in mind is the principal cause of the continuous mingling of good and evil in the life of the average person. The troubles and the worries of the day are taken into the subconscious at night, along with those thoughts and feelings that have better things in view, and the subconscious, consequently, continues to work for more good things on the one hand and for more troubles and worries on the other.

It is the truth that any person may emancipate himself completely from all the ills of perverted life by refusing absolutely to permit a single undesirable thought, feeling or desire to enter the subconscious.

To prevent the wrong from entering the subconscious we must, during the waking state, never think, with feeling, of that which is evil, imperfect or wrong, and before going to sleep the conscious mind must be cleansed completely from every undesirable thought or impression that may have entered unconsciously during the day.

The imperfect will not impress itself upon the subconscious during the waking state unless we think about it in deep feeling, but everything that is in the conscious mind when we go to sleep will enter the subconscious and produce fruit after its kind.

To cleanse the conscious mind before going to sleep, enter a state of perfect mental poise; be still in the deepest sense of the term; forget what you do not wish to retain by entering into the very life and essence of that which you desire to awaken, unfold and develop. Then concentrate upon the subconscious with the deepest possible feeling and the strongest possible desire.

The Great Within

What you wish to remove from mind may be removed by directing the subconscious to create and express the opposite, though no thought should be given to that which is not to be retained. When you know what you wish to remove, forget it by giving your entire subconscious attention to that which you wish to create and realize instead.

To carry into the subconscious those ideas that we wish to develop is not all that is necessary, however, as we go to sleep; the subconscious should be given the best possible conditions in which to work.

The subconscious is in close touch with all the functions of the body as well as the actions of the mind, therefore, the entire system must be in harmony and order before sleep begins or subconscious action will be confused and misdirected.

Before going to sleep the body should be in harmony, the mind in peace an d the entire personality relaxed. The circulation should be even, and no part should be too warm nor too cold. Digestion should be practically finished and there should be nothing in the system that might disturb any of the functions during sleep.

When physical functions are disturbed during sleep the conscious ego is drawn back to the outer mind, either fully or in part, and its work in the subconscious is interrupted. Such interruptions usually misdirect the subconscious actions to such an extent that the very opposite results to what were intended are produced.

This explains why such detrimental results are frequently secured, even when our intentions were the best and our plans carried out with the greatest of care. It also proves that the entire system must be kept in order if every action, conscious or subconscious, is to produce the results desired.

Chapter 15

Sleeping on Difficult Problems

WHEN the conscious ego, which is you, yourself, enters the subconscious during sleep, there are two objects in view. The first object is to carry into the subconscious the new ideas that have formed during the day and the second object is to recharge the system with life, power and energy.

The subconscious supplies the life and the energy that is required to perpetuate the existence of the mentality and the personality, but to receive this energy the conscious ego must enter the subconscious, and should remain there, uninterruptedly, for six or seven hours out of every twenty-four, to secure the full measure of power. When sleep is interrupted the personality does not receive as much life as may be required to keep the system in the fullest and most perfect action; personal efforts will, therefore, become inferior.

When all the conditions are provided for properly recuperating and recharging the system during sleep, and the subconscious is directed to steadily increase the supply of power, the personality will become stronger and more vigorous from year to year; instead of going down to weakness and age the personality will go on to greater strength, greater capacity, greater ability and greater power the longer you live.

To go to sleep properly is to wake up feeling refreshed, but to go to sleep with all sorts of impressions in the mind and all sorts of conditions in the body is to wake up feeling stupid and depressed.

To enter the subconscious with adverse impressions is to return to consciousness with similar conditions. Like causes always produce like effects.

To aid the mind in purifying itself before going to sleep, attention should be concentrated upon the purest purity and the highest worth that can possibly be imagined, and to place the entire system in a state of peace, concentrate the thought of peace upon the brain center while gently drawing all the finer forces of mind toward that center.

To think, with feeling, of the finer forces of mind during this process will produce immediate results.

The practice of "sleeping over" difficult problems before definite decisions are made is a practice of great value, especially when the subconscious is properly directed in the matter, because the subconscious can "turn things over" more completely during sleep than during the waking state.

To secure the best results hold clearly and serenely in mind the elements involved in the problem just as you are going to sleep and desire deeply, but without anxiety, to receive the correct answer upon awakening.

The higher and the clearer the conception that is formed of the problem during the waking state the more readily can the subconscious work it out during sleep. The same is true in the various ideas that are formed during the day and that are taken into the great within either at sleep or during waking states of deep feeling.

It is therefore extremely important to form the highest possible conception of everything that we think of during the day, and whatever attracts our attention should be considered from the very highest point of view.

Live in the upper story of mind and give *soul* to all your thought; you will thereby form ideas with real quality and worth, and as those ideas are taken into the subconscious during sleep they will cause greater quality and worth to be developed in you.

No person can afford to take a commonplace view of anything, nor to indulge in cheap thinking at any time; to do so is to place inferior seeds in the garden of the mind.

The Great Within

There are days when the average person feels as if he amounted to practically nothing; his personality lacks energy and his mind is dull, stupid and confused. Cheap, superficial thinking a day or two before is the cause.

Give inferior ideas to the subconscious, and the subconscious will, in the near future, not only cause you to feel incompetent and inferior, but your mind will temporarily be placed in a state where it actually becomes incompetent and inferior.

To produce worthy ideas it is not necessary to always continue in profound or serious states of mind; the thought of worth is the thought that mind creates while attention dwells in the life of quality and soul, and while consciousness is thoroughly permeated with the desire to realize quality and soul in everything.

Such thinking can be taken into all thought and all life, even into every pleasure.

To try to enjoy pleasures while mind skims over the surface of life and thought is to fail to receive the joy that is joy, or the satisfaction that does satisfy; but when pleasures are entered into with the feeling of quality and finer life, even the simplest of joys become founts of supreme joy.

Everything that we thoroughly enjoy we impress upon the subconscious; therefore, to enter into pleasure while mind is in the attitude of cheapness or inferiority is a mistake to be avoided under every circumstance.

However, our pleasures may be used as channels through which the subconscious may be impressed and directed along lines of superior attainment, and pleasures that are employed in this manner will invariably give the greatest, the most satisfying and the most wholesome joy of all joys.

Chapter 16

Sleep on the Superior; The Ideal

THE entire human personality is being constantly renewed; there is nothing about mind or body that can possibly become old, except the appearance, and the appearance of age is caused by a wrong subconscious process.

The process of perpetual renewal is carried on by the subconscious, but it is what the conscious mind gives to the subconscious that determines both the quality and the appearance of the personality.

To constantly give the subconscious better ideas, better desires, better thoughts and better mental states is to cause the improvement of character, mentality and personality to become perpetual.

To provide better material for the subconscious, the conscious mind, before going to sleep, should eliminate everything but those ideas, thoughts and desires that have quality and worth, and every effort should be made during the waking state to form the most superior ideas possible on every subject with which the mind may come in contact.

Never go to sleep discouraged, nor with the thought of failure in mind. To fear failure while going to sleep is to impress the subconscious with the idea of failure, and the subconscious will respond by producing conditions in the system that are failures; the system will, consequently, fail to be its best, and will lose ground, more and more, until real failure takes place.

To go to sleep discouraged, disappointed, worried or depressed, is to impress the subconscious with weakening tendencies; these will cause the subconscious to express conditions of weakness in every faculty and in every part of mind or body.

The Great Within

The tendency downward in any career originates invariably in depressed subconscious states, the majority of which are taken into the subconscious as the mind goes to sleep.

Every tendency upward and onward toward higher attainments and greater achievements, originates in constructive subconscious states and it is possible for anyone to produce such states at will.

By going to sleep with strong, clear ideas of health, harmony, power, advancement and success, clearly held in mind, the causes of those things will be formed in the subconscious and the effects will invariably appear in external life. Your health will at once begin to improve; more power will appear in mind and body; capacity will increase; all your talents and faculties will be filled with the spirit of success, and will consequently, do far better work than ever before.

To continue, for weeks and months, the practice of giving superior ideas of all kinds to the subconscious, upon going to sleep, will cause the character, the mentality and the personality to improve to such an extent that, in comparison with your former self, you will actually become a superior being.

When the subconscious is given something special to do every night sleep will become more restful; the subconscious always works during sleep, but will work more orderly when given something definite to do.

After the subconscious has been properly directed no anxiety should be felt as to results; perfect faith in the law, with that quiet assurance that knows, will give the law the proper conditions through which the desired results can be produced.

When we go to sleep in states of discord the mental material becomes confused and incoherent mental formations are produced; these are sometimes remembered as disagreeable dreams.

All such formations are produced by confusion among the subconscious creative energies and indicate that the true state of sleep was not entered completely, also that the subconscious was not properly impressed the night before.

Orderly and coherent dreams may indicate what tendencies are at work in the subconscious and whether desirable or undesirable conditions are being formed, because a dream is always a partial memory of what is taking place in the subconscious.

By noting this fact, undesirable conditions may be counteracted and removed before they advance sufficiently to produce tangible results.

An undesirable dream should always be counteracted at once by impressing the opposite, desirable conditions and qualities upon the subconscious; tendencies, however, that are indicated in good dreams, should be given added power. This can be done by directing the subconscious to work more thoroughly for the promotion of the greater good at hand.

Every good dream is a prophecy; that is, it indicates what the subconscious can do, what it is ready to do, or what it is about to do along certain lines, and this prophecy can be made to come true by directing the subconscious to proceed along those lines with greater power and determination than ever before.

These directions should be given to the subconscious as frequently as possible during the waking state, as well as before going to sleep.

Every desirable indication among the greater, interior life forces, whether it be discovered through dreams or intuition, should be taken advantage of at once, and all the forces of mind should be concentrated upon the goal that the vision has placed within reach; a successful termination will invariably be the result; the dream will come true, the prophecy will be fulfilled, the ideal will be realized.

Chapter 17

Awaking the Great Within

THE subconscious mind is not a second mind; to think so is to place an artificial barrier between the outer person and the limitless within. There is but one mind; the outer phase is the conscious or the objective; the inner phase is the subconscious or the subjective.

The subconscious is within the conscious, and, being unlimited, both in power and in possibilities, is appropriately termed the great within.

To awaken the great within is to bring into action the powers and the possibilities that are latent in the subconscious, and since the powers of the within are limitless, and its possibilities numberless, this awakening may be promoted indefinitely, increasing without end the worth and the greatness of man.

The awakening of the great within is promoted directly through a perpetual increase of conscious action upon the subconscious, and the power of the conscious mind to act upon the subconscious will increase in proportion to the practical use that is made of every added expression that appears from the within.

The fact that the within is limitless, and the fact that the greatness of the within can be brought forth into expression in greater and greater measure through the proper action of the conscious mind upon the subconscious proves conclusively that man may become as great as he may desire to be, and that his ability, his talent and his genius may be developed, not only to a most remarkable degree, but to any degree.

Personally, each person is only as much as he has, consciously or unconsciously, directed the subconscious to produce, and he will remain what he is so long as he does not direct the subconscious to produce more; but he may

The Great Within

become more, as much more as his highest aspiration can picture, by awakening the great within.

To train the conscious mind to act upon the subconscious with the greatest efficiency, a clear idea of how the two phases of mind are related to each other becomes necessary, and this idea is readily understood when we realize that mind is an immense sea of soul forces, all of which move in circles and spirals.

The circumference of each circle is acted upon by the conscious ego during the waking state, therefore, the sum total of all the circumferences of all the mental circles may be termed the outer mind, the objective mind, the conscious mind, the wide-awake mind.

During sleep the conscious ego withdraws from the circumference of the mental circles and enters the mental field within; that is, the subconscious.

While the mind is in state of deep feeling the conscious ego acts partly upon the conscious side of mind and partly upon the subconscious; it is possible, therefore, while in that state, to impress upon the subconscious what we think or feel in the conscious.

To secure the best and the largest results from every mental action the conscious ego should, during the waking state, act constantly both upon the conscious and the subconscious. To be in constant touch with the limitless powers of the within will add remarkably to the capacity as well as the quality of the faculties that may be in use, and every conscious desire will enter the subconscious at once, so that an immediate response may be secured, if required.

The strong mind is the mind that is in such close touch with the great within that the limitless powers of the within can be felt at any tune.

The capacity of such a mind will be practically unbounded; weariness will be absent; mental brilliancy will ever be on the increase, and instead of going down with the years, as the average mind does, such a mind will steadily advance in higher attainments and greater achievements the longer the person may live.

The mind that has presence of mind at all times, and under all circumstances, is in perfect touch with the subconscious. In fact, if the subconscious is impressed every day, or better still, several times a day, to guide the outer mind so perfectly that the right step will always be taken at the right time, the conscious mind will intuitively know what to do to secure the best results from every circumstance, action or event.

When the powers of the subconscious are realized one's ideas will become much higher than before, and there will be a tendency to form ideals that cannot be realized with present states of development, but since the proper direction of the subconscious can promote development to any degree desired, it is not justice to self to remain content with the lesser while the greater is in view.

However, no desire should be entertained that cannot be fulfilled through the complete application of present ability, nor should present demands go beyond what present capacity is known to be.

The proper course is to first increase the capacity, then desire what the increased capacity has the power to fulfill.

The small mind must not desire the realization of ideals that the great mind alone can possibly make real; such a course would be a waste of time; it would be schooling oneself to desire only what cannot be secured, while doing nothing to so increase one's power that the object in view could easily be secured.

The subconscious can make the small mind great, as great as may be necessary to realize any ideal, but greatness does not come from dreaming about the ideal, nor from

The Great Within

concentrating upon that which is beyond our present capacity to produce.

Develop greatness by awakening the great within, and that power that can produce anything and realize anything will be gained.

Development is gradual and does not simply consist in the unfoldment of added power and capacity, but also in the full tangible use of that power and capacity.

To proceed orderly toward greatness direct the subconscious to express what may be necessary to take the next step forward; concentrate all the forces of mind upon that step, and do not scatter mind over realms and spheres that are beyond that step; do now what you are doing now, and be satisfied to realize what can be realized now.

Proceed with the second step in the same way and, likewise, with the innumerable steps that are to follow.

This is true progress; it is concentrating the whole of attention upon the present advancement, and there is no other advancement. To move forward we must advance in the present, and in the present only.

To move forward now is the purpose, and he who continues to move forward now will reach any goal he may have in view.

The subconscious should, therefore, be directed to turn all its superior powers upon the present forward movement and should be daily impressed to desire, not the ideals of the distant future, but the ideals that can be realized today.

This forward movement, however, should not be confined to anyone phase of existence; all things in the physical, the metaphysical and the spiritual nature of man should be developed simultaneously and perpetually.

The Great Within

It is the greatness of everything in man that gives man the greatness that *is* greatness, and the perpetual awakening of the great within will produce this greatness, because to the powers and the possibilities of the great within there is no limit, neither is there any end.

The Mind Cure

The Cure of Nervousness

IT IS a well-known fact that a considerable majority of the people in this country are addicted more or less to nervousness in one or more of its many forms; and as nervousness is the direct cause of all mental ills, and the indirect cause of a great many physical ills, organic as well as functional, there are few things that would be more important than that of finding a method through which health for the nerves could be secured. How to cure this malady has long been a problem. Medicine as a rule avails but little, and the various forms of other therapeutic systems reach but a limited number. It is therefore that the discovery of a remedy that could reach all cases, or nearly all cases, would easily be considered one of the most remarkable discoveries of the age. We may safely state that when people learn to keep the nervous system in perfect order there will be very few cases of insanity, if any, and physical diseases will be reduced at least one half. In addition to this, the power and capacity of mind will be increased to a very great degree. The majority of the fine minds in the world fail to do all they are capable of doing, because their talents are interfered with by nervous troubles of some kind, and these troubles not only tend to reduce the amount of mental energy, but also confuse the intellect and almost invariably misdirect the imagination. There is scarcely a mind living of exceptional ability or genius that is not addicted to nervousness of some form, and that any mind can do its best under such conditions is impossible.

The fact is, if nervousness were completely removed from the race more than half of the physical ills, and nearly all the mental ills, would be removed. The strength and endurance of the body would be increased remarkably, and the capacity of the mind would in most instances be practically doubled. That a perfect remedy for nervousness would therefore prove

The Mind Cure

a great boon, to say the least, is evident; and a remedy has been found that fulfills all the requirements, because from its very nature it simply cannot fail. This remedy will give health to the nerves in every case where it is used, and it is so simple that all who will apply it can do so successfully.

That this remedy will remove nervousness in every instance may seem impossible, but when we examine the nature of the remedy we find that its never-failing effectiveness lies in its power to remove the remote cause of what may be termed the immediate cause of this ailment. That condition of the system that we call nervousness comes from discord in the nerve fluid, or what may be called confused vibrations in the electromagnetic energies of the body. This is the immediate cause; but back of this cause there is a remote cause; that is, that condition that originally produces the confused vibrations in those energies. The nerve fluid we speak of may be termed human electricity, as its nature and actions correspond exactly with electrical currents, though, of course, it is much finer in quality than ordinary electricity. The human brain may accordingly be termed a dynamo, because those fine currents are generated there; and the nerves may be termed the wires that carry this fluid or electricity to every part of the body.

The functions of this nerve fluid are many. Every thought, state, condition or action produced in the mind is carried all through the body, over these nerves or wires, by the force of this fluid, and in return everything that is taking place throughout the system is conveyed to the brain by the same process. The nervous system is therefore a human telegraph system through which the mind is constantly kept informed concerning the events of its own world, and constantly giving directions with regard to what is to be done in every part of its world; and we can readily understand how false news or information can be transmitted, and how urgent news can be delayed in its passage, should these finer electrical currents be disturbed.

When a person is suffering from nervousness he is frequently deluded concerning the conditions of his system, the reason being that he is getting false news because the telegraph system is not in perfect order. In like manner, such a person may fail to get the exact facts concerning his conditions. There may be conditions brewing in his system of which he is not aware, because the news is lost on the way.

The same state of affairs, however, is frequently brought about by drugs. When you take drugs to stop pain, you do not remove the pain; you simply deaden the nerves so that the sensation or news of the pain cannot be carried to the brain. Occasionally such a process may be permissible, but if we interfere too much with the news-carrying function of the nervous system we will cripple it to such an extent that most of the sensations received will be false or magnified. When people imagine that they have ills that do not exist in their systems a crippled or perverted nervous system is generally the cause. They are getting false news about their own conditions, and they think it is true because it seems so real. Not everything is true, however, that seems real. The fact is that the more disturbance and perversion there is in the nervous system, the more real will also its false impressions appear to be; and the reason is that a disturbed nervous system is abnormally sensitive.

The Mind Cure

ANOTHER function of the nervous system is to transmit creative energy to every part of the body. Every cell in the system is constructed or repaired by creative energy, and this energy is conveyed by the nerve that enters the locality of that cell; consequently when the nervous system is out of order the process of repair, or cell construction, will be retarded in many places. When this process is interfered with, or the normal activities of the process are disturbed, the system will not only be left in bad repair, but false growths may be produced. When the creative forces are disturbed or misdirected in any part of the system they cannot continue in normal cell construction, but will in many instances begin to produce false cell construction. In this manner tumors, cancers, goiters, cataracts and all sorts of unnatural growths may originate.

And in this connection we should remember that practically all abnormal growths in the human system can be traced back to nervous conditions of some form. Perfect health for the nerves, therefore, if maintained all through life, would absolutely prevent all such unnatural growths in the human system. When the creative energies of the system continue in their normal activities no unnatural growth can possibly be formed, and to keep those energies in their normal state of action the nervous system must be in order; that is, every nerve must be in good health.

To go into details and outline fully the various effects that follow the actions of the nerve fluid would lead us into every phase of physiological psychology, and volumes would be required. It is not our purpose, however, to present a full treatise on this vast subject in this connection, but simply to present in the briefest manner possible the practical application of an effective remedy for the nerves. The various effects of the nerve fluid in all its functions will be right when the cause is right; and the cause is right when the vibrations of the electricity of the body are normal. To produce and maintain such normal vibrations must therefore be our purpose.

It has been stated that confusion among the vibrations of the nerve forces is the immediate cause of nervousness, and also that this force is generated in the brain; therefore, to find the cause of this confusion we must go to the brain, or rather to the mind. When we analyze the mind we find that every mental attitude produces a corresponding action in the brain and modifies to a degree the forces that are generated in the brain. As the brain is the dynamo generating nerve forces, or the electrical forces of the nervous system, it is evident that a disturbed mental state producing a corresponding action in the brain will confuse the vibrations of the forces generated in the brain during that particular state of mind.

To remove every confused attitude or disturbed state from the mind would, therefore, seem to be the perfect remedy; but this would constitute complete prevention, and not necessarily a remedy for effective use when actual nervousness was present. To prevent all nervousness one must become master over his thoughts and feelings and learn to create only those mental states that have a harmonious and wholesome effect upon the body; but this requires a thorough understanding of metaphysics, and also considerable time. In fact, it would necessarily be a steady growth. Besides, many of the disturbing mental states are in the subconscious, and cannot be removed until the entire mentality is renewed. To renew and perfect the subconscious as well as the conscious mind, should be the constant purpose of every person; but while he is changing his mind, his thought and his life, he must have some method to emancipate himself from those conditions, the adverse causes of which have not been removed.

The Mind Cure

Though we may be working for complete prevention, still while this work remains incomplete we need quick and ready remedies to remove the results of our mistakes, past or present. If we continue to work for complete prevention we will soon arrive at a place where our mistakes will be reduced to a minimum; but until we reach that state we must have remedies or methods that will remove the mistakes at once, so that no other ill effect may follow.

Then, again, there are thousands that have not the power to remain undisturbed in the midst of the world's confusion. They are constantly meeting discord, and need help present help to prevent such discord from producing detrimental effects. We therefore need effective remedies for the present, as well as a system of thinking and living through which we may gradually provide complete prevention.

The Mind Cure

WHEN we analyze the various conditions that disturb the nerves, we find that a disturbed state of mind is the remote cause, therefore peaceful states of mind must be the remedy. Disturbed states of mind will disturb the electric energies generated in the brain, and as these energies follow the nerves all through the system, the entire system will be in discord accordingly. On the other hand, peaceful states of mind will cause the electric energies generated in the brain to become calm, serene and harmonious, and as those energies are, so will be the entire nervous system. When we create only peaceful states of mind there will be no discord whatever in the system, and when discord disappears nervousness will also disappear.

When disturbed mental states have already been produced, they can be counteracted before they enter the nervous system, and their undesirable effects avoided. The process is simple, and may be applied effectually by anyone. In the first place, life and thought should be made as calm, serene and peaceful as possible; and, secondly, every cause of disturbance or nervousness, either acute or chronic, conscious or subconscious, should be removed by cultivating serenity and peace. While the nerve force is still in the brain you can modify its vibrations by changing the actions in the mind, but after this force has entered the spinal cord it will continue in its original vibrations until it has permeated the system. This force, therefore, must be acted upon before it enters the spinal cord, and since it responds readily to every action of mind, a complete change can be made if produced in the proper place.

To reach the energies of the brain directly, the mind should act upon the brain center, a point exactly midway between the opening of the ears. Draw an imaginary line from ear to ear through your brain, and divide that line in the center. At this point you will find the region of the brain center. In the region of the brain center the energy or nerve force that has been generated in the brain is transferred to the spinal cord, from whence it goes to every part of the system. To change the vibrations of this force, therefore, before it enters the spinal cord, the mind must act upon the brain center, and must produce through that action the very condition that is desired in the nervous system as a whole. That state of mind that is impressed upon the brain center will cause all the nerve forces coming from the brain to be identical with the mental state itself, both in nature and action, therefore to impress upon the brain center a mental state of perfect harmony, calmness and poise, will cause the nerve force as it proceeds from the brain to become calm, harmonious and poised, and will accordingly convey calmness, harmony and poise to every part of the system.

When these calm nerve currents begin to pass through the system, every form of nervousness will begin to disappear, and relief will be felt at once. All weak actions of the heart will also cease and normal action be secured, because all heart troubles, practically, come from disturbances in the nervous system. To concentrate upon the brain center in the attitude of peace will cause the heart to become normal in its actions in a few moments, and if this method is employed several times every day for five or ten minutes, what is usually spoken of as heart disease will disappear without giving the least thought or attention to the heart itself.

To apply this method perfectly, turn your attention upon the brain center and concentrate gently upon this point while you are thinking calmly but deeply of poise, peace, serenity and harmony. Try to feel at the time that everything at the brain center is still, perfectly still; that all is quiet, easy and at rest. And here we should remember that while this method is being employed we should not think of mind or body in the least, but all thought should be directed upon that peaceful state that we imagine is being produced at the brain center. If you can focus your whole attention upon the brain center at the time and feel that all the energies of mind and brain are moving gently toward the brain center, you are going to realize perfect harmony throughout your system, even in a few seconds. This peaceful state of mind will soon penetrate the entire region of the brain center, and all the energies that are passing from the brain to the spinal cord, and thence to the nervous system, will change and become calm and serene, as that condition is at the brain center through which those energies always pass. And as these are the only energies that act directly through the nervous system, all nervousness must disappear when those energies themselves become serene.

When this method is being applied it is best to be comfortably seated, or better still, to lie down with the mind and body relaxed, eyes closed, and all attention withdrawn from outer things. Then have but one purpose in view to penetrate the brain center with a mental life of absolute peace and calm. The more quietly and the more easily you go about this practice, the better you will succeed; and to try to draw gently the finer mental forces toward the brain center as you think of the finer forces of your mind, will aid remarkably in producing immediate results. It is well to breathe deeply, but gently, during the exercise, which may be continued for five or ten minutes, and repeated several times every day. To combine physical breathing with this exercise, in any particular manner, will be found very helpful, and to this end proceed as follows: While you inhale physically, try to draw the finer forces of mind and brain toward the brain center, and while you exhale physically, try to feel that those finer forces are moving with calmness and peace down through your body toward the feet. To combine physical breathing with what might be called inhalation and exhalation of the finer forces of the mind will, when carried out effectually, be found to be a method of incalculable value in all conditions of nervousness or mental disturbance. Everyone, therefore, will find it profitable to practice this method until it can be carried out to perfection. When results begin to appear, an inner comfort will be felt that is delightful, and every nerve in the system will be quiet.

In this connection it is well to remember that the quiet nerve is the only nerve that is doing its work properly. Whenever you feel excited, agitated or disturbed, apply this method and immediately harmony will be restored, thus preventing both ills and mistakes. It will compose the system, restore the heart to its normal action, and give the creative energies that perfect poise that is so necessary to the keeping of the system in purity and repair. This method will also remove weariness and the tired feeling, because both mind and body are invariably recharged with energy when they are placed in perfect poise. When this method is employed daily and properly nervousness in every form will disappear, perfect health for the nerves will be secured, and the system will be placed in a higher degree of harmony a state that is most valuable in the promotion of physical or mental development.

To try to feel the finer essence or life of mind while concentrating in poise upon the brain center is very important, because when the finer life is felt the subconscious will be impressed; and when perfect peace is conveyed to the subconscious the good work is done. When the subconscious becomes calm and serene in all its actions every atom in the system will work in perfect harmony, and every action, no matter how rapid or how strong, will be absolutely calm and serene.

The Mind Cure

AN important essential in the cure of nervousness is to remove the tendency to think or act unconsciously. Unconscious action that is, doing one thing while thinking about something else will produce a divided attention, and a divided attention leads to a decrease in the power of self-control. So long as the attitude of self-possession and self-control is perfect, nervousness will be impossible, but the moment the mind begins to lose its hold upon the various functions of the system, nervousness will begin.

What is called nervousness is nothing but confused action among the nerve energies, and as the mind is the original cause of every action that takes place in the human system, confused action anywhere in the system must come originally from confused mental action. The fundamental cause of confused mental action is divided attention, and divided attention comes from having several things on the mind at once.

One thing at a time should be the law. You may have a thousand duties to perform every day, but give direct attention to only one at a time. Train yourself to do this, and you will be absolutely free from nervousness all your life. A breakdown in the nervous system does not come from overwork, but from the scattering of your forces, and it is only through the dividing of your attention that your forces can be scattered. The dividing of attention, however, may be produced in a number of ways. To try to do too many things at once is one cause; living a complex life is another cause; though the principal cause is usually found in the reckless use of the imagination.

The majority do not know how to apply the imagination constructively, and therefore its actions are, as a rule, helter-skelter. The result is confused mental action, to be followed later by confused actions among the nerve forces. The same is true in all forms of life and thought where imagination is carried off, so to speak, into all sorts of abnormal states through excitement or various forms of mental intoxication. Mental confusion is the result, and when the forces of the mind are going helter-skelter the forces of the nerves will do the same, because the nervous system is directly connected with the brain in general, as with every individual action that takes place in the brain.

When the energy of the system runs low every function of body or mind, including the imagination, is crippled to a degree in its effort to continue normal actions. The result is abnormal or confused action, which may be followed by sickness of some kind, or by a nervous breakdown; but the original cause of a lack of energy in the system is not always physical. Physical dissipation, burning the candle at both ends, will reduce the energy of the body; and there is also such a thing as mental dissipation, some of the chief elements of which are anger, worry, excitement, mental depression, despondency, discouragement, reckless thinking and reckless imagination. Energy may therefore be wasted, both physically and mentally, but every action of waste comes originally from the mind, because the body can do nothing unless the mind originates the action. To remove the cause of nervousness, there are two factors to be considered. First, the vital energy of the system must be kept full and strong at all times. When vitality is insufficient, normal action becomes impossible. To cease normal action is to begin abnormal action.

Abnormal action leads to confused action, and confused action leads to nervousness. Second, mental disorder in all its forms must be removed completely; and this is accomplished by removing the habit of dividing attention. In brief, to remove the cause of nervousness, train yourself to give your whole attention now to whatever you may be thinking of or doing now, and so think and live that your system will be brimful of energy at all times. When you are constantly full of vital energy, and are constantly using your energy in the actions of harmony, poise and self-possession, you will never be nervous. Abundance of power in all your actions, and perfect poise in all your actions these are the two secrets.

The Mind Cure

TO secure abundance of power, you need not generate more than you are generating now. All that is necessary is to prevent what you are generating from being wasted. In brief, learn to use all your present energy so that all waste may be avoided completely. The power that is wasted is lost, but the power that is used produces increase. The power we use today will reappear in the system tomorrow, because everything that is properly used is like a seed sown in rich soil; it will reproduce itself, and will not only reappear with the original amount, but with more.

The first essential in the proper use of the power we possess is to have some definite purpose in view for every thought and action, and to give that purpose our undivided attention. When we think, we should think with a purpose, and should think of only one thing at a time. In that way all the power of our thought is put to work, and none of it is wasted. In this connection it is well to remember, and to repeat again, that weariness comes from the waste of power; never from power that is put to work. Power that is put to work reproduces itself, therefore no loss of power can follow; and it is only when power is lost that weariness can be felt in the system.

When you work, do not think of the next step or try to plan for the next step while the work of the first is being finished. Take special moments for laying new plans. In this way you will not only work out the best plans, but you will avoid dividing your attention or confusing your mind. Do not let your head run faster than your feet; and do not live mentally in the future while you are working in the present. Where the body lives, the mind should live also, and the energies of both should work together in building up the life of the present moment.

The Mind Cure

When you read, do not try to read the second paragraph before you are through with the first, and do not skim over an article with a view of getting the substance out of it in one-tenth of the time it takes to read it. The habit of skimming over things is one of the worst mental habits in the world, and should be eliminated completely. We may think we gain time by skimming over things, but we lose energy and power, as well as mental brilliancy, and in the end it is all loss and no gain.

In your living, avoid the same mistake. Do not try to get all there is in life by hurrying through life. The majority, however, are addicted to this habit, but it leads directly to nervousness, and is the direct cause of more than ninety per cent of the nervous breakdowns that are produced. In the meantime, this same habit brings much destruction, depression and unhappiness. Learn to live in the present. Plan for the future during special moments selected for that purpose, but refuse absolutely to live in the future. Refuse to do in your mind today what you expect to do in the reality tomorrow. Thousands have this habit. In consequence their minds are nearly always confused, while they scatter their forces continually. If you are going to take a journey tomorrow, make your plans today, but do not take that journey a score of times in your mind today; or, if you are going to undertake something special tomorrow, get good and ready today, but do not mentally pass through the details of that work today.

Get ready the bricks for the building of tomorrow, but do not lay the bricks in your mind today. Never do with your mind today what you are to do with your hands tomorrow. Do not live over in your mind in the present the experiences you passed through in the past, or the experience you expect to pass through in the future. Such a practice will scatter your forces and divide your attention. The result will be

The Mind Cure

confused mental action, to be followed by confused nervous action. This practice will also decrease your power of concentration; and without concentration we can accomplish nothing. The peaceful contemplation, however, of past joys or expected future joys, will produce nothing but good effects, provided we do nothing else while we indulge in such contemplation. In fact, to give special moments to such contemplation every day will prove beneficial. It matters not what we may be thinking about during our spare moments whether it be the past, the present, or the future so the thought is pleasant and attention is undivided.

To prevent completely, or permanently cure, nervousness, therefore, we should always bear these two things in mind: To avoid divided attention and to avoid the energy of the system running low. In other words, so live and think that your system will be brimful of energy at all times, and give your whole attention now to whatever you may be thinking of or doing now.

The Mind Cure

THE following exercises or methods may be employed most profitably, both in the prevention and in the cure of nervousness; and where faithful application is continued, the most perfect results will positively be secured: Place yourself in a calm attitude for a few minutes several times every day. See how quiet you can be in mind and body during those moments, and see how fully you can realize the deep stillness of your entire nature. By making it a practice to be deeply quiet for a few minutes several times a day, you can check completely any tendency toward nervousness. Besides, those moments will serve to recuperate your system, and you can do more and better work during any given period of time.

During those quiet moments, relax mind and body completely. Let go of every muscle and every thought. Just be still, and think only of how delightful it feels to be perfectly still.

Aim to increase and deepen your consciousness of harmony. Think of the real meaning of harmony at frequent intervals, and try to inwardly feel that real harmony. In other words, make it a practice to turn your attention upon the idea of harmony itself, with a view of getting your system into the very life or soul of perfect harmony. You will soon begin to feel more harmonious, because we always tend to develop in ourselves every state or condition to which we give constant thought and attention. Mentally see yourself calm. Whenever you think of yourself, think of yourself as being calm, masterful and self-possessed. Every mental picture that you may form of yourself should appear in the attitude of calmness, and whenever you think of yourself as being in any position in which you expect to be placed, picture yourself as being calm and poised while in that position. You thus produce a tendency toward calmness, and you are daily becoming more and more serene and self-possessed until you place yourself in that masterful attitude that is both deeply peaceful and immensely strong.

Whenever you feel deeply, proceed at once to feel peaceful. You thus impress peace, harmony and calmness upon the subconscious mind; and the more you impress peace upon the subconscious the more peaceful you will feel throughout your interior nature. The undercurrents of your life will become harmonious and serene in their actions. You will feel peaceful and calm on the inside, in the depths of your real life and thought; and it is the man who feels calm and serene in the depths of his interior nature who also feels the greater power of his interior nature. Such a man is strong and masterful. Such a man has real will power. Such a man has full possession of himself all that is in himself; and he has not only gained the power to be well, but the power to do things worthwhile. Always remember the great law: The deeper your consciousness of peace the greater your possession of power.

Refuse to be sensitive. Never say that you are sensitive. Never think that you are sensitive. When you are on the verge of feeling hurt, say to yourself that you can stand anything, and resolve to make good in that respect. Refuse to be offended at anything. Refuse to stoop to the petty position of being insulted, and refuse to accept any form of indignity that may be intended for you. Have too much respect for your nervous system to feel badly about anything that may be said or done, and have too much good sense to waste energy brooding over troubles when you know that that same energy, if put to good use, could put all your troubles to flight.

Never dwell mentally on anything that is unpleasant. To do so is to rob your nervous system of its very life. To brood over misfortune, trouble or loss is to steal energy and life from the nerves and organs of your body for no other purpose than to keep alive the ugly and distressing memories that those misfortunes have impressed upon your mind. When you do this, you are simply starving your nervous system in order that you may perpetuate the existence of mental monsters. The result will be nervousness, then nervous breakdowns, and in many instances the loss of mind or life. But all of this can easily be prevented. Refuse absolutely to remember the unpleasantness of the past or dwell on the dark side of anything that may exist in the present. Turn your attention at once to the richer and greater possibilities that every experience may contain, and enter positively into the very spirit of those possibilities. You will soon realize that your gain is greater than your loss, and that you have the power in the coming days to multiply this gain any number of times.

Never think of nerves. Never say that you are nervous, and never give conscious thought to any condition that may exist anywhere in your system. When you feel that something is wrong proceed to make it right, and the less you think of the wrong, or the organ in which the wrong may exist, the better. Think of your entire body as being wholesome all the way through, and live constantly in the life, the health and the strength of that thought. When you wish to change physical conditions, do not act mentally upon the physical body, and do not concentrate attention upon physical organs. The course to pursue is to produce the desired cause in the subconscious mind, and the desired effect will shortly appear in the physical personality. Do not permit for a moment any form of the high-strung attitude of mind. If you are addicted to this habit or tendency, cultivate relaxed calmness by frequently letting your whole system go into the feeling of deep calmness. To accomplish this, try to picture the inner world of deep calmness in which you live, and move, and have your being. Then simply let yourself go into the serene life and deeper soul calmness of this world. Also employ the special method given in the first part of this lesson whenever your nerves are on the verge of being strung up. That method will invariably produce relaxation, and besides, is quieting, soothing and recuperative to an exceptional degree.

Cultivate poise, wholesome mental states, and be deeply joyous at all times; but let your joy be of that nature that tends to produce a peaceful contentment. Avoid joyous attitudes that tend to excite the nerves, or that may produce an overwrought condition of mind. It is the deep, calm happiness, the happiness that becomes deeper and sweeter, as well as more peaceful, the longer it is enjoyed, that we should seek under every circumstance. This form of happiness cure should be taken every hour. Then be at peace with all things. Take plenty of sleep, and live in faith that all things are working together for greater and greater good.

The Mind Cure

Good Health for the Mind

TO secure and maintain perfect health and wholeness of mind, these important facts should be carefully considered:

1. In the prevention and cure of ailments that are almost wholly mental in their nature, there are two tendencies in particular that must be avoided, and these are the tendency to deplete the energies of the mind through the wrong use of mental action, and the tendency to intensify, under certain strained circumstances, the actions of those energies.

2. When the life and the energy of the mind is weakened to a point where there is not enough power to carry on normal thinking, the mind ceases to a degree to function according to its true nature, consciousness becomes so dull that no experience is correctly interpreted, and those mental conceptions that are formed at the time are mostly illusions. It requires energy to think and know, just the same as it requires energy to walk or move physically. When the body loses too much energy it becomes too weak to walk; and when the mind loses too much energy it becomes too weak to think. But inability to walk is not always produced by a lack of physical energy; nor is inability to think clearly always produced by mental weakness.

3. The mind may be full of power, but when that power is abnormally intensified we find that harmonious and consecutive mental actions are interfered with, and clear thinking becomes impossible. Such a mind usually thinks a good deal, and is constantly in a worked-up condition; but the thinking will be disconnected, and false beliefs and ideas, and even hallucinations of every description, may result.

4. A close study of those ills that are mental in their nature proves clearly that when overworked conditions and worked-up conditions are avoided the mind will never become abnormal, unbalanced or disturbed. Overworked conditions, however, do not come solely from too much mental exertion; but may also come from worry, depression, grief, fear, anxiety, and the like. These states of mind deplete the mental forces by using up energy in destructive thinking, while ordinary mental work consumes energy in performing what may be useful. Occasionally a person may work the mind so hard that too much energy is consumed, and we may have in such cases mental troubles coming directly from overwork. But such cases are very rare, as by far the greater number comes from worry and anxiety. An hour's worry will use up more mental energy than ten hours of steady brain work; and the same is true of fear, grief, depression and similar wrong mental states. It is usually the worry that goes with the work that makes a person feel exhausted after the work; and there are few who do not worry about something while at work; but this is a habit that not only can be but should be overcome completely.

5. When a person studies he imagines that hard study is wearing on the mind, and accordingly the mind is used up more or less during such work; but he is mistaken in his idea. Study will use up a certain amount of mental energy, but not enough, even after many hours of continued study, to produce mental weariness. It is the anxiety that most students combine with their study that wears on the mind. When study is taken up for a certain purpose, the student is usually overanxious to fulfill that purpose, and frequently there is fear lest failure should come, or depression on account of mistakes that already have been made. All of these misuses of the mind exhaust the mind so that the study cannot be carried out with satisfaction, while the study itself hardly ever exhausts or wearies the mind.

The Mind Cure

6. To prevent the mind from becoming weak we should establish faith in the place of worry, fear and anxiety. That mind that dwells, thinks and works in faith will always be strong. This is one of those great truths that we should always remember; and to live in that truth is to provide the mind with a protection that has no equal.

7. Worked-up conditions of mind come principally from anger, excitement, intense action of mind or body, or from nervous rush; though any forceful mental action or any strained action will produce the same condition. In this condition the mind is strung up, so to speak, and throws its energies out of their normal spheres. They are therefore misdirected and finally lost, but on their way to complete loss they usually produce all sorts of illusions, and this accounts for the fact that a mind that is out of harmony with itself usually produces illusions along several lines without being conscious of doing so.

8. When the mind dwells too much on one isolated subject, or is forced too long in one direction, a similar condition is produced, and mental equilibrium is lost. In this condition one part of the mind will be overworked, while the other parts will become practically dormant. The overworked part, therefore, will be unable to think clearly on account of its exhausted or intensified condition, while the dormant parts will be unable to think clearly on account of their state of inactivity. The result will be that the various states of mind produced at the time will be wrong, and wrong states invariably lead to ill health, both of mind and body.

9. To avoid the tendency to apply the mind too much in anyone direction, everyone should make it a habit to engage in what may be called mental variety; that is, there should be change of mental action, mental work, and interest at frequent intervals. This practice is most important when the system is more or less in nervous conditions. During such conditions sensitiveness is very keen, and every deeply-formed impression will tend to carry the mind away along any line that may be indicated by that impression. At such times, therefore, the tendency to cause the mind to act in one direction only is very marked, and should be avoided completely at the very outset. Whenever a tendency is felt to move in anyone mental direction exclusively, attention should be turned at once upon something else, so as to call into action the other parts of the mind, as the mind will usually return to wholesome action when every part of it becomes active. It is a splendid practice, in this connection, to study all kinds of subjects that have worth, in addition to what may engage one's attention in his vocation, and also to exercise all the functions of body, mind and soul as completely and harmoniously as possible.

10. All forms of fanaticism and prolonged actions of enthusiasm must be avoided completely, and no part of the mind should be permitted to run in a groove. It is a well-known fact that whenever anyone begins to become a fanatic, his mind becomes more or less unbalanced, and he becomes unable to see more than one side of any subject that he may consider. When this condition is prolonged it leads to intense mental action along a single line, which will finally produce the conditions just mentioned. A fanatical mind is never a healthy mind, and is wrong on nearly all subjects, as well as being unwholesome in most of its usual mental states. As soon as a tendency to isolate action of mind is discovered in any part of thought or thinking, a new experience should be sought at once; and when we find ourselves completely absorbed in certain places, persons or things, we should immediately proceed to look for superior qualities in other things.

11. To prevent worked-up or overwrought conditions of mind it is necessary to cultivate perfect poise. All, therefore, who have a tendency to use the mind in such ways should proceed at once to acquire poise. In a few minutes, or even in much less time, the normal action of mind and body will be restored perfectly, and a great deal of energy will be added both to physical and mental action.

12. The mind must never permit itself to go down into any of the depressed states of feeling, as such a tendency invariably leads to mental ill health. To overcome this tendency, a sunny disposition should be cultivated, and the habit of fixing attention on the larger, the better, the superior, and the ideal in all things should be made a permanent factor in all lines of thinking. The fact that cheerfulness and ascending attitudes of mind add a great deal of power both to mind and body, is important; and it is well to remember in this connection that a cheerful, optimistic, ascending state of mind can be made so strong that no experience we may encounter can possibly make us depressed or discouraged. In connection with this phase of the study we shall find it profitable to refer to what was stated on mental tendencies in a previous lesson.

13. The importance of avoiding the downward tendency of the mind will be realized when we understand that all depressing conditions invariably take the mind down nearer to that point where clear thinking becomes impossible; and, conversely, that all ascending or elevating attitudes of mind invariably cause the mind to act in those higher and clearer realms of thinking where all thinking functions, so to speak, in a world of mental light. In other words, the higher the mind ascends in conscious action the more light it will receive on any thought, and the clearer will all thinking become, accordingly.

14. To eliminate adverse conditions of the mind the first essential is to become mentally quiet, and the second essential is to provide more life and energy for the entire nervous system. To make the mind quiet the special method given for nervousness in the preceding lesson should be employed; and to provide more life and energy for the mind and nervous system, the various energies of the mind should be redirected so that they may proceed along new lines. When the energies of the mind proceed along new lines they will call into action other parts of the mind, and consequently bring forth the dormant mental power. The full power of the mind will thereby be restored in a short time, and perfect health and wholeness of mind will invariably follow.

The Mind Cure

The Cure of Despondency

THE fields and the gardens in the without require sunshine before they can bring forth their richness and beauty, and it is the same with the gardens of the wonderful within. Recent discoveries in psychology have revealed the fact that no mental talent or faculty can grow to any satisfaction unless the mind realizes an abundance of brightness and joy. There must be sunshine in the mind if the mind is to develop, and so long as this mental sunshine is continuous, development will be continuous provided the mental soil is made rich through rich thought, and well cultivated by being and doing. Rich thought, however, is not out of the reach of the average mind, neither is the effort to be and to do lacking among the majority; but the art of living continuously in a world of mental sunshine that is something that is lacking almost everywhere. But it is a lack that must be supplied before we can become and achieve as we should.

To be happy is profitable. This is one of the new thoughts of the new age, and it will prove a great thought to all who receive it in the right frame of mind. To cultivate cheerfulness is just as necessary as to cultivate ability and skill. So, therefore, the prevention or cure of despondency is just as important as the prevention or cure of any physical disease. The despondent mind is a sick mind, and a sick mind is more of an obstacle to human welfare than a sick body. For this reason no one can afford to live on any other side than the sunny side. All other sides mean sickness, failure and premature death. If our object in life is progress, growth, advancement and perpetual increase we must eliminate despondency in all its phases, and permanently establish in its place a state of perpetual joy. Happiness is the normal state of mind. When your mind is in perfect health it is always happy. In fact, a healthy mind cannot be otherwise than happy. Therefore, when you are not happy your mind is sick and needs attention. And it needs attention, first, because a sick mind may produce both moral and physical disease; and second, because a sick mind cannot do its work properly. Thousands of cases of intemperance and crime can be traced to sick or disappointed minds. And tens of thousands of failures had their beginnings in the same way. To overcome despondency, therefore, and all phases of unhappiness is a matter of the greatest importance.

When we study the subject closely we find that there are two kinds of despondency, each one having its own causes and requiring its own special remedies. The first of these will require but little attention, as it can hardly be called a mental ailment, being rather a symptom of disordered thoughts and wrong viewpoints. It usually rises from unpleasant experience such as disappointments from failure or defeat, and is therefore easily removed by training the mind to count everything joy, and by resolving to go in to win, no matter what present conditions may indicate.

When we look at life from the higher viewpoint, from the viewpoint of the real greatness of man, we will lose neither hope nor courage though we fail repeatedly. From this viewpoint we discover that every failure can be made a steppingstone to success, and we proceed to use failure in that way whenever it appears. If we are to use failure in this way, however, we must never permit ourselves to fall into despair, but must meet every occasion in the attitude of complete self-mastery. Every failure is simply valuable energy gone astray, and if we approach this misdirected energy in the right attitude we can regain its possession and cause it to work for our advantage.

Therefore, those forces in our present circumstances that may seem to be destructive can be changed and made constructive. The reason why is simple. If we can change the direction of our forces or circumstances by wrong action we can also change the direction of those forces through right action, and thus cause those forces to work according to our purpose and plan. In consequence, when failure comes we should not give up in despair, but should cheerfully and masterfully gather together the scattered forces and redirect them toward the construction of greater success than we ever knew before. The man who knows that his possibilities are unlimited will never give up to defeat, and therefore will never become despondent. He knows that he will win sooner or later if he continues as he has begun. And he also knows that every great difficulty that he overcomes invariably means added power to the victor. Such a mind can never be disappointed even though he should lose and fail in many places. He knows that he has destiny in his own hands and must inevitably attain whatever he has in view.

When we understand metaphysical laws we know that we cannot afford to become disappointed at any time, no matter how wrong things may seem to go, for the fact is that if we continue to be cheerful, hopeful and full of faith we are in that attitude through which we can apply our powers and talents successfully in causing all things to go right. In consequence, the despondency that comes from failure or defeat can easily be overcome or prevented by looking at life from the higher point of view. When we know our own possibilities and are constantly learning more thoroughly how to master and control our fate we shall never mind a few reverses. They are but temporary, and under the hand of the mind that knows, will soon give way to order, advancement and greater achievement. We may therefore pass this form of despondency without further consideration, knowing that the mind who understands his powers will never get sad or depressed from defeat any more.

The Mind Cure

THE second form of despondency is actually a mental disease, and must be dealt with as such. It is produced in various ways and at times comes from the conditions mentioned above. As a rule, however, it originates in other ways. People have chronic despondency who have everything that heart can wish for, and who never knew disappointment or defeat. Sometimes this form of despondency is called melancholy and is the principal cause of insanity. Here it is well to remember that no mind can ever become insane that is always happy a great truth that should be well considered and thoroughly applied under every circumstance.

The chief causes of chronic despondency are as follows: First, exhaustion of nerve force or mental vitality; second, the misdirection of the emotions; third, disturbance in the chief nerve centers, especially the solar plexus; and fourth, disordered physical activities. The first cause is easily prevented, and the conditions that arise from this cause can be removed through very simple methods. There is usually sufficient vitality generated in the human system to supply all requirements, and unless this vitality is misused there will be no exhaustion whatever of mind or body. But discord, worry, anger, fear and similar states of mind tend to waste vital energy and, consequently, may bring about exhaustion. Regular work, however, will never produce this condition, as it has been conclusively demonstrated that work alone never does exhaust the vital forces of the human system. Despondency from exhausted vitality comes suddenly as a rule, and even when everything in your life seems conducive to harmony and joy. Under such circumstances the experience is mysterious. You can find no definite cause. Everything seems all right in your world, but you feel all wrong, and the conditions may last for hours. The temptation to seek remedies among stimulants is very strong at such times, and it is a well-known fact that nervous exhaustion has been the original cause of many a life gone wrong through the liquor habit. Instead of seeking artificial remedies, however, we should look for the cause and try to remove it directly.

When you feel fagged out, so to speak, in mind or body, you may know that the cause is low vitality. The first step to take when you make this discovery is to practice deep, full breathing, as there is nothing that will increase the vital forces so readily as right breathing.

And by right breathing we mean breathing that is deep, full and gentle, the entire chest being employed in the exercise. The average person, however, employs only the upper half of the lungs while breathing, thereby making himself liable to ailments in that part of his body, as well as tending to reduce the regular supply of vital energy. The simple science of right breathing is to breathe with the entire chest and to make all breathing orderly. When you feel the vital energies of the system running low breathe more, and if you have the opportunity to be perfectly quiet for a few minutes, trying at the time to realize that you are the vital center about which all the forces in your world tend to accumulate. And this is true. You are a vital center of all the elements and forces in your world, and when you concentrate your attention upon yourself as a vital center of life, you begin to accumulate more life until you are actually filled with more energy than you ever felt before. To hold yourself in this attitude for a few moments is to recharge your system, and instead of feeling depressed you will soon begin to feel happier and better than you have felt for a long time. When concentrating upon yourself as a living center, hold yourself in perfect poise, realizing that you live and move and have your being in an infinite sea of life; then gently desire to accumulate all the energy you can appropriate and remain silent for a few minutes in that attitude.

The results will be far beyond your expectations. A number of despondent states are produced by misdirected emotions, and the chief cause of misdirected emotions is found in the practice of entertaining desires that cannot be realized at the present moment. When energies accumulate in certain parts of the human system, where they cannot be employed at the time, the effect is always disturbing and depressing upon the nervous system, which in turn produces mental despondency; in other words, whenever unused forces accumulate anywhere they tend to aggravate the nerves in that region of mind or body, and this disturbance perverts the feelings and the emotions. So long as there is a strong tendency to express energy of any kind in any direction, a great deal of energy will move in that direction, and if it is denied expression it will accumulate, and this accumulation will produce abnormal conditions in that part of mind or body, the reaction of which always produces a disagreeable feeling in mind.

To prevent this we must learn to entertain only such desires as can be realized at the present time, and also learn how to transmute our energies so that all that energy that cannot be employed in certain functions at the time may be drawn into other functions where more energy can be used to advantage. We should never permit the existence of a desire that cannot be realized at the time. When such desires arise we should turn our attention at once to something else. This turning of attention will tend to draw the energy connected with that desire toward other parts of the system where practical use can be realized. In this connection a few illustrations will be found valuable. If you cannot honestly satisfy your desire for elegant clothes, change that desire and desire a beautiful soul instead. If you cannot afford to satisfy your desire for rich food, train yourself to desire rich thoughts instead. If you cannot at present satisfy your desire for physical progeny, turn your attention upon the mind and create great talent instead. Any number of similar illustrations can be given to bring out the idea intended, and all who will apply this idea will find it an easy matter to prevent all this physical and mental disturbance that may arise in the system when our energies are not permitted to express themselves along the original channels.

In gaining more perfect control over the energies of our system so that we can apply them whenever we may like, we should proceed in the realization of the fact that all energy, whether physical or mental, can be drawn into any organ, any function, or any faculty where we may need extra energy at the time; and as that realization becomes strong and vivid we shall find that a mere desire to cause our energy to accumulate in any particular part of mind or body where present action is taking place will cause all the surplus energy of the system to flow directly toward that place without delay.

The Mind Cure

ANOTHER cause of misdirected emotion is found in uncontrolled feelings. When we permit our feelings of joy to become what may be called hysterical ecstasy or permit our enthusiasm to take us off from our feet, we are preparing the way for a great fall of the mind. Despondency will follow. Every feeling and every joy must be held in poise, and enthusiasm has its greatest power when perfectly controlled. That form of enthusiasm that runs away from people invariably produces abnormal states of mind, and this is one thing we must do our best to avoid. Whenever a certain emotional state through lack of control goes so far in a certain direction that it usurps the whole attention of mind, more energy will accumulate in that place than can be used. This accumulation will depress the mind because it becomes a burden, while those other parts of mentality that have been depleted will experience a feeling of emptiness; and here you find the reason why you feel as if you had neither force, ability, nor ambition whenever you feel depressed.

When we are never overjoyed nor over-enthused, when we never permit the existence of desires that can never be satisfied, and when we never permit any feeling to go beyond our control, we shall prevent entirely all depression that may arise from the misuse of emotions. But should despondency come from any source whatever we can remedy the matter in a few minutes by concentrating attention upon the brain center as outlined in the remedy for nervousness in a previous lesson, proceeding at the time to practice deep and full breathing. Through these methods we shall restore the equilibrium in the nervous system and at the same time increase the vital energy all through the system. When we come to consider those forms of despondency that arise from a disturbed solar plexus we are face to face with a problem that sometimes appears to be mysterious, the reason being that the solar plexus is considered by many to be the connecting link between the physical and the metaphysical sides of the human system.

Those who accept this idea naturally believe that a great deal of extra energy would be liberated if the solar plexus were made more active, but this is not true. The fact is that the less conscious attention we give to the solar plexus the better. Disturbances that arise in the solar plexus invariably come from imperfect digestion, and when the solar plexus is disturbed it tends invariably to disturb all our feelings, both physical and mental. We find, therefore, that despondency coming in this way has its original cause in an imperfect digestion.

For this reason we shall find that some of the most severe cases of despondency are not premonitions of terrible disasters near at hand, as many people sometimes think; but have no other source than the stomach. In fact, it can be safely stated that more than three-fourths of the cases of despondency have their origin in a poor digestion. A good digestion, therefore, especially if reinforced with a well-poised harmonious nervous system, will prevent the larger part of the despondency that may come to the average individual. And knowing this, we realize the folly of taking despondency with so much seriousness. If we would make it a practice instead to look upon those conditions as of no particular moment, and then proceed to place our digestion in order, we should go very far toward restoring mental health and wholeness for all time.

Those cases of despondency that come from physical disturbance are found only among people who have strong psychical tendencies, but who do not know how to use those new forces that have arisen in their deeper mental life. Whenever a new power is awakened the knowledge of how to use it should be at hand, and there will be no serious mistakes in this application. This being true, no one should attempt to use a new power, whatever it may be, until well informed as to its nature and right use. That form of despondency, however, that comes through psychical disturbance is usually of a serious nature, and everything possible should be done to prevent it completely. To prevent this condition there is but one safe course to follow, and that is to have nothing whatever to do with psychical phenomena or psychical experience until you understand fully the psychological and metaphysical laws that underlie the phenomena, or until you have attained perfect mastery over yourself. To a great many minds, however, these requirements may seem too stringent. In fact, if one should comply with these requirements it would be impossible for anyone to engage in psychical research; and though this is practically true, it is also true that most of us will find it greatly to our advantage to give no attention to psychical research whatever. The subject of despondency, however, is one that should receive our best attention, and every method that we can find, in addition to those presented above, should be employed if such methods will remove the tendency of the mind to become depressed. We know that the growing mind as well as the healthy mind needs continuous sunshine, and knowing this we shall certainly do our best to provide this sunshine under every circumstance. Our object is not only health, but the power to do greater things in the world. And as the realization of both of these objects demands a growing mind, we shall find it most profitable to provide that mental sunshine that can cause mental growth to be continuous.

The Mind Cure

The Prevention of Mental Depression

IN addition to what has been said on this subject in preceding pages, we find two special causes that frequently result in chronic mental depression. The first cause is found in the presence of certain adverse mental states that have become so deep-seated that they affect the subconscious life, and the second cause is found in the presence of awakened subconscious forces that cannot find a full and natural expression.

There is many a person who is suffering from mental depression simply because the genius within him is trying to force itself out in tangible action, but cannot produce such action on account of the inharmony existing between the objective and the subjective states of mind. When there is a great deal of power within that wants to act, but cannot find an opportunity to act, an unnatural pressure will be produced in various parts of the mentality, and mental depression will usually result. This depression, involving more or less gloom, disappointment and even despair, may continue for years, and this accounts for the fact that there is many a genius, or possible genius, who is unhappy almost constantly. The outer mind of the average person has not been trained to respond to the power and the genius of the subconscious. Therefore, the genius within is held in prison, so to speak. It is not permitted to come out and act. It is confined behind the bars of objective limitations and refuses to reconcile itself to such a fate. In some minds the power within, not being very active, is seldom felt, while in others the powers of the great within are constantly clamoring for freedom and expression.

It is this that produces unrest, dissatisfaction, mental depression and that seemingly hopeless longing for the ideal that sensitive minds find so difficult to bear. When the objective mind is placed in such a complete harmony with the subconscious that the power of the within can come forth and do what it wants to do, we have the peace that passes understanding, the harmony that touches the very ecstasy of the soul, and the joy that cannot be measured. At such moments the individual is in the now, all that he can be in the now, and his life is complete. But such moments come rarely to the average person, the reason being that his outer mind is not in a condition to give expression to the life and the power that is being awakened in the great within.

The average person is not trained to give expression to the genius from within. It is simply trained to remember what others have said and to imitate what others have done. In the meantime the genius within is held in prison, and in trying to gain freedom produces much confusion, much depression, many mistakes and many moments of mental despair. A great deal of the unhappiness that comes to most ambitious people originates in these very conditions. The mental household is divided against itself. The inner mind wants to produce the greatness and the joy of the full individual life, while the outer mind wants to live a superficial life and do only what the senses in their limitations may desire to do. The objective mind, however, was not created to act at variance with the subconscious. It is generations of unscientific training that has given the outer mind this tendency, but there can be neither real peace nor real greatness in the mind of man until this tendency is removed.

The two minds must work together in harmony and for the same purpose. The objective mind should daily impress the subconscious with its highest thoughts, aims, desires, and should respond perfectly when the subconscious brings forth the power with which those aims and desires may be fulfilled. The objective mind should constantly expect more

The Mind Cure

and more power from the subconscious, and should constantly hold itself in that calm, well-poised receptive attitude which is so necessary to the full expression of the greater power from within. To cultivate this attitude is to place the two minds in harmony, and as the objective mind is daily directing the subconscious to produce more life, greater intelligence and greater power, this harmony will enable the subconscious to come forth and do what it has been directed to do. The majority of those who suffer from mental depression, discontent, chronic despondency, or an inclination to live on the dark side of life will find complete emancipation from those conditions when the greater power within them has been given full freedom to act. To place the conscious and the subconscious in harmony is to give the entire power within an opportunity to express itself, and relief will come at once. In addition, the entire personality will be recharged with new life, the body will become more vigorous, and the mind more brilliant.

When chronic mental depression comes from adverse mental states, the remedy is to train the objective mind in exact scientific thinking. That is, the mind should live on the sunny side, the constructive side, the growing side, and every thought should be formed in the exact likeness of the highest ideals that can be created. When we concentrate our attention upon our ideals, and deeply feel at all times that we are moving toward those ideals, we will proceed to rise out of depression, darkness and discontent into the world of light, freedom, peace and joy. There is an upper region in the mind of man where happiness is perpetual.

To enter this upper region the first essential is to place the two minds in harmony, and the second essential is to keep the eye single upon the heights of all that is true, all that is perfect, all that is lofty, all that is beautiful, and all that is sublime.

The Mind Cure

How to Remove Fear

SO long as there is a tendency to fear it is not possible for any mind to do its best, and as it is absolutely necessary for every mind to do its best in order to live the life of peace, health, freedom, and attainment, we must proceed to remove fear completely. The real origin of all human ills can be traced to retarded growth, and we know that growth is retarded whenever we fail to do our best.

Everything, therefore, that interferes with the being of our best must be removed; and there are many things that interfere in this manner, but the attitude of fear is one of the most pronounced. It is possible to demonstrate that fear has prevented more natural-born great minds from applying their greatness than all other adverse states of mind combined; and it is also possible to demonstrate that fear has produced more disease, trouble and misfortune than any other cause. To remove fear, therefore, would be doing something that would be extraordinary, to say the least.

There are many methods that will remove fear temporarily, but to remove it permanently we must find its fundamental cause. This cause has been sought far and wide, and has been found in what may be termed the outer time of the present moment. Reduced to its last analysis, fear is simply a state of mind arising from the seeming uncertainty of the immediate future. If we knew that everything in the coming days would be exactly as we wished it to be there would be no occasion for fear at any time; but it is in this uncertainty with which we come in mental contact nearly every day that gives origin to every form of fear. To remove fear, therefore, this state of uncertainty must be overcome; and it is good news to know that this is possible. This feeling of uncertainty gives origin to a number of forms of fear, and one of the most pronounced is possibly the fear of death. We fear death because we feel an uncertainty with regard to the life beyond; but if we positively knew that death was simply the open door to a larger and more wonderful world than this, the thought of death could never produce fear in the least.

Another phase is that of calamity. We live more or less in the dread of calamities, because we do not know whether we shall escape safely or not, nor do we always know what precaution to take that absolute safety may be secured. We fear poverty because things in this world seem so uncertain. Our friends everywhere meet unexpected misfortune, and we imagine that the same fate is quite likely to come to us. If we could master our circumstances we should think differently about this particular phase; but the art of mastering circumstances is not clearly understood, consequently the majority continue to fear the possible misfortune of the future. We fear disease because we are almost daily brought face to face with threatening symptoms, and we see people all about us going down to the grave through the continued actions of what at first seemed to be but insignificant symptoms. There are scores of other conditions and things that we fear more or less, and for the same reason; that is, we are uncertain as to the outcome.

The outcome may be good or ill; we do not know, and we fear that it may be the latter, because we have not acquired the power to produce the former at will. It is therefore evident that all fear comes directly from uncertainty as to the immediate future, as to the results of what we are doing now. What is brewing in the present has frequently been brewing in the past, and in the past such indications have many times turned out badly; and the question is. Can we make everything come right this time? Most of us do not know, and that is the reason why the majority are almost in constant fear concerning the events of the near future.

The Mind Cure

That fear comes from uncertainty, and from no other cause, is easily demonstrated; but the question is what it is that produces this uncertainty. When we analyze that phase of the subject we find that the cause of every form of uncertainty is produced by the fact that similar things under similar adverse conditions turned out badly before, and we have nothing to prove at the present time that we can cause all things to come right in the future; that is, the majority have nothing to prove that the future can be made right, regardless of conditions in the present. Though the majority may not have this proof, that fact does not indicate that the proof cannot be found.

To remove fear it is therefore necessary to secure positive evidence to prove the idea that we can cause everything to come right, that we can make the future better than the present, and that we can cause all things to work together for the promotion of our highest welfare. The majority, however, may believe that such evidence cannot be secured, because they judge according to appearances and think of human nature as weak and incompetent, even at its best.

But those who understand the great law of cause and effect, and understand the real power of man, know that appearances do not reveal the exact truth concerning anything, and they also know that man has it in his power to change his whole life, his entire nature and his own destiny. This world is not a world of aimless chance; neither do events just happen. When we look at the confused surface and see how many things move in some helter-skelter fashion we may think that it is entirely useless to attempt any orderly readjustment; but when we discover that every adverse effect comes from some adverse cause, and that man himself produces those adverse causes, we find it necessary to take another point of view.

The Mind Cure

The confused surface of the world is produced by the confused and misdirected actions of the human race, just as an upset household is produced by disorder among its members. The inside of every house is the exact likeness of those who have charge of it. An orderly person will have everything in harmony, and neatness will prevail even though the house itself be ordinary, and everything in it be ordinary and inexpensive. But the newest and finest house and the costliest furniture can give the appearance of utter depravity if placed in charge of a disorderly mind.

The same law rules everywhere among the smallest things and the largest things in the world. The world itself and its many parts are like the people that are in charge. The good things in the world come from good causes; the other things come from adverse causes; and all causes come from man. Man, however, can produce any cause he likes; therefore the future is in his own hands.

To change the condition of the world in general, the human race in general must be changed, and this is possible. For a long period of time the race has been told to be right and good, but we have not been told clearly how to proceed. The race is most willing to change for the better; in fact, the great majority are constantly praying for the required knowledge and truth on the great subject of human betterment. All that is necessary, therefore, is to provide this greatly desired information which is already at hand, and the world will begin to change.

The world in general is the direct effect of the actions of all its people, while the world of the individual is the result of his own actions plus those actions of the general world with which he may come in contact. But he can change his own actions and also adapt himself to the actions of the world in such a way that the very results he desires can be secured in

The Mind Cure

each instance. In other words, each individual can produce in his own world what he may desire; and he can so change those things that come into his world from the world in general, that they become identical in nature and action with what he himself is producing for himself.

To understand the real nature and the real power of man, is to know that he can determine what he himself is to produce, and that he can also determine what the world in general is to produce in his individual world. He is therefore complete master of the situation, and this being true, the entire subject is reduced to that of pure mathematics. When we are working out a problem in mathematics we do not dread the answer; if we know the principles, we have no fear as to the outcome. If we are good mathematicians we know positively that the answer will be correct, and there can be no fear or dread where one positively knows. The good mathematician, however, is not free from fear in his calculations because he is superior to others; he is superior only in this respect that he knows the principles involved. He lives in the same mathematical world as does the stumbling student.

The two are not different in kind. The only difference is that the one understands the principles and the other one does not. The good mathematician gets the answer he wants; he makes the future of the problem just what he wishes it to be. He wants the outcome to be right, and understanding the principles, he gets what he wants.

His simple secret is this: He knows what principles to apply in solving the problem, and he applies those principles in every problem. Accordingly, he gets the results desired. The problems we meet in everyday life can be dealt with in the same manner. They all have a mathematical basis, and if we apply the principles of life correctly those problems can be worked out so as to produce the right results in every case.

The Mind Cure

WHEN we know that the future is the direct outcome of the present there can be no fear concerning the future so long as we correctly apply the principles of life to everything that we may be doing in the present. Then we should remember, in addition, that the man who is living constructively every day is building for himself a future that is larger and better and more perfect than his present. He is positively convinced that the outcome of his present efforts will be good, and will produce the greater, because he knows that he is daily placing in action causes that are productive of better and greater things.

That such a man can have fear is simply impossible. There is no uncertainty in his mind, therefore there can be no fear in his mind. He has no fear of poverty, because he is daily improving himself, daily rendering better service to the world; and it is invariably the law that the better our service the better our recompense. There may be occasional exceptions to this rule, but these exceptions are seeming, and are due to certain violations of the laws of life that we do not happen to see at the time.

There are many who may be using certain principles correctly and misusing other principles. The results in those cases will therefore be uncertain, and fear may arise; but when we apply all the principles there can be no uncertainty and no fear, because the result will be as we desire. That man who has ability, and who properly relates himself to the needs of that sphere through which his ability may be fully expressed, will be in constant demand, and his recompense will steadily increase. When great minds are not appreciated in their own time, they themselves are to blame, the fault being that they do not adapt their genius to the needs of their own times. Anyone, however, no matter what his ability may be, can adapt himself to the needs of his own day, and thus not only receive full appreciation from his own generation, but fully apply in the most successful manner all the ability he may possess.

Those minds that are doing their best today have no occasion to fear provided the law is understood, because so long as they are doing their best they are becoming better, and will advance steadily. To such minds the future is bright. They are daily creating good causes, and the future will be more and more abundantly supplied with good effects. This is the law, therefore he who applies this law has nothing to fear.

To this statement everyone will agree; but with the average mind the problem is how to create good causes, and good causes only, and how to know whether or not living is constructive. There are thousands who mean well, and who are actually trying to create only the best, but they are living almost constantly in trouble and misfortune. The cause of this condition is found in the fact that they have not been taught how to apply the principles involved in those particular problems that come up in their lives.

To proceed, we must bring our life out of this chaotic condition and establish absolute order. Then upon this orderly foundation, no matter how small or insignificant it may be, we must begin the construction of a new mansion of life. Before we begin, however, the plans of the new structure must be clearly fixed in mind; that is, we must form our ideal. The first essential is to live in the peaceful, serene, well-poised attitude of mind, because the forces of life must be brought into the harmony of constructive action.

The second essential is to take life into our own hands by constantly holding life in the consciousness of our own possession; that is, we should always think of life as being absolutely in our own possession, and before long the power to completely govern our own life will become second nature. The third essential is to have one predominant purpose, that is, to make yourself and your work better and better every day, to build constantly for greater things both in your own nature and in your own environment. In this connection we must learn to see all things in our imagination as being made more and more perfect, because to keep the mental eye single upon the better side, the strong side and the superior side of everything, is to give the creative forces of mind a superior model; and these forces always create in the exact likeness of the model. When we think constantly of the superior, and keep the mental eye single upon the superior, we therefore create the superior in our own natures.

On the other hand, when we think of the dark side, the weak side, the troubled side, the sick side, and the failing side, we tend to create all those conditions in our nature and in our world; and when we fear we always think of those inferior sides, thereby causing that which we fear to come upon us.

When we concentrate our whole attention upon the construction of a superior life, and work with a constantly increasing knowledge of the art of using all our faculties constructively, we shall bring the whole of life into a perfect system of action, wherein all things will cooperate in producing for us the greater, the better and the superior. When all our energies are organized into an army of skilled builders there is only one effect possible, and that is the perpetual increase of everything that is desirable in human life. He who employs all his energies in this manner will therefore have nothing to fear, as in his life the very cause of fear will have been removed completely. It is therefore evident that the problem of removing fear is solved through the art of using all our faculties and forces in such a manner as to build more nobly in the present than we did in the past, and this we may accomplish by learning to use the principles of life with mathematical precision. There are many things that we are afraid of, but the principal ones are undoubtedly poverty, disease, calamity and death; and when we learn how to remove the fear of these four we shall also be able to remove the fear of all minor conditions that are not desired. To remove the fear of death it is only necessary to become convinced of the fact that life is continuous, and that the future life of each individual is the natural outcome of his present life.

The development of what may be termed the consciousness of soul, or the realization of the I AM and the perfection of the I AM, will demonstrate conclusively to any mind that the life of every individual is continuous and endless; in fact, to become conscious of the I AM is to know that the I AM and life are identical, and we know that life is indestructible. Then add to this the great fact that you, the real you, constitutes the I AM, and you have an exact basis upon which you may demonstrate to yourself through pure reason that you shall continue perpetually to live.

The Mind Cure

THE understanding of the laws of cause and effect will demonstrate that you can create your own future and your own destiny, not only in the present sphere, but in future spheres of existence, and that you can make your future existence as beautiful, as marvelous and as gorgeous as your imagination can possibly picture. The law is, that he who is living nobly in the present is creating for himself a better future, both in this life and in the life to come; therefore he who applies the principles of that law, which simply mean the principles of right living and right thinking, has nothing to fear, neither from death nor from the future. In fact, death to him will simply mean the gates ajar to a far richer, far better and far more beautiful world than this; and the future to him will mean attainments, achievements and enjoyments so far superior to what anyone has realized in this world that words cannot possibly describe them.

In this connection it is interesting to know that they who have no fear of death always live the longest lives, the best lives and the happiest lives upon earth; and it is also a well-known fact that they who know they are doing their best in the present are not afraid to leave this planet at any time. They dread no change, because they know that every change must be a change for the better. These people have inner conviction based upon the fact that they are applying principle in their lives; that it always will be well with those who do well; and we know that such a conviction will remove fear completely. When we learn how to live we shall lose all fear of death, because when we begin to actually live we know that we shall live a very long life, a very interesting life and a very beautiful life; and we also know that what is called death is but an open door to a still more beautiful life more beautiful because a beautiful present invariably produces a more beautiful future.

The Mind Cure

What we have earned, that we shall receive and enjoy. This is the law, and therefore he who so lives that he earns much, will have much to receive and enjoy in days to come.

When symptoms of disease appear, we know that we have violated some natural law; but if we understand life we also know that the pain is a good friend coming to inform us that something needs readjustment; and if we proceed to right the matter, which we can readily do when we know how to think and live, there will be no disease whatever. When we know how to remove all threatening symptoms at once we shall never fear disease; and when we know how to create health in greater and greater abundance, the fear of disease will become impossible. So long as we create health we cannot be sick; and every person who is living a constructive life who is applying the principles of life to his own living, as the mathematician applies principles to his problems is creating health in greater and greater abundance.

The fear of poverty will disappear when we learn that ability and power can be developed more and more for an indefinite period. We know that competent men and women are in great demand everywhere, and when we know that we can become competent sufficiently competent to fill the best places in the world we shall live in the assurance of perpetual increase, and all fear of poverty will therefore disappear. You cannot have any fear of poverty or loss when you know that your earning power is increasing every day, and that the demand for your services in the world is increasing every day.

To eliminate the fear of calamities, accidents, catastrophes and the like, may seem impossible because it is generally believed that the individual cannot control the causes through which those things are produced; but when we look closely at the matter we find that we meet those unpleasant events because we fail to do the right thing at the right time. When we live according to principles, we will learn more and more to do the right thing at the right time; and we shall also develop those finer senses as we grow in mind and soul, through which we can discern readily the course to pursue in each case, and thus avoid what might not prove agreeable. Then in this connection we should also remember that though we may not be able to control all the causes of calamities in the world, we can so well control ourselves that we can go out of the way of the actions of those causes. In other words, we can avoid the path that leads to calamity, and take those paths that are always safe.

What is Truth

What is Truth

Table of Contents

Foreword	131
Chapter 1 - The Meaning of Truth	133
Chapter 2 - How to Know the Truth	144
Chapter 3 - How to Seek the Truth	154
Chapter 4 - Where to Find the Truth	166
Chapter 5 - Where We Get Our Ideas	176
Chapter 6 - The Two Sides of Truth	185
Chapter 7 - Striking Illustrations of Half Truths	197
Chapter 8 - The Subconscious Factor	206
Chapter 9 - The Real and the Unreal	216
Chapter 10 - In Reality Everything is Good	225
Chapter 11 - Causing the Best to Happen	230
Chapter 12 - The Truth About Right and Wrong	236
Chapter 13 - The Truth About Freedom	245
Chapter 14 - The Royal Path to Freedom	252
Chapter 15 - The Truth Beyond Truth	257
Chapter 16 - Discernment of Absolute Truth	266

What is Truth

FOREWORD

To formulate a complete and final definition for truth is not possible, the reason being that the truth in itself, or in any of its expressions, cannot be circumscribed by the human mind. The truth is too large to be described by any definition, however basic or comprehensive it may be. The best we can do, therefore, is to define our highest conceptions of truth. And moreover, we shall find this to be sufficient.

To define and understand our highest conception of truth is to know, in the present, as much of the truth as we shall find necessary to gain that freedom that invariably comes with the truth. And as we continue to seek higher and higher conceptions of truth, as we advance in life, we shall accordingly find that greater measure of freedom which must necessarily accompany the more advanced stages of human existence.

The purpose, therefore, of this book is not to present a clear-cut definition of truth, nor to give an answer to the question. What is truth? that would stand the test of all thought and experience.

No, indeed, for such a course would defeat the aim we all have in view — the finding of more and more truth, and would make the search of truth far more difficult. The reason for this will be evident as we peruse the following pages.

Our purpose in this work is rather to present a plan or outline by which any individual may guide his mind in the attainment of higher and higher conceptions of truth in all its phases, and thereby understand the truth for himself at every stage of advancement which he may reach in his own sphere of life, thought and action. And this is the only rational course to pursue, for each individual must understand the truth for himself if he is to know that truth that brings freedom; but in order that he may understand the truth for himself he must seek and find the truth for himself. The only truth that is of any value to us is that truth that we have gained through our own individual efforts to actually know truth and inwardly realize the presence and power of truth.

This being true, all wide-awake and progressive minds will agree that the aim of this book, which is to present practical and effective methods through which anyone may find more and more truth, instead of trying to give a final and complete system of thought supposed to contain all the truth, which is impossible — all such minds will agree that this aim is the only aim, in this connection, that can possibly be rational in its process and practical in its application. And it is for such minds that this book is written. We feel, therefore, that every page will be fully appreciated, and that every statement will be thoroughly understood.

Chapter 1

The Meaning of Truth

No aim can be higher than that of seeking truth, and no reward can be greater than that of finding the truth. In fact, it is now considered by everybody that the greatest virtue of all virtues is to have an intense and ceaseless desire for truth. And the greatest good of all that is good is to realize a greater and greater measure of real truth.

The necessities of life are many, but there is nothing that man needs so much as more truth. To possess the truth is to possess everything that we can use now, and also to possess the key to everything that we may require for the future. The great objects of every normal person are invariably emancipation and attainment. To be set free from the imperfect and the lesser and to attain the perfect and the greater — this is what everybody is consciously or unconsciously working for; and truth can accomplish this, but truth alone. To know the truth is to secure complete emancipation; and to know the truth is to ascend into higher and higher attainments.

The awakened minds of every age have realized that the knowing of truth was the one great secret that could unravel all other secrets; and they have given their lives trying to reveal to mankind what truth really might be. Nevertheless, the race does not know, and the universal question still continues to be, What is truth? To answer this question, however, is not difficult, but it is difficult for most minds to comprehend the answer. The human mind too often believes its own conception of a truth to be the truth itself, and here is where the difficulty lies. This is the one great mistake of every age.

What is Truth

Truth is one thing, but man's conception of truth is quite another thing. Truth is eternal, unchangeable and complete, while man's conception of truth is temporal, mutable, and incomplete. To absolute truth nothing can be added, nothing taken away, but man's conception of truth is frequently wrong, even when it may appear to be absolutely right.

The truth is infinite and immeasurable. No one, therefore, can know the whole truth. To claim that you have found the absolute truth, or that you have discovered the perfect path to absolute truth is, in consequence, to delude yourself. The truth is so large that no one can ever find it all. We may devote an eternity to the finding of more and more truth, and yet, what we have found is insignificant compared to the immensity of the whole truth itself.

The truth is everywhere, therefore there is no one perfect path to the truth. Every mind is in the truth, literally filled and surrounded by the truth, but no mind can contain the whole truth. It is possible to discern truth and know truth, but it is not possible to actually comprehend the truth. It is possible to understand the mental conception of truth, but it is not possible to understand truth itself.

The truth may be defined as an eternal state of perfect being; therefore, to know truth is to know that real being is perfect, and also that the perfect state of real being is eternal. To obtain a larger and a larger mental conception of eternal perfection of real being, or fundamental reality, is to grow in the truth. To grow in the truth is to find more truth, and to pass into the larger, the better, and the superior.

To accept a mental conception of truth as the truth itself is to bring all growth to a standstill, but this is what mankind in general has been doing and is doing. And because of this the majority remain in mental darkness, bondage and inferiority. An age that worships someone mind's conception of truth invariably becomes materialistic, no matter how lofty that mind was that originally formed the conception of truth that is worshiped. A materialistic mind is a mind that lives in the effects of previous efforts and that does nothing to rise above such conditions as heredity has handed down.

Growth, however, comes from the breaking of bounds, from the leaving of the lesser and perpetually pressing on toward the greater. The materialistic mind is like the stagnant pool; it is inactive or practically dead, no matter how active or beautiful its surroundings may be. At the present time we find materialistic minds everywhere surrounded by the highest culture and the most beautiful in art, and on account of those surroundings we fail to discern the uselessness, and in many instances the detriment, of the materialism thus hidden from view. We may believe the stagnant pool to be a pond of living water, because it is found in a garden of roses. In like manner we may believe that minds found in the midst of art, learning and culture must surely be living, growing, aspiring minds; but when we draw very near in either case we are disillusioned. In this age the most detrimental form of materialism is practically hidden within circles of enchanting music, fascinating rituals, elegant rhetoric and royal garments. Accordingly, materialism itself is not discerned by the many, and they follow blindly, continuing in sickness, sin, and death.

Truth alone can give emancipation, but we cannot find the truth so long as we humbly worship what someone has said about the truth. In this age many efforts have been made to formulate the truth in some definite system, but how can we place that something into system that is infinitely larger than all systems? To follow a system of thought is to worship some mind's conception of truth and to ignore the real truth itself. A system, however, may be employed if it is employed solely as the means to higher conceptions, but as soon as we look upon a system as authority, our eyes will not be able to see the truth any more.

Systems of thought, as well as systems of action, are necessary as a means to higher ends, but the higher ends will not be reached unless we constantly look through the system and keep the eye single upon the infinite, unchangeable and immeasurable truth. When using systems in this manner, however, we must remember that it is not possible to know absolutely any part of the truth upon which our mental eye may be directed. It is not possible, even for a mind that is ever becoming larger and larger, to comprehend the limitless at any time. All that we can do now is to form the largest and highest conception of truth that our present mental capacity can permit, and then proceed to enlarge that conception perpetually.

True wisdom comes through mental ascension into the unbounded truth, and not through a studied belief of what we now accept as the truth. That knowledge that has power is gained through the constant enlargement of mentality; that is, through the expansion of consciousness as the mind grows in the truth, and not from the accumulation of relative facts. Emancipation comes through ascension, and in no other way; that is, the ascension of the mind into a larger, a higher and a finer understanding of the truth. The mind that is perpetually passing into the greater is constantly being emancipated from the lesser. And the mind that is forever growing better is daily being set free from the ills of error and imperfection.

In this connection it is important to realize that the only cause of bondage is found in a settled or inactive condition of mind. There are many minds that think they have secured

What is Truth

freedom through the acceptance of a certain system of thought, but the freedom they have received did not come from the system of thought itself. Freedom never comes from the acceptance of systems, but from the mind's ascension into the new and the larger. If a certain system leads you away from the imperfection of your present life you will be emancipated from that imperfection, but if you give the system the credit, you will worship the system. You will dwell in the mental conceptions upon which that system is based and your mind will not move any further toward the realization of larger truth.

In this very place millions have brought their lives to a standstill; they having accepted various new systems as the whole truth discovered at last.

and they have settled down in that belief. When they first accepted the new system of thought their minds naturally gained a higher place, and they were set free to that extent; but when they began to worship the system as the great emancipator it ceased to be a means to higher things, and became a prison which they dared not leave lest they fall back into their former condition. A new system of thought if worshiped as the truth will prevent you from ascending further into truth, and will, therefore, in due course of time make your mind just as materialistic and as limited as it was in the past.

The fact that you have health, peace and contentment does not prove that you have found absolute freedom, or that you have realized absolute truth.

There are thousands who have health, peace and freedom who do not follow any system of thought at all, and who do not claim to have found a single absolute fact. For here we should remember that whenever we accept a new system of thought our minds are changed in a measure, and a change of mind always tends to eliminate adverse conditions of the system, both physical and mental.

Our great purpose, however, is not simply to realize peace, health and attainment, but also to develop our own individuality. And if we continue our individual development, health, peace and attainment, and all other blessings will follow.

This being true, we must not permit anything that will in any way hinder our fullest individual expression. But the fact is that there is nothing that hinders individual expression and the development of individuality more than the acceptance of a fixed system of thought as the absolute truth itself. No matter how well it may be with you in your present condition, physically, mentally or financially, if your belief makes you dependent upon any person, institution or outside authority, your individuality is being kept down. And instead of moving forward, as you may think, you are actually on the path to retrogression.

The experience of all ages proves this fact, and what has crippled individuality, or caused man to deteriorate in the past, can do so again. It is the evidence of history that every fixed system of thought has made mental and spiritual dwarfs of "its most faithful followers. We all understand the reason why. No individual mind can know the truth through the understanding of some other mind; therefore each mind must not only be permitted, but encouraged, to develop its own individual capacity for knowing the truth, and nothing must stand in the way of the perpetual ascension of the soul into new conceptions of truth every day.

The understanding of truth is promoted through individual research in all domains of life, and in the use of all the systems of thought available as means to an end in the furthering of all research. It is therefore evident that individuality or the power of each mind to stand upon its own feet is indispensable in the search of truth. Fixed lines of action may be necessary in the systematic search for truth, but these lines should not be limited in number, nor confined to certain spheres of action.

Thousands of minds, otherwise intelligent, keep themselves in mental darkness because they refuse to seek truth outside of the usual lines. They forget that the lines now looked upon as usual and regular were once upon a time very unusual, and even considered dangerous. The fact is, however, that any line of research will lead to truth, and nothing is dangerous that will bring us more truth. We may therefore lay aside all fears, open wide all doors to all realms, and place our minds absolutely out in the open.

In the search of truth it is of the highest importance to be able to discriminate between truth itself and our mere mental conception of truth, and also between those conceptions that are true and those that are not. When you are dealing with a mental conception you are dealing with something that your mind contains, but when you are dealing with truth itself you are dealing with something that contains your mind. A mental conception of truth is limited — it is something that mind can measure, but the truth itself is not limited, and therefore cannot be measured.

False conceptions of truth, however, will not form themselves in your mind when you view the truth as infinite, and when the mind invariably ascends or tries to rise higher in the scale of understanding while attempting to realize more truth; in brief, a conception of truth is true as far as it goes if the mind expanded while that conception was formed.

What is Truth

This is a simple rule and will be found to contain the greatest secret of all in the realization of more and more truth.

The fact is, that the aspiring or expanding attitude of the mind is the only attitude through which more truth can be gained, for no mental conception of truth is true unless it is superior to the conception that was formed before. And here it must be remembered that to know the truth is to know more truth. The very act of the mind in knowing the truth involves the act of knowing more truth at that particular time.

Whenever the mind is trying to know the truth it must try to know more truth in order to know truth at all. We are not moving forward unless we are moving forward. For the same reason we are not knowing truth unless we are knowing more truth, because the truth is limitless, and every act of the mind that is attracted toward the knowing of truth must of necessity be attracted toward the knowing of all the truth. This means that every effort to know the truth must be a forward movement in the mind.

What was truth to you in the past is not truth to you now because that alone is truth to you now that you discern through your own present mental capacity, which is necessarily larger than your capacity was in the past. What we call truth is our present view of infinite truth, therefore if our present view is not superior to the past view we are still living in the past view; and if we are still living in the past view we are worshiping a system of outgrown beliefs; therefore do not see the truth at all.

The mental conceptions we form while in a stagnant state are not conceptions of truth; they are simply varying beliefs concerning the size and the structure of our prison walls; that is, the walls of the system in which we have incased ourselves.

When you are confined in a system you are standing still, you see the bounds and the limitations of the system, but you do not see the boundlessness of the truth itself. And since we cannot form conceptions of truth unless we have our eyes directed upon infinite truth, the fact that your present conception is not superior to its predecessor proves that you are not viewing the truth. Accordingly, that conception cannot be true. The truth invariably lies in the line of an ascending scale of thought or mental action, while the untruth is formed when the mind is at a standstill, or is in the line of retrogression.

The understanding of truth is never fixed. A fixed understanding is no understanding, because to understand is to go deeper and deeper into the unfathomable states of the absolute; in brief, it involves an action of the mind. And any action of the mind that aims to understand must necessarily move toward the greater truth. We therefore see how impossible it is for any form of understanding to be fixed and stable. Comprehension does not comprehend unless it perpetually enlarges itself, because when the mind ceases to expand it ceases to act, and when it ceases to act no comprehension can take place. To comprehend is to go around, but if we are not going there necessarily will be no comprehension.

We therefore realize how necessary it is that every effort to know truth must be an effort to comprehend greater truth. The mind either goes out into the larger or remains at a standstill, though frequently when it remains at a standstill it is actually being contracted into a smaller mental sphere. When the mind remains at a standstill, or deteriorates, it does not act upon anything that is larger or superior to its past belief; and consequently the act of comprehension does not take place.

A mind that is belittling itself is not on the way to the realization of greater wisdom. The mind can know only through the act of ascension or expansion; that is, the rising in the scale of thought, feeling and consciousness. When the mind ceases to ascend it ceases to know, because the act of knowing is a forward movement of those mental processes that are involved in thinking, reasoning and similar acts of the mind.

Therefore, when the mind ceases to ascend it begins to dwell in mental darkness, and from mental darkness come all the ills of life. To find the truth and to know the truth it is necessary to view the truth as infinite and immeasurable, and to ascend perpetually into a larger and a larger consciousness of that infinite view of truth.

When you think of things as entities, and try to know the truth concerning them, it is always necessary to turn the attention upon the limitless truth that is back of appearances. We cannot gain the truth about anything unless the mind expands into the consciousness of the all that is contained in everything. And we cannot ascend in this way unless we direct our research into the vast realms that are beyond all appearances.

There will always be a beyond, but the beyond of today should be the tangible and demonstrated realities of the days succeeding. What is hidden today should be proven fact tomorrow. This is possible when we search for the truth, not in the world of appearances, but in the wider realms just beyond present appearances.

What is Truth

But our object in seeking the truth is not simply to possess the truth — it is also to find greater means for growth, progress and ascension. Emancipation and attainment are the two great aims in real life, and both are the results of knowing the truth. To know the truth is to ascend perpetually into the infinite domains of truth, thus leaving behind the lesser and forever entering into the greater. In this way we pass out of and rise above everything that has served its purpose and enter constantly into the marvels and splendors still in store.

What is Truth

Chapter 2

How to Know the Truth

The discovery of the subconscious mind and its extraordinary powers over the outer mind and the body is turning new light on many subjects. And we can safely predict that the understanding of the subconscious will in the near future practically revolutionize all thought and all methods of mental, moral and spiritual training. The fact that you can impress anything upon the subconscious and that all such impressions will react as corresponding expressions, is creating the most profound attention among all progressive thinkers, not only because it pens to the mind an immense field of most fascinating study, but also because it explains hundreds of phenomena that have hitherto baffled all attempts at solution.

Among the many mysteries that are explained by subconscious study, few are of greater interest than that of the origin of ideas or what might be termed beliefs and convictions. Many a person asks himself daily why he believes what he does, and why he is convinced that certain things are true when he has no evidence. If our convictions always proved themselves to be true this matter might not attract much attention, but the fact that so many convictions sooner or later prove themselves to be untrue or mere illusions makes the subject one of more than passing importance. What we believed yesterday we frequently discard today, and what we believe today we are quite liable to discard tomorrow, possibly with a few exceptions. Nevertheless, while the beliefs of today remain, we are so thoroughly convinced that they are true that practically nothing can change our minds. In fact, our present beliefs sometimes have such a powerful hold upon our minds that we have absolutely no desire to think differently from what we do. And what is more, those very beliefs, as a rule, refuse to be examined.

It is certainly mental bondage with a vengeance when a mind dare not examine the credentials of its own beliefs, and is so completely under the control of its own convictions that it is unable to question their genuineness or authority.

But what we want to know is what places the mind in such a condition, and also what might constitute the path to emancipation. These are great questions when we realize the fact that there are millions of minds that are more or less in such a condition. The subconscious mind, however, explains the mystery. Our. convictions, that is, those things that we feel to be true, are in most instances mental expressions from the subconscious.

When these expressions are very strong they invariably color all views, desires, motives, feelings or intentions of the outer mind. Sometimes these convictions, or subconscious expressions, are so strong that even a liberal university education will have to obey and color its ideas accordingly. We frequently ask, "How can that well educated man believe as he does?" The fact is that he is compelled by his own subconscious convictions to believe as he does. Those convictions are so strong that they bend, twist and color his education so that the education itself is made a servant of mere belief, and is not infrequently compelled to use its power to prove the genuineness of that belief.

But in the face of these facts, how are we to know that truth is truth? How are we to distinguish between a real principle and an opinion which is simply the reaction of some idea or belief that was previously impressed upon our minds?

What is Truth

How are we to determine when a law is a law and when it is simply the tendency of a strong expression from the subconscious? To know these things is highly important, because the truth is the cause of all that is good, while the untruth is the cause of all that is not good.

To distinguish truth from error we have usually depended upon logic, or upon scientific evidence, but a study of the subconscious proves that logic is not always safe, and also that scientific evidence may be so colored and modified as to prove the very opposite as to what happens to be fact. An expression from the subconscious, if very strong, can so modify the logical process that reason is literally compelled to act along certain lines only, and wholly ignore certain other lines which if considered would change the conclusion decidedly. We have any amount of this sort of reasoning going on all about us, and it is responsible for a great many false views as well as half truths.

In addition to the twisting process, which is constantly applied to logic or reason by prejudice, strong personal feelings and contradicting subconscious convictions, there is another process originating wholly in the subconscious, which makes logic still more incompetent to prove that truth is truth.

The logical process is based upon premises, and the conclusion is true only when the premises are true.

If one or both of the premises are false, the conclusion will be false, even though the reasoning employed be absolutely sound in every respect.

The process of logical reasoning is similar to the working out of a mathematical problem. If one of the original figures were wrong, the final answer will be wrong, regardless of the fact that the figuring be entirely correct all the way through. In logic it is therefore necessary to have correct premises at the beginning, but how are we to know that they are correct? A strong, preconceived subconscious conviction may color or modify any premises which we may formulate, and make it appear true when it is false, or vice versa. What is more, a strong subconscious conviction may influence the mind to form all of its premises so as to harmonize with that conviction, thus forcing the logical process to prove that the subconscious conviction is true, even though it may be the most impossible illusion. A great deal of this is done; in fact, there are few minds that are absolutely free from it.

Again, a great many impressions concerning the nature of life in general, and this or that in particular, may establish themselves so firmly in the subconscious that they are accepted as absolute facts; and these may be employed as fundamentals in the formulating of principles, laws, premises, and so on.

Upon these fundamentals we may construct an immense system of thought which may seem to be plausible, reasonable, and logical, and we may gain thousands of followers even though there may not be a single truth at the bottom of the system.

In this connection we must remember that any idea which seems plausible may impress itself upon the subconscious as a fact. And since we naturally accept what comes from the subconscious, provided the subconscious expression be very strong, we will believe this plausible idea to be a fact even though it may be nothing more than a mere illusion. It is the nature of the human mind to feel that whatever comes from the subconscious is true; that is, every expression from the subconscious feels as if it were real, and what we feel to be true or real we accept as final, usually asking no questions. But we must not blame the subconscious for such phenomena. The subconscious only responds to impressions from without. The conscious mind acts, the subconscious reacts, and the two actions are always similar.

When we accept an idea from another mind, or from our own study simply because it seems plausible, we will permit that idea to impress itself upon the subconscious, provided it is deeply felt. Later on that same idea will come back from the subconscious as a strong conviction; and we shall not only be forced to accept it as true, but in addition it will color all our thinking; in fact, it may become so strong that we do not care to be free from its absolute control. There are many illustrations of this very thing, as there are quite a number of people who are in such complete bondage to the mental control of the beliefs they cherish that they actually take pride in being under such absolute control; in brief, they frequently declare, "I AM completely in the hands of this system of thought and I AM glad of it."

The cause of this strange state of mind is easily explained, however. The absolute slave, be he physical or mental, does not wish to be free, because if he IS an absolute slave he does not have sufficient freedom of thought to distinguish between bondage and emancipation; in brief, he cannot appreciate freedom. Therefore, it appears to him to be something that will deprive him of the privileges he may enjoy in his bondage. He would rather endure the present state, even if that state happens to be undesirable, than risk the uncertainty of that of which he has not the slightest conception.

There are a large number of minds in this condition; they are afraid to change their minds, because their bondage is so complete that they have not sufficient individuality or

What is Truth

freedom of self-assertiveness to stand upon their own feet should they be called upon to do so. They may be miserable where they are, but they are wholly unable to express a desire for change. They believe what they believe because that belief has become a deep-seated subconscious habit and their minds are completely under the control of those habits. Their habits of belief may have been formed in childhood under the strict discipline of "authority for truth"; or they may have changed later, accepting a new belief and permitting this new belief to sink so deeply into the subconscious that it colors all thought and prevents the mind from thinking anything which does not conform to this belief.

But the question is, if there need be any truth in a belief in order that it may gain such full control over the mind. That there may be some truth in all belief is possible, though from the nature of the case, the larger part of it will be untrue. We realize that any system, no matter how untrue, may gain complete supremacy in the mind and compel the mind to accept it as true. Therefore, the mere fact that our belief seems to be true proves nothing, nor does the fact that we are satisfied with our present belief prove anything in its favor.

Many a serf is satisfied to be next to nothing, and many a mind knows so little that it looks upon its ignorance as a virtue. In fact, it was only a few years ago that ignorance was considered a virtue among a large percentage of people. Those people, however, were not to blame; in fact, no one is directly to blame. Nevertheless, the fact that all these things exist in our very midst but adds importance to our subject.

The great question before us is, "How are we to know the truth; that is, how are we to know the truth when we see it?" Thus far there is only one way through which we may know the truth, and that is what is called "the scientific method." This method has been applied by students of the physical universe for half a century or more, and they have in that way made modern science a marvel. But the same method can be applied in any department of thought or research, and must, if we are to distinguish the truth from what is not truth.

The scientific method is based upon the principle of permitting truth to demonstrate itself; or in other words, acting upon the statement, "By their fruits ye shall know them" When we proceed according to this principle we find that truth always demonstrates itself when permitted to do so; and also, any belief which does not prove itself to be the truth, proves itself through the same process to be the untruth.

In this age, one of the reigning desires is to find the truth; in consequence, wide-awake minds may be seen in large numbers going here and there and everywhere in search of the precious jewel. But how many of them know what the jewel looks like?

Are we sure that most of us have not passed it by thousands of times, thinking it was something else?

It has been said that "All is not gold that glitters' but we can with equal propriety declare, that all is not truth that dazzles the mind with the colorings of plausibility, though the average truth seeker is entirely too prone to accept the plausible as truth without further evidence. The ideas thus accepted invariably become subconscious convictions of more or less power, and we have a repetition of the old process until the new belief becomes a habit and controls the mind as it was controlled by the habits of belief which went before.

What is Truth

Knowing that subconscious convictions can so dominate judgment and reason that the true may appear to be false, and vice versa, it is wholly unsafe to accept anything as true until we have seen the fruits. We should therefore demand that every idea demonstrate its genuineness before it is made a part of the mind. No idea should be permitted to impress itself upon the subconscious until it has proved itself to be true, because the subconscious is like k fertile field. Anything will grow there if you simply drop the seed.

"As a man thinketh in his heart so is he"; and the thought of the heart is invariably that thought which is rooted in the subconscious. The thoughts, ideas, desires and convictions which enter the subconscious will wholly determine what we are to do, think or become. Whatever enters the subconscious will express itself in the personality, and whatever we accept with implicit faith will enter the subconscious. Since ever seed that is sown in the subconscious will positively bear fruit after its kind, and since what we accept as true will enter the subconscious, we cannot be too cautious with respect to what we think of as the truth; and should therefore require all ideas to prove themselves before we receive them.

But here we may ask what we are to do with all those beliefs that the race has for ages looked upon as sacred? Will it be necessary to take all these beliefs out and demand that they demonstrate themselves through the scientific method to be absolutely true before we reinstate them in our minds? The answer is, this is the course we must take. All truth is sacred, and nothing is sacred unless it is the truths The fact that we think a certain belief to be sacred does not make it so, even though it has been held sacred for a thousand centuries. We can easily get into the habit of thinking the most ordinary illusion to be a sacred truth, and finally be completely controlled by that belief. If a belief is true it will produce the fruits of the truth, which means all good things for life here and now. And if so, it is sacred. But if it produces no fruits or produces results that are undesirable, it must be examined.

It may simply be a habit of thought that poses as sacred truth, and we want to know. Truth is for us, and if there is any idea in our minds that has all these years deceived us, we want to get rid of it at once, no matter how sacred it may have appeared in the eyes of ignorance.

The fact that we have to discard a few of the old beliefs when we begin to search for the truth need not disturb us in the least. We shall not be left empty-handed. The truth is everywhere. There are millions of great truths all about us, above us, beneath us, within us, and we have the power to know them all; therefore, we are perfectly safe in changing our minds in a few respects when we find that such changes will be conducive to a much larger understanding of the truth. To eliminate the useless will give place for that which can add more richly to the welfare and the beauty of life.

Concerning the demonstration of truth we must remember that we are living in the great eternal now, and in consequence can take interest only in those ideas that deal with the present. We cannot demonstrate anything concerning the future; therefore it is a misuse of the mind to try. It is also wrong, for the same reason, to fill our minds with beliefs which deal solely with future states of existence. To understand the life that we are living now is the problem, and to live this present life in the truest and most beautiful sense possible is the purpose. To fulfill that purpose we must know the truth about present existence, and must live the present life according to that truth. I And here we should remember that to make the present good is to make the

What is Truth

future better, because what is to happen in days to come will be the natural result of what we are doing now.

Chapter 3

How to Seek the Truth

In this age thinkers are becoming numerous, and all thinkers are seekers of truth. At any rate they try to be, but they are not all successful in this respect, the reason being that the principle upon which all search of truth must be based is not clearly understood. To the majority truth is a something that can be received from some other mind; therefore it is sought from those who are supposed to know or who claim to know. And this is the real reason why there are so few who really understand the truth, or who are actually growing in that understanding.

In the strictest sense of the term truth cannot be taught. One mind cannot teach the truth to another mind. And in the same sense the truth cannot be learned. It can only be realized, and realization is a process that no two minds enter into exactly in the same way. Methods for finding the truth may be given by one mind to another, but each individual mind must employ such methods as his own present conception of truth, life and reality can apply.

We all occupy different positions in life. Therefore we all shall have to begin differently in taking any step forward. And if this step is taken in our own best way it will invariably be a forward step.

In like manner, since we all have different conceptions of the real we must seek to perfect our own conceptions. We cannot enlarge upon something in our own mind that never existed in our own minds. Therefore we must develop our own view of truth in order to obtain a better understanding of truth.

What is Truth

Before you can take a step from a lower position to a higher you must have a lower position upon which to stand. And that lower position must be under your own feet, not under the feet of another.

To obtain a larger realization of truth each individual mind must begin by unfolding the truth that he already perceives through his own present realization, no matter how crude or undeveloped that realization may be. He must enlarge upon that which he himself is in possession of. He must begin his development with his own present state of development, and not try to imitate the understanding, the realization or the process of growth in another.

No progress is possible so long as we try to see truth through the eyes of another, or try to imitate the understanding that a more advanced mind may possess. This very thing, however, nearly all seekers of truth are trying to do, and in consequence they do not succeed in knowing truth. To believe the truth is one thing. To know the truth is quite another. The former is possible to anybody, but it is only the latter that makes man free.

The average beginner in search of truth believes that his own conception of truth is wholly wrong.

At any rate, he is usually told so by those who imagine they have discovered the only truth; but in this respect they are quite mistaken. No conception of truth is wholly wrong. There is some truth in every belief that you may now entertain. Therefore begin with that tiny truth and continue to unfold it and enlarge upon it until it touches the universal on all sides. And when this process of growth is entered into you will find the way to perpetual growth in the absolute truth itself.

What is Truth

To develop the truth that may exist in your present conception of life and reality, the first essential is to open the mind on all sides. Realize that the truth is the soul of everything, and that something good can be gained from everything by opening the mind to this soul wherever it may be found.

Whenever a person declares that there is nothing in this or that, or that such and such is impossible, he places obstacles in the way of his own understanding, and therefore closes the door more or less to the truth. There positively is something in everything, and to find the truth about everything you must recognize this something in every phase of existence. This, however, is not possible so long as you continue to close your mind to everything that does not appeal to your understanding at first sight.

Everything that exists or that appears has some reality back of it or within it. Even so-called illusions are mental clouds that hide some light of truth. Therefore, instead of ignoring the mere appearance as worthless, the hidden truth that is certainly back of those things should be sought directly and with persistence. By tracing an illusion back to its origin you may make a great discovery. This very thing has been done a number of times. In fact, most of the greatest discoveries made in the world have been made exactly in this manner.

The man who refuses to investigate what does not appeal to him at first sight will never find real truth, nor will he become an original thinker. He will continue to remain a follower and will blindly believe what custom has made safe and respectable.

To say that there is nothing in this or that is to close the mental door to that something that is there, thus depriving

What is Truth

yourself of a truth that might be the very truth you are seeking now.

All truth is valuable and extremely important, but the truth that we actually need now is usually the truth that is hidden beneath the common misconceptions of everyday life. But we usually judge according to appearances and conclude that there is nothing in these things; therefore we fail to find what we want. Back of every truth there are scores of other truths and larger truths. It is therefore evident that when we close the mental door to those that are nearest we separate ourselves from a universe of rare wisdom.

To declare that this or that is impossible is to limit the power of truth, and when we place a limitation upon the power of truth we place a limitation upon our own power to understand truth. The mind that lives in the faith that all things are possible is the mind that opens itself more and more to the truth and that power from within that can make all things possible. In consequence such a mind develops daily in capacity, ability, understanding and power.

In this connection the proper course is to believe that there is something in everything, and to resolve to find it. Believe that everything is possible and resolve to prove it. Through this attitude your mind will expand in every direction, gaining light, wisdom and power from every source. To open the mind to truth on all sides is to bring consciousness into touch with an infinite sea of truth. The mind therefore will live perpetually in pure light, and will constantly gain a larger measure of this light.

Never say, "I do not believe this." You draw down one of the shades by so doing thereby excluding some of the sunlight of real truth. Say rather, "I believe the truth that is back of everything, therefore I respect everything, and will penetrate everything so as to find all the truth, and thus grow perpetually in the realization of all truth."

Do not attempt to gain truth by absorbing the views of others. On the other hand, do not attempt to gain truth by secluding yourself from the views of others. Proceed to develop in yourself the understanding of truth and you will find that the views of advancing minds will become nourishing food for that understanding. But so long as you have no real understanding of truth, or if your present conception of truth be undeveloped, the more advanced ideas you try to absorb the more confused you become.

When you have begun to understand the truth, that is, when you have begun to unfold your own present conception of the truth, you will find that every person, every book, every idea and every belief that you may come in contact with will prove to be an inspiration, and will help to open your mind to higher conceptions and deeper realizations.

In the search of truth we must remember that instructions from others are valuable only, in so far as we are able to interpret the inner meaning of the tangible facts presented. And this ability develops by our trying to feel and understand the soul of every idea that enters the mind. Knowledge becomes a power in us only when we feel within us the real soul of that knowledge.

The real truth seeker must try to interpret the meaning that underlies all phenomena, all experience, all events and all ideas. He must constantly keep the fact in mind that there is something back of everything. And he must seek this something in everything that is met in life. We shall find in this connection that the perpetual growth in truth will naturally follow the effort to realize the inner or soul existence in everything with which we may come in contact.

What is Truth

Truth is found directly by seeking to understand the interior essence of life through one's own interpretations of life and through the development of one's own insight into principles, laws and things. In other words, when we enlarge our own present conception of truth we gain a larger interior conception of all truth as all truth appears from our present point of view.

With most minds too much time is given in trying to find truth in the outside world, and not enough time is given to the development of that power within us that alone can know the truth. To receive a message of truth from some great mind is not sufficient. You must try to understand the spirit, the life and the real soul of that message by entering mentally into the deepest conception of that message that you can possibly form in your own consciousness. Truth will not come to you through any message or form of instructions if you make no attempt to go beyond the literal statements.

It is the inner life of things that contains the truth. Therefore, to understand the truth you must develop that insight that can discern the interior, the seemingly hidden, or the very soul of existence. The great secret in finding truth is to enter more closely into harmony with the interior soul life of everything, thereby developing the higher consciousness that actually knows truth.

We should make it a point to listen to everyone who has a reasonable message; that is, a message that deals directly with truth, unsystematized truth; but we should learn to interpret that message through our own conception of truth. We should welcome the thoughts of others on all subjects, but we should not accept those thoughts as final statements. We should not take the literal meaning, but look for the inner meaning of every word that is spoken. We should analyze the thoughts of others, but do our own independent thinking. Though we must not imagine that we have begun our own thinking simply because we have discarded one system of belief and adopted another.

We should pay no attention to a message that deals simply with doctrines and opinions. It is life in all its manifestations that we wish to understand. And when we understand life we shall also understand everything that pertains to life, or that comes from life. A message of truth invariably deals with life and the living of life now. Therefore we can readily distinguish between what is claimed to be a message of truth and one that actually is a message of truth.

What we are thinking at the present time is very important, therefore every thought of the present should be created in the likeness of truth; but it is equally important that we move constantly into larger thought, superior thought and higher conceptions of true thought. A message that presents a fixed system of belief; that is, a belief supposed to contain the truth, is of no value to the truth seeker.

To adopt a fixed system, no matter how good it may seem to be is to cease to be a seeker of truth.

To seek the truth is to seek constantly a larger and larger understanding of truth; that is, to enlarge upon one's present conception of truth and enter again and again into new truth. But neither new truths nor larger truths ever spring from a fixed system. To gain the understanding of larger truth and steadily grow into the absolute truth the mind must constantly expand. But the mind that adepts a fixed system will remain fixed, therefore cannot expand.

What the truth seeker wants is methods that promote individuality and originality, methods that lead the mind upward and onward in every direction. It is not something to believe that is wanted, but something that we can use in developing the mind so that we can understand the very foundation of all belief. We do not want ideas that will simply satisfy the intellect. We also want methods that will expand, enlarge and develop the intellect.

We do not want a religion or a philosophy that we can accept as authority. We want a science of living that will so develop man that the man himself can speak as one having authority. Truth does not come through believing something. It comes through the use of that something that unfolds, develops and elevates the mind.

A great many truth seekers believe that it is necessary to work independently in order to promote originality of thought, and therefore they have a sort of fear of personalities, systems and institutions. But this is a mistake, because nothing can hold you in bondage unless you fear that bondage.

On the other hand, all things may at times serve as means through which a higher conception of greater truth may be attained. And here we should remember that more mental bondage comes from the fear of institutions than from the institutions themselves. The real truth seeker is friendly to all minds, to all beliefs, to all systems and to all institutions, because he knows that back of them all there is some truth, and through friendly relations that truth may be found. He also knows that when we are friendly with all things all things will be with us, and what is with us will help us on to greater things.

This being true, we should eliminate the critical spirit and encourage the analytical spirit. In brief, we should try all things and hold fast to the good.

What is Truth

The critical mind may have plausible opinions, but it is not possible to realize the truth while we are in critical or antagonistic states of mind. This is a fact of enormous importance, a fact that should be so deeply impressed upon every mind that it will never be forgotten. The mind that is looking for the truth that is back of all things will not criticize anything, because to such a mind all things are paths to greater truth and therefore to the greater goal we may have in view.

In our search of truth we must remember that it is not sufficient simply to seek the truth. We must also live the truth. If we fail to live the truth that we have found we will soon lose that truth, and also close the door to new truth. By living the truth that we now understand we open the mental door to more truth and larger truth, for the fact is that when we apply what we know we gain the power to know more. This is especially true when we live in the. aspiring or the spiritual attitude. And we live in the spiritual attitude when our mind is open to the best from all sources.

As we proceed in the application of any particular principle, we shall so enlarge the mind that other and more important principles will be comprehended. The application of all of these in turn will expand consciousness still farther, and so on indefinitely, until a universe of wisdom is held in the grasp of the mind. To apply the truth in its present limited phases will develop the understanding of larger phases. Any mind, therefore, may begin with the most limited understanding of truth, and in the course of a few years have an understanding that cannot be measured.

Nothing should be accepted as truth that does not appeal to reason. The idea presented may be true, but if it does not appeal to your reason you cannot apply it now; and what you cannot apply is of no present use to you. However, do not criticize or condemn what you cannot accept. There is truth back of it because there is truth back of everything, even though you may not see it now. Therefore suspend judgment for the present and proceed to develop a finer insight and a finer mind so that you may in the future see what may be hidden in the present.

Although all truth must appeal to reason before it can be applied, reason must not be depended upon exclusively in finding the truth. It is the finer perceptions and insights that occupy the most important position in the discovery of truth. Therefore if you are a truth seeker proceed to develop those faculties by using them constantly wherever your attention may be directed.

If all these perceptions and insights were universally developed, we should all see the truth so clearly that there would be practically no disagreements concerning what is true and what is not true about this sphere of existence. However, our object must not be to try to agree, but to develop the power to understand the truth, for when this power is developed perfect agreement among us all will come of itself.

In the search of truth the imagination must be held under perfect control. The majority, however, among the truth seekers permit their imaginations to form all sorts of ideas and conceptions, and they frequently accept these as true, regardless of evidence. This is one reason why illusions and half truths are so numerous.

Another essential is to keep the emotional nature in poise. Our emotions tend to excite the imagination, and a number of artificial ideas will be impressed upon the mind. Many of these will be so deeply impressed that they appear to be true, because when the mind is in an intense emotional state nearly every idea formed at the time will be deeply felt. And what is deeply felt we usually accept as the truth whether it is or no.

One of the greatest essentials in the search of truth is the spiritual viewpoint; that is, to examine all things from the principle that the soul or the reality that is back of all things is absolutely perfect and absolutely true. The purpose of life is perpetual growth in the realization of perfection.

Therefore we must stand upon the principle of possible perfection in all things, and deal with all things according to that principle.

The understanding of truth does not mean the acceptance of a fixed idea that has proven itself to be true, but the perpetual unfoldment and enlargement of that idea through the constant growth of the mind in the realization of truth. The process of understanding is not a fixed attitude of mind, but a constant deepening and widening of mind as consciousness grows deeper and deeper into the very soul of reality, and expands in every direction toward the wider comprehension of reality.

You may think you understand the deep things of life, but there is still a larger universe beyond what you may understand. And to understand this the mind must constantly enlarge and deepen its understanding toward greater depths of truth and wisdom. Every idea that is found contains truth, or the possibility of some unfoldment of truth; therefore by entering the soul of every idea and enlarging the present conception of that soul the hidden truth will be found. In addition many paths to other truth will be revealed.

What is Truth

Higher truth is discovered through the higher consciousness; therefore to try to compel people to believe what is beyond their present state of consciousness is a violation of mental law. Instead, we should teach man to develop himself and he will gain the greater understanding of life. He will also through this higher development learn to seek truth, learn where to find truth and learn how to apply truth.

The real secret of the truth seeker is to begin with his present conception of truth and develop himself in mind and soul through the perpetual enlargement of that conception; in brief, develop your power to understand greater truth by using the truth you now understand. This will positively give you the power to understand more truth and higher truth, and this is the great purpose we have in view.

What is Truth

Chapter 4

Where to Find the Truth

The search for truth is becoming more and more extensive, and the desire to know truth for the sake of knowing is increasing with remarkable rapidity.

For the same reason the number of new systems of belief are also increasing in proportion, as it is the general opinion that it is only through special systems of thought that the truth can be found. And the supply along any line of desire is always equal to the demand.

But the demands of the human mind are not always properly placed. Therefore we find many minds who desire systems based upon the latest conceptions of truth instead of upon the truth itself.

This state of affairs causes rivalry among the various systems, and the question with them becomes not how to find more truth and live more perfectly according to the truth we know, but instead, which system is correct and which one is not.

Opposing systems, however, cannot all be correct, but since the advocates of each system believe their own to be correct they finally come to the conclusion that their own is the only true system. This conclusion is perfectly natural, because if you believe your belief to be correct, all other beliefs that do not agree with your own must be incorrect from your point of view. You therefore feel perfectly justified in declaring your own belief to be the only one through which the truth may be found.

What is Truth

The average mind looks at things only from his own point of view. He has not enlarged his consciousness sufficiently to know how it feels to be on the other side, therefore has nothing but his own limited experience upon which to base judgment.

Accordingly, he cannot be blamed for what he thinks about his own favorite ideas. Though we must remember that no matter how convinced he may feel as to the exactness of his own conclusions we must not accept them until we have compared them with others and found them to be superior.

When we study the nature of the mind we find that the tendency of the average person to think that his system of belief is the only system through which the truth can be found, comes from the general tendency to worship systems of thought instead of the all truth that is back of every system. When you know that all systems are but varying interpretations of one absolute truth you will never say that your own system constitutes the only field wherein truth may be found, because you will know that all minds, even the most ignorant, know some of the truth. If they did not they could not continue to exist.

The very fact that a person continues to live and continues to secure certain results in providing for the essentials of life, proves that he is possessed of a considerable portion of the truth. If a person had no truth everything that he had would be false at its foundation, which would make his own individual existence impossible. This is a fact that we must well remember.

Another fact equally important is that no person can secure results in any field of action unless he applies the truth in that field. An action based upon mere falseness can produce nothing. Such an action cannot even enable a man to walk across the floor. To walk at all you must apply certain laws correctly. And to apply any law correctly you must have a correct conception of that law, conscious or unconscious. And to have a correct conception of anything is to know the truth to that extent.

The true use of anything can alone produce results, and the true use of anything is the application of a certain phase of the truth that lies at the foundation of that particular thing. Our conception of such truth may be subconscious only, but it exists in our minds. We possess it, and when we apply it we have results.

There are a great many things that we do not understand objectively, but the fact that we use them successfully proves that certain parts of our minds know the underlying laws and can, at least to a degree, apply those laws. According to these facts we realize that everything that lives must necessarily be in contact with the truth somewhere.

If it were not it would produce a misstep at every turn, and nothing can continue to exist that produces missteps or mistakes only.

The average person deplores the fact that he makes so many mistakes, but when we stop to consider how many things we do that are not mistakes we conclude that things are not so bad after all. We have formed the habit of taking special notice of our mistakes just as the press of the world records mostly what is not good or desirable, because such things are exceptional, therefore constitute news. Normal and wholesome actions in the social world do not constitute news. They are too numerous. And being normal they can be found in every nook and corner in the world. It is the normal, that is, the right and the good, that constitutes the rule of action in the world. It is the abnormal, or the bad, that constitutes the exception.

A man may act like a gentleman sixty minutes out of the hour and we pay no attention to that fact. However, should he act contrary to the principle of right for one minute the fact would be noted by everybody. And if that particular act was striking it would be wired all over the world.

In his case the good would be sixty times as large as the evil, nevertheless, it would be the latter only that would constitute news, being so exceptional.

In like manner we may, as individuals, act according to the truth as far as we see it, and every minute of the hour. And no one pays special attention to such an unbroken series of good acts, unless, of course, those acts should be very striking or extraordinary. However, the very moment we make a mistake attention is aroused at once. If we make many of them our attention is very much concerned because we know by experience, if not by insight, that when the abnormal outnumbers the normal the end is near at hand.

Since a person can bring physical existence to an end simply by causing the abnormal actions to become more numerous than the normal ones, we can readily understand that he could not exist at all if all of his actions were abnormal. In fact, conscious existence could not even have a beginning under such conditions, and organic life would not be possible for a second. A life where every act was a mistake would be absolute chaos, and a state of absolute chaos is nothing. Therefore, so long as a person lives at all it is evident that his normal actions are more numerous that his mistakes.

What is Truth

And a normal action is always a right action. A right action is the application of a truth in one or more of its phases, because nothing can be right unless it is based upon the truth. This proves that every existing entity knows consciously or unconsciously certain portions of the truth; And that therefore there can possibly be no one system through which all truth may be found.

The problem that confronts us all, however, is how to so relate ourselves to the all truth about us, that we may find as much truth as we may need now in order to make every action right that we may express. We know that the ills of personal existence come from mistakes or from abnormal actions. We understand, therefore, that if we could prevent all mistakes we could prevent all ills.

To accomplish this some advocate this system and some that, each one believing that his system is the one that contains the secret. The fact, however, that all systems produce results has led to the belief that results secured through the system of another were secured through the aid of evil power. But here the question arises, how can an evil power make correct use of the laws of life; and again, how can evil power know the truth obtained from those laws? For it is a fact that evil in every instance is the opposite, or rather the absence, of truth.

To build a bridge you require mathematics.

Without mathematics you cannot build that bridge.

Therefore, whoever can build bridges or who does build bridges, understands mathematical principles.

And for anyone to say that such or such a person builds bridges with the aid of an evil power — a power that would

What is Truth

naturally tend to eliminate the truth of mathematics as well as remove mathematicians from their positions, is to make a statement too absurd to be considered for a moment among scientific men. Nevertheless, when we come to mental, moral and spiritual fields we make statements every day that are equally absurd; and we even try to prove that such statements are inspiration.

The fact in this connection, however, is simply this, that it is only the good that can produce good results. And it is only through the understanding of certain phases of truth that we can apply the good. We conclude, therefore, that any man, no matter what his beliefs may be, who secures good results in any field understands the truth to that extent.

The whole universe is based upon absolute law.

If it were not, space would contain nothing but chaos, and nothing could exist. Therefore everything that is to be done must be done according to law. We cannot go outside of the law if we wish to construct bridges or engines. Neither can we go outside of the law if we wish to build character or make real the ideal. We cannot perform a single good deed without using some of the laws of life.

We cannot convey our ideas through language without using some of these laws. We cannot do anything and produce the same results under the same conditions without using one or more of these laws. And to use the laws of life correctly is to use understanding a certain phase of the truth.

Every person is producing certain results in his life. Some of those results are great and others small, but they are results. Therefore everybody knows some of the truth, as it is only through the application of truth that results can be secured.

We thus see the folly of claiming anyone system to be the only channel through which truth can be found.

The truth is just as universal as life, and in fact is the very essence or soul of life. Therefore everything that lives, lives some of the truth — as much of the truth as present consciousness can comprehend.

Every constructive action of the mind opens the way to greater truth. But no mind can act constructively to good advantage as long as a certain interpretation of truth is accepted as final. The fact is that when you accept anything as final you bring your mind to a standstill in that sphere of action. And the fact that the whole world has accepted certain spiritual and metaphysical ideas as final is one reason why real spirituality is found so rarely. The same is true, however, in various fields of mental and intellectual realms. Therefore no matter how remarkable a discovery you may make, if you accept that as final in its own field you stop there; progress is suspended; further growth is retarded along that line.

And after the new discovery has become a system and lost its life, as all truth does when formulated into a system, we are just as much in mental or spiritual darkness as before; for we must bear in mind that every discovery that we look upon as final in its own field loses its soul; that is, it dies, leaving us the shell of mere belief only. This is natural because all belief comes from within. And as soon as we formulate a number of truths into a fixed system, we begin to worship the system, thereby ignoring the life and the spirit of the within. To ignore the within, however, is to turn away from the source of all truth, all life and all power, which

What is Truth

means that we separate ourselves from those very things that we wish to secure in greater abundance.

In this connection we should also remember that the very moment we look upon a truth as final we cease to rise in search of more. It is only the rising mind that receives the life, the substance and the spirit of things. And it is only that mind that is ever in search of more truth that can really understand truth. We know the truth only while we are steadily moving upward and onward into more truth.

Truth is everywhere, and truth alone does things.

Therefore everything that produces results in its own sphere of action demonstrates truth. And whoever has results has truth. Every demonstration is the result of truth, be it in the healing of disease by any method whatever, or the building of a beautiful mansion by any method whatever.

Every method that produces results or that emancipates, builds, constructs, beautifies or elevates, is based upon truth and employs truth. This is natural because truth is everywhere, so that every method can touch truth, be fixed or rooted in truth, and be a constant expression of truth.

If every demonstration was not the result of truth some demonstrations would be the result of untruth, which is impossible. The false cannot take away pain at any time. The false cannot invent and construct machinery. The false cannot develop a child into a musical genius. The false cannot write a poem, nor cause barren waste to become a garden of highly developed roses. In brief, the false cannot do anything.

The laws of the body are just as much in the hands of truth as are the laws of the mind or the soul. Therefore a man who builds a house or perfects his physical form, employs the truth just as well as the man who builds character or unfolds cosmic consciousness. All life is good. Everything is sacred, and the truth is the foundation of the entire universe. Thus we understand that the only truth is the universal truth; and the only way to find universal truth is to live in conscious touch with everything that gives expression to life or truth in any form or manner.

Universal truth is not encased in this religious system or in that philosophical belief. Universal truth is the spirit of every atom, of every flower, of every creature, of every entity in existence.

There is no special path to this truth because every path leads to this truth. It can be found everywhere and in everything. Everything that lives is moving into more and more of this truth, because to live is to move forward, and to move forward is to enter a larger measure of the all truth.

Every mind lives in the truth and actually breathes the very life of truth. Therefore to find more truth we must live more, and not search for truth in any particular system, but to try to enter into closer mental touch with the all truth as it lives and moves in all things.

Your method for finding the truth you may need now; it may be the only method that works for you at present. In like manner the methods that others employ may be the only ones that they can use now.

Therefore we must never say that our method is the only method that will work for everybody, or that everybody can find truth now in the same place as we are finding truth now.

In this connection, however, we must watch a certain tendency that is present more or less in all minds. When we find a new method that does the very thing that we have never succeeded in doing before, there is a tendency to exaggerate or overvalue the merit of that method. This tendency intoxicates the mind, so to speak, and magnifies the new discovery, so it appears much larger than it really is. Naturally, we conclude that it is the best of its kind. In fact, must be the best to our view of thinking, because our view at the time is so magnified.

From this belief of the best there is only a tiny step to the belief of the only; and the tendency that produces the former will also produce the latter.

Whenever a mind declares that his is the best he is on the way to the belief that his is the only. And if he is not thoroughly balanced he will soon enter the latter view. The reason the mind acts in this way is easily understood when we become familiar with psychological laws. But those who think they have the only way to truth do not study psychological laws, because their belief has limited their minds to the idea that they have found the one only law. However, the very moment that any mind begins to study psychological laws the "only truth" idea will vanish like the darkness before the light.

When we all understand the mind, and also why we think what we think, all systems of belief will be discarded. Then we will all seek the truth itself directly, and seek it everywhere. The result will be perpetual growth into the truth. We shall then find the truth that gives freedom to the whole life of man — the truth that develops every part of the being of man for a higher and truer use. Accordingly, the life more abundant will follow. And from such a life comes everything that mind may desire.

Chapter 5

Where Do We Get Our Ideas

Ideas do not come to us from the without. The belief that we are living in a world of readymade ideas upon which we may draw as we like is not true. The human mind is not a mere receptacle into which ideas may flow from some outer source.

The ideas that exist in the individual mind are created by that mind, and by that mind alone. The belief that all ideas come from some external source — that we simply have to open our mind to receive them — makes the mind a mere channel through which something may pass from one place to another; or it may make the mind a mere automaton upon which any force from without may act for good or otherwise. This belief, however, is very common, and it is one of the principal obstacles to originality and greatness, as well as to the finding and knowing of real truth.

The belief that man develops by opening more widely his mind so as to receive a greater number of ideas from the cosmic fields about him, tends to prevent the further development of the mind.

While the realization of the fact that man develops by creating more and more original ideas of his own will tend to promote further development.

Any system of thought or belief, therefore, that compels the mind to accept the ideas of others will retard the progress, not only of the individual but of the race. On the other hand, anything that teaches man how to create his own ideas and do his own original thinking will promote the development of greatness.

What is Truth

It is a well known fact that every form of greatness comes from original thinking, and those who understand the natures of mind and soul know that original thinking is the direct result of man's power to create consciously his own ideas according to his highest conception of what is truth. The mind that can create ideas has begun to exercise its own creative powers. And when those powers are mastered anything can be created or recreated. Through these powers man can recreate his own personality, his own character and his own mentality. He can recreate his own mental world, change all his exterior surroundings, and create his own destiny.

Man has the power to become a master in the largest sense of that term. And the first step is to create consciously and intelligently his own ideas.

To begin, the fact that ideas do not come from without must be realized. We may receive impressions from external sources, but we do not receive ideas from those sources. The only ideas that exist in any mind are the ideas that that mind itself has created.

In this connection we must remember that an idea is not a belief about something, but the result of your own mental conception of that something.

You may accept any number of beliefs about things without actually thinking about those things. But when you try to understand those things from your own point of view, you form a mental conception of your own, and the result is ideas of your own.

These ideas may be crude, nevertheless, you have begun to exercise your own creative power, and may so develop that

What is Truth

power that the future may find you in advance of the greatest minds of the age.

To exercise this creative power try to form mental conceptions of everything that may enter your mind; that is, try to understand all things of which you are conscious by looking at those things from your own individual point of view.

Do not ask what others may think about this or that, but ask yourself, What do I think? How do these things appear to me while viewed through the eyes of my own mind? Your conclusion may be imperfect at first, but you are arousing your own creative powers; you are forming mental conceptions in your own mentality; and you are creating ideas of your own. You are therefore developing originality and have entered the path to greatness as well as the path to the higher and better understanding of greater truth.

To bring your mental creative power into full play the more impressions from the without that you admit in your mind the better, provided those impressions have quality and worth; because to form conceptions we must have something about which to think, and both quality and quantity should be sought from every source. Impressions come through the senses, and indicate to consciousness the fact that there is something real back of those phases of life that are represented by the impressions thus received.

When you look at something you gain an impression. But that impression is not at first an idea.

The impression simply indicates the existence of something without giving any definite information as to what that something might actually be. If you accept that impression as final on the subject you fail to form any idea of

What is Truth

your own with regard to it. Thus your creative power is not brought into action through the coming of that impression, and no original thought is formed. On the other hand, if you proceed to form some definite mental conception about that something, the existence of which was indicated by the impression, you will form an idea of your own, thereby developing the power of original thought

The same impressions, however, do not originate the same ideas in different minds; nor is this necessary. The purpose is that each individual mind is to form ideas of his own in connection with every impression that is received so that the power of original thought may be developed. To a materialistic mind the sight of a forest may simply suggest lumber and profit; but to a lofty mind the same forest may suggest the beautiful idea of God's first temples; and he may enter to worship in states more sublime than he ever knew before. What ideas we shall form therefore from impressions thus received will depend entirely upon our own attitude and purpose in life. Though if we actually form ideas according to our present capacity we shall take real steps in the right direction.

Our interpretations of things may differ for a time, but if we use these interpretations for the purpose of creating original ideas we shall all reach gradually but surely the same high goal, even though our several paths in the beginning were not the same. We realize therefore the folly of criticizing those who differ from us in their ideas about things, because so long as they are creating ideas of their own they are moving forward, building both mind and character; and accordingly deserve only the highest praise.

We want everybody to become much. We want everybody to live the largest and best life that is possible in their present state of development. And since we know that

What is Truth

original thinking is the secret of greater things, we must invariably rejoice whenever we discover an individual who has begun to create his own ideas. The fact that his ideas may differ from our own should not disturb us, because when a mind begins original thinking that mind will become larger and larger, and will ere long gain just as large an understanding of truth as we have, and possibly much larger still in the course of time.

In dealing with people, therefore, our object should not be to persuade them to accept our system of belief. On the contrary, we should try to encourage them in original thinking. We should try to present methods through which they may become so great in mind and soul that they can understand the whole truth for themselves. The mind that becomes larger and larger will know the truth and live the truth without being persuaded by others.

Therefore all our efforts for the race should be directed upon the development of larger minds and greater souls. To promote this purpose original thinking along the lines of seeking, finding and knowing the truth is the one great essential. Let people believe what they like for the present, but do your best, by all means, to stimulate the desire in all minds to create their own individual ideas about everything.

The truth is everywhere. We all can see it if we have sufficient mental capacity; no one has the monopoly; nor is it necessary for us to gain our understanding of truth through certain persons or systems. All minds are equal before the Infinite Mind. And each individual mind must understand the truth through his own mentality. We can know only by using our own power to know. And that power develops through the constant use of creative capacity, that is, original thinking, or the creation of our own ideas about everything about which we may think.

What is Truth

If we wish people to see as much of the true and beautiful as we see, we should help them to develop the same high states of mind. The same mental altitudes produce the same points of view, the same points of view produce the same mental conceptions, and the same mental conceptions produce the same ideas. In consequence, when we reach the heights of great souls we shall see life as they see it; we shall think the same thoughts that they think; and the peace and the joy that they feel we shall feel also.

Do not criticize what you do not understand, or what does not appeal to you. Instead, develop your mind more and more; and what you do not understand today will be simplicity itself tomorrow. We are wasting too much time trying to change each other's belief. If we would all use that time helping each other on to greater heights of understanding and power we should ere long become so highly developed that we all could see all things from all points of view. Then we should all agree in all things without even trying to agree.

We cannot find the truth by following this system or that, but by using the best systems and methods in the development of a superior understanding; and in the use of methods we must remember that impressions or beliefs have no value except as indicators pointing the way to some hidden reality or truth. Therefore those who receive the wisdom of the past, or the impressions of the present, as something to have and to hold, gain absolutely nothing.

However, those who try to form original mental conceptions of everything that enters the mind from any source, will not only develop originality and greatness, but will sooner or later form those very ideas that have always produced the greatest things in life.

What is Truth

We are changed, improved or transformed through the renewal of our minds. And this renewal is the result of our creating superior ideas of everything about which we may think. To form superior ideas it is necessary to improve constantly upon all of our mental conceptions; in brief, to accept no conclusion as final, but to try to see all things through a larger and a larger understanding The greatest mistake that can be made in this connection is to accept ideas from other minds without trying to improve upon those ideas in our own minds.

The ideas we think we receive from other minds are not necessarily ideas, but usually only impressions of those ideas, because the only ideas that can exist in any mind are the ones that that mind creates itself. Those impressions, however, that are received from the ideas expressed by others may become instrumental in forming ideas of our own if employed for that purpose; but if they are simply accepted without further thought they are valueless.

Originality comes not by accepting beliefs, but from the creation of superior ideas about all things that are represented by our beliefs. And the more numerous our beliefs or impressions are the better, provided we select only the best. There are some who are trying to develop originality by refusing to listen to other minds, thinking that they must depend wholly upon their own conclusions. But originality does not come by ignoring the thoughts of others. Originality comes by improving upon those thoughts. And since we must know the best thoughts in the world today in order to create something better, we should familiarize ourselves with the best ideas and the best minds everywhere. Then we should try to form superior ideas in our own minds.

We may not succeed at once in forming ideas that are superior to those of the master minds, but we will in the

What is Truth

effort create ideas of our own, thus taking the path to greatness and the path to greater truth. And by continuing in this path we shall soon rise to those heights from where we can give the world something better than has ever been given before.

To form superior ideas look at the subject under consideration from as many viewpoints as possible and enter into the finest grades of mental life during the process. Learn to feel deeply whenever you think, and try to see the very soul of all thought.

All such effort, however, must be gentle, though filled with a strong, penetrating desire that gives the whole attention to the spirit of perfection that permeates all things. Refine the mind by training yourself to think through the feeling of your finest conception of refinement, and hold attention centered upon your highest realization of what may be termed cosmic substance. This substance is the perfect substance from which all substance is formed. Therefore it is the highest and finest that we can think of. It is the least material, and by thinking about it your mind enters into a finer consciousness through which superior ideas will invariably be formed.

Having realized this fine mental life, take up your various beliefs and try to form superior ideas about the principles or realities which those beliefs represent. You will have results almost from the beginning. Then search everywhere for ideas that are superior to your own in order that you can improve upon them all. Whether you do or not you will at any rate improve upon your own power of originality, and to continue in that improvement is to reach those heights in the course of time where you can improve upon almost anything. Through this practice discoveries and inventions of great value may appear to you at any time. In fact, you are liable to do greater things than ever were done before, no matter how insignificant you may be today. By creating your own ideas about all things you begin the development of creative power and there is no limit to what this power can do.

Chapter 6

The Two Sides of Truth

Everything in life has two sides. When we view anything from the one side only the result is a half truth. But when the same thing is viewed from both sides the result will be a whole truth. The physical scientist who ignores metaphysics has therefore nothing but half truths to present to the world. And the same is true of the metaphysician who ignores the physical side of that which he attempts to study and understand.

A half truth generally seems plausible, in fact so plausible at times that only a few can detect its incompleteness. But the conclusions of the half truth invariably mislead the mind at every turn. A half truth, however, not only misleads the mind, but gradually eliminates the power of discrimination so that the mind finally becomes incapable of finding the truth when real truth does appear.

That person that has followed half truths all his life is unable to know real truth when face to face with it. And as the majority are more or less in this condition this phase of our study of truth becomes extremely important.

Every modern system of belief is filled with half truths, but it will not be necessary here to analyze them all. A general analysis of the most striking illustrations will be sufficient, as through such an analysis anyone will be able to detect the flaws in the others. One of the most striking of these illustrations in the thinking of half truths is found in the statement that mind is the only power.

What is Truth

At first sight it may appear that the mind is the cause of everything, and that it does everything, but a deeper study reveals the fact that the mind is only one phase of the only power. There is but one power in the universe; that is, one fundamental force of action, but this power differentiates itself into a vast number of phases, and anyone phase is as real as any of the others.

We have recently discovered the fact that the mind exercises great power over the body. And for that reason many have come to the conclusion that the mind is the only power that effects the body.

But this is a half truth and comes from viewing the subject from one side only. Many people who accept this view go so far as to say that it is wrong to use anything else but mind whenever we wish to relieve or effect the body. But those who follow half truths are never consistent; and in consequence, while affirming that mind alone can help the body, they continue to protect the body with physical clothes and feed the body with physical food.

As a rule, people who follow half truths forget that it is the same power that has created everything, and that therefore the things that are seen are just as real and good as the things that are not seen, and, of course, vice versa. In brief, all things are real in their own sphere of existence, and all things are good in their own proper places.

In this connection we must remember that the mind always acts through agencies; whether these be muscles, nerves, senses, intellect or thought, they are agencies of mind; and one agency is not inferior to another. If it is right for the mind to use thought in removing a physical condition or disease, it is also right for the mind to use muscle in

What is Truth

performing a surgical operation, should it be wise and necessary to perform such an operation.

In both instances it is the mind acting upon the body through an agency. On the other hand, if it is wrong to perform a surgical operation when some simple remedy would avail, it would also be wrong to waste precious mental energy in overcoming physical ailments that could just as easily be removed by some simple or natural method.

The question is, not what to discard entirely and what to use exclusively; the question is, to determine what means or methods will produce the best and the quickest results now under present conditions. Use any power when that particular power is needed, and use it well, because every power is but an expression of the one Supreme Power. All is good in its place, and all is made for the service of man; therefore all things can be used in adding to the welfare of man.

When you believe that mind is the only power, you limit yourself more and more to such powers as may be expressed on the mental plane. In consequence you will be compelled to depend almost entirely upon mental force, and will be helpless when that force is weakened, which frequently happens with those who neglect the development of everything but mind. So long as you believe that the mind is the only power you open the mental door to mental powers alone. You eliminate all others and cannot come into possession of those marvelous spiritual powers that alone can make man great.

A study of people who believe that mind is the only power, reveals clearly that their work is conducted entirely upon the mental plane; and in too many instances gives expression to the narrowest phases of mentality. When you carry this idea of the allness of mind to its extreme conclusion, you eliminate all the expressions of the mind to that of what may be called mental force or mind vibrations.

You will depend upon such actions of mind for everything. You will expect those vibrations to act upon things directly and to do anything desired without the use of agencies. Ability, mental capacity, character, intelligence, talent and, in brief, all the natural functions and powers of the mind will be neglected. All development, therefore, will be retarded, as the whole of attention is centered upon the efforts of mental vibration; that is, the mind acting with a certain purpose in view without the use of agencies through which to act. Finally the mind becomes so dull that it is even incapable of retaining conscious control of its own mental vibrations. In fact, by narrowing itself down to one thing it becomes so small that even that one thing is neither understood nor controlled.

It is therefore evident that by thinking that the mind is the only power, your mind will become so small and so superficial that it will be incapable of original and individual thought. It will be unable to stand upon its own feet and will have to depend wholly upon some fixed system.

Life is complex and gives expression to many powers. Mind is one of these, but only one of many. And if we would develop the power of the mind we must train ourselves to give a larger and a more perfect expression to all the other powers as well. We add to the power and the capacity of every single function by increasing the power of all the other functions. And the leading faculty of any mind will have the greatest ability and capacity when backed up, so to speak, with a number of other faculties that are also strong and highly developed.

What is Truth

Another statement heard frequently among those who see only the one side of truth is this, that everything is all right if we think so. This idea, of course, is founded upon the belief that wrong thought is the only cause of evil or imperfection.

But if we should follow this belief to its extreme and inevitable conclusion, we would have to say that thought is everything, and that all else is nothing. If your thinking makes things right or wrong the things themselves can have neither power nor qualities. And if this were true things could not even have existence, because, to exist, a thing must have powers and qualities of some kind.

According to such a belief the cheapest clothing would be rich and rare if we only thought so; the most homely face would be charmingly beautiful if we only thought so; the most ordinary music would be simply inspiring if we thought so; and the worst meal that was ever prepared would be perfectly delicious if we thought it was. Thousands of other conclusions equally absurd would naturally follow our attempt to describe things according to this belief. But this is always the case with half truths.

They seem plausible as long as they are not closely examined.

If we should adopt the belief that everything is all right if we think it is, we would soon be unable to distinguish between degrees of perfection; our judgment would become so poor that we could see no difference between the common and the worthy, between the homely and the beautiful, between the false and the true. To us everything would be lovely, but loveliness would mean nothing more to us than the most superficial sentiment. We would say that all things are good because we think so, but we should be unable to understand what goodness actually means, therefore would fail to grow in the realization of goodness.

The whole truth in this connection is that when things are wrong your thinking they are right will not make them right. But you can through the proper use of your thought cause things to change and become right. The way you think, when in the presence of wrong things, will determine to a very great extent how you are to be affected by those things, and also how much those things may be changed by your action under the circumstances.

But the things themselves, as well as their present conditions, are just as real as your thought, though they will obey the power of your thought completely if that power is properly employed.

You may listen to the most beautiful music, but you will fail to enjoy it if you are in a critical frame of mind. The lack of enjoyment will in this instance come not from things, but from your perverted thought about things. Your wrong thought, however, had no effect whatever upon the music.

The music was good in spite of what you thought, but your own thought prevented you from getting any good out of the music. On the other hand, you may listen to music that is full of discord, but if you refuse to be disturbed by discord you will remain in harmony. The fact, however, that you remain in harmony will not make the music harmonious, proving conclusively that under such circumstances your state of mind affects only yourself, and does not affect those things that exist outside of yourself.

However, you may try to think that inharmonious music is actually sweet and lovely, and may wholly succeed through this suggestion in rendering yourself unconscious to the

What is Truth

discord. You may in consequence enjoy the music to some extent, but your judgment of music will suffer. Should you practice this method frequently the best music would after a while fail to give more enjoyment than ordinary music, and you could not possibly enter into the realization of the soul of music itself.

If you undertake a certain work and think you are going to fail, the confusion of mind and the scattering of forces produced by such a frame of mind, will almost invariably produce failures. On the other hand, if you think you are going to succeed you will concentrate all your forces on success; accordingly, those forces will work together for success and will place success within reach, though of course work and ability must be added before results can be secured. The fact that you think you are going to succeed will not alone produce success, but to think that you are going to succeed is one of the essentials. In fact, it is quite indispensable.

A number of ambitious people at the present time who have no ability, and who do not care to develop themselves, believe that everything will come to them if they simply think success. Success, however, does not come in this way. If you wish to succeed you must have ability and you must apply it thoroughly as well as wisely. You must have confidence in yourself and faith in abundance.

You must press on with all the determination that is within you, working constantly in the right states of mind, and turn all the forces of thought, talent and ability upon the goal in view.

The way we think affects to an extraordinary degree everything we do and everything with which we come in contact. But mere thinking is not all that is required to make things right, nor will things turn from bad to good simply because we think they are good. There are methods through which all things can be changed, but such methods will not be employed simply by our saying or thinking that things are what they are not.

If we try to make ourselves believe that things are what they are not, we not only delude ourselves, but we carry on a sort of mesmeric process that will sooner or later make invalids of our minds, and so weaken all our faculties or talents that we will soon be incapable of achieving anything worthwhile.

The real student of life takes things as he finds them, regardless of what they may be. If things are not right he admits it, and goes to work doing something to make them right. On the other hand, if they are good he is fully able to enjoy them to the fullest extent because his appreciation is not clouded by self delusions. The strong soul is never disturbed or made unhappy when meeting things out of place. He does not have to suggest to himself that all is well, when it is not, in order to keep himself composed. He knows that he is ready for any emergency, that he is equal to any occasion, that he has the power to overcome any adversity, and that he has the ability to make all things right. He is therefore composed in the presence of wrong and fully ready to do something definite to make the wrong right. Such a mind can see the whole truth about the subject of right and wrong. The undeveloped side or the exterior side, with its possibilities, is recognized and understood. And that power within that can develop these possibilities is recognized and applied. Thus the imperfect is changed into some degree of perfection, and evil is transformed into actual good.

The mind that meets life in this way will constantly make things better and will develop superiority in himself through

What is Truth

that mode of thinking alone. On the other hand, the person who thinks that everything is lovely will leave things the way they are, improving nothing, not even himself; thus he will continue to remain in the same small self-deluded state. He may have health, peace and happiness in a measure in his little world, but how small that little world will be. And nothing in the world at large will be better off because he has lived.

In this connection we must remember that it is of the first importance to recognize and learn to apply the immense power of thought, but that power is not applied simply by thinking that things are as we wish them to be. The power of thought works through methods; that is, through the living of what we think, and through the doing of those things that make for growth, quality and worth.

Another half truth that has deceived thousands of well-meaning minds is expressed in the statement, "If you see evil in others it is because you are evil yourself." There is, however, some truth back of this idea though this truth would be better expressed if we should say, "There is a tendency of the human mind to believe that others have the same weaknesses that we have." Though here we must remember that this is only a tendency and is by no means the rule in every mind. We know that if a man is selfish he finds it difficult to think of

Others as unselfish; but the cause in his case is simply a narrow viewpoint.

So long as we live in a certain mental attitude we are inclined to look at all things through the colored glasses of that attitude; in consequence our judgment is biased. However, when the judgment is unbiased and the mind can see all things from all points of view, all things will be seen as they are.

Such a mind can see the wrong in others without being wrong himself, because he can see all things from all points of view. The higher we ascend in the scale the more clearly we can see the mistakes of the world and the less mistakes we ourselves will make. But we not only see the mistakes, we also see the cause and the remedy; and we do not condemn.

Though we see all wrong we can forgive all wrong because we can see the cause of it all, remembering the great truth, "To know all is to forgive all." Thousands of well meaning idealists condemn themselves for seeing evil in others, believing that they are in bondage to the same wrongs, but this is simply a delusion coming from viewing only one side of the truth in the matter. When you can see everything, you can see the imperfect as well as the perfect, both in others and in yourself. It is not wrong to see the mistakes of others, but it is wrong to condemn. For it is certainly a fact that when we condemn wrong we perpetuate wrong, and also tend to produce that same wrong in ourselves.

When you actually believe that you have a certain failing you tend to create that failing through your own thinking. The mind has the power to create any sort of condition in the system and employs all deep seated beliefs, ideas or impressions as models. Therefore, by believing that you are a sinner you make sin the pattern for your thinking, and all your thoughts will be created more or less in the likeness of sin. When we understand this law we understand what a horrible mistake it is to think of ourselves as sinners; and we also discover why the majority continue to remain weaklings from the cradle to the grave.

What is Truth

If you wish to eliminate sin, evil and worry from your life study metaphysics and psychology. Learn to give the creative powers of your life more ideal patterns. Learn to create your thoughts after the likeness of purity, truth, goodness, strength, wholeness and virtue. You will gradually become more and more like those thoughts because, "As a man thinketh in his heart so is he."

The belief that we have the same sins or evils that we see in others is a belief that is self-contradictory at every point. For if we see evil in others simply because that same evil is in ourselves it is the evil in ourselves that we see. If that evil was not in ourselves we would not see it in others: but if it is only in ourselves it does not exist at all in the others. And if this be true, why do others see sin in us? They must according to the theory be just the same kind of sinners as we are. The fact that they see wrong in us proves that the same wrong exists in them, while according to our belief the wrong does not exist in them, but exists only in ourselves.

We must admit, therefore, that the wrong we see is not simply in ourselves, but also in others, otherwise the belief would not hold good all around.

Nevertheless, if we admit this we contradict the very idea upon which the belief is based, proving that the whole thing is but an illusion. We may imagine that others have certain wrongs that they have not, but the fact that we imagine these wrongs existing in others does not prove that these wrongs exist at all, either in others or in ourselves. For, suppose we see in others what is not there; suppose we imagine others having certain failings because we have them; suppose some of us at times do this; does that prove that the pure mind is unable to see what is not pure? It does not. It simply proves that when the imagination is not under control we may imagine many things that do not have existence anywhere.

When your eyes are open you will see everything that is to be seen, be it black or white. And the mind that is pure certainly has the same power to see with open eyes, that the mind has that is not pure. In fact it is only the pure mind that sees all that is good and all that is evil. The impure mind is partially blinded. However, when we realize that evil in itself is not bad, but simply an undeveloped state, we conclude that it is no more of an evil to see evil than it is to see a green apple.

The green apple is undeveloped. It is not ready to be eaten, but it is not on that account bad of itself, though it would produce undesirable effects if it were eaten in its present condition. The same is true of all other things that are undeveloped.

We think they are evil because we have found it painful to use them in their undeveloped state. We have not realized that the pain came, not because the fruit was bad, but because we tried to eat it before it was ripe.

Chapter 7

Striking Illustrations of Half Truths

Everyday experience has demonstrated the fact again and again that when we look for trouble we usually find it. And also that when we look for health, peace, harmony and abundance we almost invariably gain possession of those things in a greater or a lesser measure. This fact has led a number to believe that we meet only what we look for. But this conclusion is nothing but a half truth.

We know that we meet a number of things in daily life that we never looked for, and many things that we even never thought of. Almost daily we come in contact with conditions that do not belong to us and that have no legitimate place in our world.

Therefore to say that we meet only what we look for is not to speak the truth.

Besides, when we live in the belief that we meet only what we look for, we condemn ourselves for many times as many wrongs as we are responsible for. And to condemn ourselves for any wrong is to impress that wrong upon the subconscious.

What is impressed upon the subconscious will bear fruit after its kind; therefore when you condemn yourself for any wrong you sow a seed in your mind that will later on produce more wrongs of the same kind. This is a fact of extraordinary importance and clearly explains why it seems so difficult for most people who want to be right to live up to the doctrines they profess. If we wish to emancipate ourselves from sickness, trouble and discord, want and misfortune we must not sow any more seeds of that sort. And to condemn ourselves for any wrong is to sow seeds that will produce another harvest of those wrongs.

We are living in a world where many things are imperfect. Things in general are in a state of becoming and many parts are incomplete, but those things are not incomplete because we may be looking for incompleteness. They are incomplete because the world is not finished. And so long as the world remains unfinished those things will remain incomplete whether we look for incompleteness or not. So long as we are moving about in the world we will meet the imperfect whether we are looking for it or not, but those imperfections will not do us any harm if we meet them in the proper attitude.

Green apples will not give you pain so long as they are not taken into the system. Nor will incomplete circumstances and conditions disturb you if you do not take those conditions into your mind. The fact is what things are to do to us will depend largely upon what we in the first place proceed to do with things.

When you go on a journey and find an immense rock in the way you do not ask yourself what wrong you have done in the past that you should meet this obstacle. The rock came there through causes that are entirely distinct from the causes of your individual existence, and you found that rock because you went that way. But why did you go that way?

The answer can be found, though this will lead us into hairsplitting arguments regarding the nature of motives. However, so long as you have errands here and there and everywhere you will find obstacles in the way due to the fact that the world is not finished. But instead of becoming discouraged about those obstacles you should learn to surmount them.

What is Truth

In this connection we may well ask, that if we never looked for obstacles and never expected to meet them, could we not go about our work without meeting obstacles at all? For is it not true that there is a smooth path to every place, and that he who seeks such a path will always find it? It is true that there is a smooth path to every place in the domains of life, or rather the possibilities of such a path, but this path is not readymade. Each individual must make it for himself to fit his own requirements.

The whole truth in this connection is that we have the power to make every path smooth as we go on. We can remove all obstacles and change all misfortunes, sorrows and adversities into such things as may be more desirable or more advantageous. The average person is constantly looking for smooth paths that are all ready; that is, paths that are made smooth by someone else, but such paths do not exist. You cannot use the path of another and at the same time fulfill the purpose of your own life. And though such a path may be smooth to him, it might prove the most difficult way that you could possibly undertake.

The reason why so many fail to realize their ideals is, because they are looking for readymade advantages, expecting to find them because they are constantly looking for them. But here we must remember that the only things we can use to advantage are the things we ourselves create at such times as we have greater things in mind. It is true, however, that what we are constantly looking for we tend to create in our own minds. And as like attracts life, what we create within ourselves we shall naturally attract in our external circumstances.

When you are constantly looking for trouble you will be thinking trouble — thus your mind will be troubled and confused. You will be constantly making mistakes, and mistakes always lead to real troubles in the external world. It is therefore simple to understand why the person who is looking for trouble usually meets trouble. But we all meet troubles that we never look for, that we never thought of, that we never created; which fact proves that it is not true that we meet only what we look for.

If we wish to be free from trouble, we should never look for trouble, never think about trouble, never expect trouble and never create trouble. And in addition when we meet such troubles as others have produced we should refuse to become troubled.

You do not have to eat green apples. Neither do you have to take into your mind troubles that others have produced. Be in peace, be in poise, be in harmony, be strong, be your own master and resolve to think only peace, regardless of what your surrounding conditions may be. And this anyone can do just as easily as he can move the muscles of his hands or feet.

When you meet troubles or misfortunes do not condemn yourself, whether you are to blame or not.

Troubles and misfortunes come from mistakes, and the more you condemn yourself the more mistakes you will make. When in the midst of wrong forgive yourself and forgive everybody; let the wrong go; drop it completely from your mind; rise out of it and resolve to recreate everything for the better.

You will soon be free. And you will also turn all misdirected energies to good account for the fact is all things in your life will work together for good when you desire the good, and the good only.

What is Truth

Every time you forgive yourself you decrease your tendency to do wrong. And if the forgiveness of yourself is followed by a positive ascension of mind into the higher and the better, the tendency to do wrong will be removed, and a strong tendency to do the right will appear instead. When all the tendencies of life have a tendency to do right and build the greater you will naturally do the right.

You will be good not because you try to be good, but because it has become your nature to be good.

And this is the goal we all have in view.

When you forgive yourself for everything and try to surmount everything you steadily develop that power that can surmount, transform and overcome everything. And ere long the meeting of trouble will not be a misfortune to you because you can change it instantaneously to something good.

Although we shall meet many things that we never looked for, and encounter many wrongs for which we are not responsible, still we are equal to every occasion if we continue to be our best And what is more, the things we meet in life constitute the raw material from which we may build a larger life and a greater destiny Whatever you meet, be it pleasing or otherwise, remember it is raw material.

You can take that material and turn it to excellent use in the creating of a stronger personality, a more brilliant mind and a more beautiful soul.

Man is an alchemist in his own domain. He can change the basest metals of his life into the finest gold. He can transform every element within his own existence and make it what he may wish it to be. And though it is true that we shall meet many things that we do not look for, many adversities that we did not create, still we should count it all joy because we can make good use of everything and turn all things to good account.

The fact that each individual has the power to recreate his own world has led many to believe that the individual is the creator of everything that appears in his world. And therefore it has frequently been stated as a law that we find in life exactly what we put into it. This, however, is another half truth, because no person lives to himself, for himself or by himself. Each individual finds in his life many things that others have placed there both before and after birth, though each individual is at liberty to use all these things according to his own aims and desires.

Every individual act will affect thousands of lives for good or otherwise, depending upon the nature of the act. Therefore, every individual must learn not only how to place the best in all those lives that he may affect, including his own, but also how to use those things that constantly flow into his life from other sources. In this connection we meet a most important fact, for it is evident that the person who believes that we find in life only what we put into it will naturally turn his whole attention to the art of placing the best in his own life, but will not give any attention to the art of using to advantage what comes from others.

It is therefore evident that such a person will soon find himself in a sea of problems that he cannot solve — problems that have arisen through his coming in contact with the hundreds of things that naturally flow into his life from the lives of others.

To give your best to life you must make the very best use of everything that you possess; but in the using of things, you constantly come in touch with the world in general, and you will have to know how to dispose of those things, be they good or otherwise, that invariably come into your life through this contact. However, if you are unable to overcome the adversities that you meet in the world, and do not know how to make practical use of the good things you find you will be at the mercy of your circumstances. You will gain little or nothing from the opportunities that may surround you because you have not learned the art of taking advantage of opportunities; and as you do not know how to remove obstacles you will be practically helpless. In such a condition you can do nothing, neither with the possibilities that exist within you nor with those that exist all about you. You can give nothing of value to life. You will sow nothing in your own world and you will reap nothing in your own world. And what conies from others you cannot use because you do not know how.

The whole truth on this great subject is this: We find in life what we put into life and what we take out of life. What we put into life is the result of our own individual talents, powers and possessions.

And what we take out of life is the result of our individual use of that which comes from other sources; that is, from persons, things, circumstances and events. Others may place sorrow in your life, but it will not be sorrow to you if you understand how to make all things work together for greater good. The world may place rare opportunities in your very path. In fact, the world is constantly placing such opportunities in the path of everybody, but unless you know how to take advantage of those opportunities they will be of no value to you. It is the same with all other things that may come to us from other sources. If they are good their value will depend upon how well we use them. If they are not good they will not affect us adversely unless we permit them to do so.

Every day we find things in life that we never put into life; some good, some not. The good things we often pass by not knowing their value, while those things that are not good disturb us because we do not know how to turn misdirected energies to good account. The universe is a rich gift to man.

Each individual is heir to all that the race has done, not because he has put an equal amount into the life of the race, but because he is a member of the race, and a necessary part. Each part is necessary to the whole. Therefore each individual has the privilege to take into his own life everything that he can use. And he can do this without depriving anybody of anything because there is more than enough to go around. However, nothing is of value to you unless you can turn it to practical use.

And what is important, you cannot turn your life to practical use unless you can also turn to practical use those things that come to you through the lives of others. And as others are constantly giving you things that are good and things that are not good you must understand what to do with all such gifts.

If we do not use things we will be used by things.

And if we do not learn the art of using what comes from others we shall be so completely controlled by circumstances that we shall be unable to apply our own personal talents. This will prevent us from putting anything into life, and also from taking anything out of life. Life to us therefore, under such circumstances, will be practically empty.

What is Truth

Though we have it in our power to change those circumstances and gain a life of richness and high worth instead.

Chapter 8

The Subconscious Factor

Extensive investigations along metaphysical and psychological lines have demonstrated conclusively that thought exercises an extraordinary power in the life of man. And since this power is found to act, not only in every part of the mind, but in every atom of the body as well, many have come to believe that everything in man, good or otherwise, comes from thought, and that man is as he thinks, and only as he thinks. Strictly speaking, it is the truth that man is as he thinks; but that abstract thought is the only cause of his thinking is not the whole truth. A large number of metaphysicians and idealists, however, have taken this idea as the whole truth, and have in consequence, not only been misled in every pursuit of the truth, but have failed to apply the power of thought in such a way as to accomplish what really can be accomplished through systematic and scientific thinking.

The power of thought, however, is very great, as it is the powers of mind and thought that determine what every part of the body is to do. It is conscious thought that causes the voluntary motions of the body, and subconscious thought that causes the involuntary. Before you can move a muscle you must exercise the power of the conscious mind, and before your food can be digested the subconscious mind must give action to the functions of digestion. It is the subconscious mind that controls the circulation, digestion, assimilation, the process of physical reconstruction, all functional activities, and all those actions in the body or the mind that are not originated by the will. The subconscious also controls habits and characteristics, mental tendencies, the actions of character and the scope, capacity and present power of all the faculties and talents. But the subconscious mind does its work automatically and acts according to directions received from the conscious mind.

It is therefore possible for the conscious mind to change gradually the actions of the subconscious, or to bring the subconscious back to normal action when it is not performing its functions properly.

This fact proves that man is absolute master of his entire personality. Though he must follow the laws of life to exercise that mastership.

When the conscious mind worries, the subconscious mind is thrown out of harmony and therefore fails to perform its functions properly. That part of the subconscious that controls the functions of digestion will be misdirected and indigestion will follow. That part that controls the reconstruction of the body will through perverse action create abnormally looking cells, and the body will begin to look old and ugly. Other functions are similarly affected, not only by worry, but by every other action of the conscious mind.

The subconscious also effects the chemical actions, vital actions, nerve actions and all the various forces of the personality. Though the subconscious never modifies its regular actions until impressed to do so by the conscious mind. We may therefore state it as a general law that the personal man is what the subconscious mind causes him to be. But the subconscious mind does only what the conscious mind directs it to do. And since the conscious mind is controlled by the understanding and the will each individual can determine what he wants the subconscious mind to do, thus proving the mastership of man.

What is Truth

The statement, "As a man thinketh in his heart so is he," might be transposed to read, the personal man is the result of what the subconscious mind is, thinks and does; because it is the subconscious that constitutes the heart of mentality or the vital center of the entire mental world. Since the personal man is what the subconscious mind causes him to be, and since the subconscious does only what it is directed to do by the conscious mind, the great question before us is, how to use the conscious mind in such a way that the subconscious will always be directed to do what we want to have done.

However, before we proceed further, we must remember that after the subconscious has begun to do a certain thing it will continue to do that particular thing until the conscious mind directs otherwise. After you have made the subconscious perform a certain function it will continue to perform that function not only in yourself but in your children and children's children for generations and generations, or until it is stopped by the actions of the conscious mind in any individual. What is impressed upon the subconscious in one generation will be inherited by the next. Though each individual can remove undesirable hereditary conditions by changing the action of his own subconscious mind.

Through gradual development ages ago, the subconscious mind was trained to make the digestive organs digest when anything entered the system.

It was trained to cause the eyes to wink every few seconds so as to keep the eyeball moist. It was trained to cause the saliva to flow whenever anything of an edible nature entered the mouth. It was trained to cause the gastric juice to flow when the food entered the stomach. It was trained to manufacture a certain amount of these juices in the system every day. It was trained to remove the old cells in every part of the body every few months and cause new cells to be formed in their places.

In brief, it was trained to cause everything to be done in the body that is being done in the body, and it will continue to do those things of itself. The subconscious will not have to be directed anew to do those things. It was properly directed a long time ago through the gradual needs of man. It does not require a second command. But it can be directed to do those things better. And it can be trained to do special things both in mind and body that have never been done before.

The subconscious can be trained to do almost anything. Therefore there is practically no limit to the possibilities that are latent in the human system. In the average person, however, the subconscious fails to control the physical functions as perfectly as it might. And it does not in any person bring the system up to the most perfect state of being and action. The reason is it has not been directed along those more perfect lines.

The conscious mind in the average person permits the subconscious to be the way it is or the way it has been from one generation to another The average man therefore is the way the race has been thinking because he thinks the same way. His life and his actions are the result of the sum total of the habits that have been inherited in generations past. He can, however, improve upon these habits, tendencies or inherited conditions through the training of the subconscious mind to do its work better than that work has been done in the past.

That this is possible we know through the fact that experimental psychology has proven the susceptibility of the subconscious to do whatever the conscious mind may direct.

What is Truth

In the average person the subconscious has been trained to create an older and weaker body every year, but it can just as easily be trained to create a stronger body and a more vigorous body every year. The subconscious has also been trained to keep the body in a limited state, and to cause those faculties actually to lose their power and brilliancy after a certain period of life has been reached. But the subconscious, if properly trained, can just as easily cause all the faculties to become stronger and more brilliant every year no matter how long a person may live. The subconscious can also be trained to do things in mind or body that no one has done before. We realize, therefore, that the individual man not only is in the present what he thinks in the present; that is, the sum total of his thought habits, but also that he may become in the future whatever he may train his subconscious mind to think and express. The problem, however, is to train the subconscious properly, or in other words to make the thought of the heart what we wish it to be.

And it is in our attempt to regulate the thought of the heart, which means the same as the thought of the subconscious, that a number of half truths have arisen in modern systems of belief. In the first place, we have believed that it was thought in general that moulds the personality of man. And we have tried to change our thought on the surface without any regard to the fact that no thought can affect the system until it becomes subconscious.

In the second place we have tried to change thought by acting directly upon our own minds without taking into consideration the environments in which we might be placed at the time. In the third place we have tried to master mind and thought by simply using will force, paying no attention to the law through which the will must act in order to demonstrate and exercise this larger self-control.

Concerning the first mistake nothing further need be stated. The preceding pages have made the fact clear that the thought of the heart is synonymous with the mental actions of the subconscious mind, and that no change can be brought about in the mind or the body until the desired change in the actions of the subconscious has been produced.

And in this connection it is well to state that every thought, desire or action of the conscious mind will, if deeply felt, become subconscious.

Another fact, of equal importance is that the personal man is not the result simply of what he thinks.

but of that thought that is placed in action. And by action in this connection we mean all action in the human system, whether that action be mental, chemical, vital, functional or muscular. Also that no thought, desire or will can produce action at any time unless it is made subconscious. We realize that every thought that is to affect the system must be created with the tendency to produce action, and must be deeply impressed upon the subconscious mind.

To produce a change in any part of mind or body the conscious mind must first, create that thought that has the power to produce the necessary change. Second, the conscious mind must will to apply that thought in actual tangible action. And third, that thought must be impressed upon the subconscious, or rather, the subconscious must be directed to carry that thought into positive action.

Why the majority of idealists have so frequently failed to demonstrate long sought for changes in their minds or personalities after they have fully changed their mode of thinking is therefore evident.

They have followed a half truth and have done their work largely for naught. In other words, they have not removed inherited subconscious beliefs and established actual truth in their places.

A group of half truths that is very detrimental has come from the belief that we can change our thought by simply willing to change our minds; and also that we can change our thought without changing our thinking. But here we must remember that thought, and thought forces, as well as mental images and ideas, invariably come from thinking. Therefore we must change our thinking before we can change our habits of thought or our subconscious thought.

To think, is to actually exercise the mind in forming definite conceptions about something; that is, to try to understand that about which we may be thinking. To change our thinking it is therefore necessary to change our conceptions of those things with which we may come in daily contact. That is, we must not only change our ideas about ourselves and about certain abstract principles, but we must change our minds about everything in our environment. We must try to gain a higher viewpoint in our relation to all things, thereby gaining a better conception and a truer understanding of all things.

In brief, we must remove the imperfect beliefs of the subconscious, because it is the beliefs of the subconscious, that cause man to be what he is, and establish a higher understanding of truth along all lines in the place of those beliefs.

What is Truth

Many metaphysicians and students of idealism define environment as a mere reflection of the mind of the individual. Therefore, according to their philosophy, environment will change immediately the individual himself changes. But that this is a half truth is easily proven; and it is a belief that has been most misleading.

To change himself man must change his thought. To change his thought he must change his thinking. And to change his thinking he must change his conception of everything with which he may come in contact. But if he thinks that his environment is simply a reflection of his own thought, his conception of his environment will constitute zero in his mental world. In fact, that conception will involve nothing, and a mental conception that has nothing in it is simply a state of ignorance.

He therefore knows nothing definite about the nature of his environment, and the man who does not understand his environment will naturally accept the conclusions of his senses, which are always more or less imperfect. Accordingly, his thought concerning his environment will be wrong thought, or at any rate incomplete. And it is not possible to improve something that we do not clearly understand.

If a man's environment is the reflection of his own mind then environment does not exist as a separate thing. According to such philosophy it becomes impossible to think of environment because you can form mental conceptions only of those things that have individual existence. This proves conclusively that the man who thinks of his environment as a mere reflection of his own mind cannot possibly know anything about his environment. And we may repeat that we cannot improve upon that which we do not clearly understand.

However, whatever we may see, or hear or believe will impress the mind. Such impressions will cause the mind to form conceptions about those external things from which the impressions come.

From these conceptions will come ideas and thoughts, many of which will affect the personality in one or more places. Therefore the man who does not try to understand the real nature of those things that exist about him will absorb indiscriminately such views as are suggested by the senses.

In consequence he will make no intelligent selection of his ideas, and his thinking will be controlled largely by such ideas as are suggested by his environment

And no man can control himself or improve himself whose thinking is controlled by environment.

But to say that the visible universe is unreal, or that tangible things are mere illusions, and that material substance has no existence, is to bring about the same effect. The man that has such views will be controlled both by environment and by such persons as he may accept as authority.

To change your own life and think what you want to think you must form a definite mental conception about everything with which you may come in contact. And this conception must be as high as your mind can possibly reach. In fact, it must be composed of a higher and finer understanding of actual truth. You are as you think in the subconscious; therefore to change yourself you must change your subconscious thought. However, you change your thought not by willing to change your mind, but by changing your mind about all things. You make the proper use of the will, not when you try to force the mind to change, but when you try to direct the mind toward higher and higher points of view.

When you begin to look at all things from the higher point of view all your thoughts will change of themselves. Then if you give this change of thought action in practical life, and direct the subconscious to act with those new ideas you will cause your entire personality to change to correspond.

And every such change will be a decided improvement, because you have eliminated in a measure the imperfect or lesser beliefs of the subconscious, and placed in their stead a larger measure of actual truth.

What is Truth

Chapter 9

The Real and the Unreal

All systems of thought have searched for the causes of good and evil, and several phases of thought have developed the belief that "It is all in yourself." But to reduce this belief to its last analysis is to come to the conclusion that there is no power in the universe outside of the mind of the individual, and therefore nothing has existence except the mind of man. The fact is, however, that every force and element in the universe does have a power of its own, but what that power has to do with the individual will depend directly upon how he relates himself to that power.

Man does not possess the only power, but he does possess the power to determine how all other powers are to be used. Therefore, final results will depend upon him. What is to be in his own world lies entirely with him. But he cannot use properly those powers that exist about him so long as he believes that those powers have no existence. We cannot study and understand that which we believe to be unreal.

To illustrate a leading phase of this idea we will say that you dislike decayed apples, which is natural. But the cause of that dislike is not wholly in your own taste. The cause lies partially in the nature of the apple, which is no longer wholesome.

You can prevent the disagreeable sensation of such a food, however, if you avoid it. But to continue to eat that apple, believing that the dislike is all in yourself, will not remove the disagreeable sensation. It may seem to be absent for a while, but that seeming absence will be due to the deadening of your sense of taste caused by strong suggestion.

The deadening effect of suggestion, however, is neither permanent nor desirable, therefore in the course of time you will have to reap all the consequences that naturally follow the practice of eating such apples.

The same illustration will hold good with respect to every element and force in existence. You cannot control or determine the effect of things upon yourself by trying to think that they have no existence, but rather by learning how to use those things. True, it is possible to imagine that certain things are disagreeable when they are not, but that is hysteria, which, of course, is all in yourself.

Hysteria, however, is an abnormal condition and we cannot understand the normal through the study of experiences that come from the abnormal.

The proper course to pursue is not to deny the existence of things, but to try to understand more perfectly the real existence of things. Through this understanding we shall learn how to use things. And when we can use things properly we have it in our power to produce what results we may desire.

The idea that all is good is, from a certain point of view, exact truth, but as usually interpreted it is not the whole truth. To state that all that is real is good would be the whole truth. But to state that all temporal conditions as well are good would not be the truth. A disagreeable condition is not good, but the original power producing that condition is good and produces evil only when misdirected.

What is Truth

Many idealists when meeting wrongs or adversity declare indifferently that all is good, and in consequence make no efforts to produce a change. They may in this way avoid evil consequences for a short time, but they do so by mentally running away, so to speak, from trouble. The troubles, however, that we try to run away from always follow sooner or later, and never fail to come upon us again in the course of time.

The habit of saying that all is good, no matter what may happen, will invariably lead to extreme mental blindness, and the judgment will become so obtuse that nothing is seen or understood any more as it really is. This habit therefore must be strictly avoided by all whose object is to find the whole truth.

The whole truth in this connection is, that everything is produced by a power that is good in itself.

It is possible, however, to misdirect anything that may proceed from that power, and a lack of knowledge on the part of man may cause these misdirections; therefore it is the understanding in man that alone can prevent them or correct them after they have been made.

To gain this understanding the mind should establish itself in the consciousness of that state of being where the good is realized as absolute good; and from that attitude deal with the conviction that the power back of things is good, and also that things can be changed to become exactly like that power. In other words, the mind should act from the viewpoint of the consciousness of the real which is always good, and thereby gradually eliminate those adverse conditions that manifest as evil or unrealities.

The discovery that the source of everything that is expressed through the personality exists potentially in the within has led many to believe that if the within were developed the without would take care of itself. But we must remember that the objective mind must be highly cultivated before the superior qualities of the subjective mind can find complete expression. To illustrate, a good musician needs a good instrument. Though all things come from the within it is necessary to apply those things upon the without in such a way that the superior qualities of the interior life produce the same superiority in the external life.

Here we must remember that there is a vast difference between being conscious of the ideal and making that ideal real. In like manner there is a difference between dreaming and acting, between visions and tangible results. The visions are necessary, but they must be carried out. They will not of themselves become tangible realities. And that is something that can be brought about only through the efforts of the objective mind. To impress the subconscious with a certain idea is to cause a corresponding expression to come forth, but that expression must be taken up and used.

The subconscious expression brings out the material, but the objective mind must go to work and use that material if results are to be gained.

Many idealists believe that they can think anything, do anything, eat anything or live in any way they like because all is good; therefore nothing can do them any harm. And the idea would be true if we were living absolutely in the real, or what may be termed the ultimate. But the human race has not as yet reached that stage. We are gradually approaching the absolutely real wherein there is absolute good; but we have not entered that state, therefore we must deal with things as they are in our present state of development.

When you believe that you can do anything at any time you will violate natural law at almost every turn. But laws were not made to be violated.

They are made to lead us into the new, the higher and the better; therefore they must be followed in every form and manner if we have greater things in view. Whenever you violate law there will be harm, injury and suffering whether you think that all is good or not. But when you live so completely in the understanding of the real and the true that you discern the purpose of all law you will never violate any law. You will have no desire to do as you please. Your whole desire will be to conform with the law of your life because you know that every phase of that law is a path to greater things.

At the present time you frequently hear the statement, "I AM able to do anything because I AM one with the Infinite." But this is not the truth if applied to the present moment. We cannot do anything at the present moment even though it is true that we are one with the Supreme, because there are only certain things for which this present state of existence is adapted. And to try to go outside of that adaptation would be to violate the law of life. We can do today only what we are ready for today, and no more. The majority, however, do not do what they are ready for. There are only a few that are always at their best.

No one can be his best unless he is in harmony with the Infinite and works in conscious unity with Supreme Power. And he who is his best in this sense can do anything that may be necessary to make the present moment complete. But he cannot do in the present that which belongs to some future moment. There are too many, however, who are living almost exclusively for the future, doing very little to make the present complete. For that reason they are never their best in the present, and fail to promote a natural and orderly advancement of existence.

In this connection it is highly important to understand that when we make the sweeping statement that we can do anything now, we tend to scatter thought and consciousness over such a wide area of future possibilities that the present moment will receive but a fraction of the power that we have the ability to apply now. It is a great truth, however, that he who lives and thinks and works in harmony with the Supreme can do everything now that is necessary to make the present moment full and complete.

Another mistaken idea that has arisen among minds who do not fully understand the relation of the real to the unreal, is that the experiences of the senses are illusions. From certain points of view, however, this idea seems plausible. But the plausible is not always true. To state that the senses always mislead, is to admit that we can know nothing and convey nothing, because we have used our senses in every effort that is made to learn facts or convey facts to others.

In brief, we have used our senses to learn that the senses do not exist, or that the experiences of the senses are illusions. But if all the experiences of the senses are illusions, then even this extraordinary knowledge would also be an illusion. To make the statement therefore that all experiences or that most of the experiences of the senses are illusions, is to contradict the statement itself absolutely.

The person who depends upon the senses to receive information and who depends upon the senses of others to have that information conveyed, must not state that the senses always mislead, for according to that very theory the information he is trying to convey will be nothing but a bundle of misleading statements. You may think that you have found the result of pure reason, that reason that knows without using the senses, but to convey your discovery to others they must employ their senses, and if the senses always mislead it would be impossible for you to teach pure reason to others.

If the senses are not reliable no one can teach anybody anything. And if this were true we would all be in perpetual darkness and could neither give nor receive information of any kind. Our effort, therefore, to lead each other out of the beliefs of sense experience would involve nothing but mental chaos. But the fact that we can talk coherently about the senses proves that senses are not always unreliable. In the world of illusion the same causes never produce the same effects, but in the world of sense the same causes under the same conditions invariably produce the same effects; which fact proves that it is not the senses that are unreliable, but that our use of the senses sometimes is imperfect. The whole truth is that the senses convey wrong information only when reason accepts certain conclusions as final before all the viewpoints have been taken.

To state along this same line that there is no intelligence in matter, is to declare that there is no intelligence in the laws of matter. But a law in order to be a law must express a certain phase of intelligence.

If there were no intelligent expression in matter your body would be vapor one moment and possibly a soap bubble the next; your clothes would be a solid one day and a liquid the next; and what might nourish the system at one meal might decompose or consume the system at another meal. If there were no intelligent expression in matter the entire physical universe would be in perpetual chaos, and none of us could stay long enough in anyone state of existence, to convey to each other the precious information that we did not exist. The very fact, therefore, that the books that claim to teach that matter has neither intelligence nor existence — the very fact that those books continue to exist in the same form proves that matter does exist and that the laws of matter do have intelligence.

The whole truth in this connection is that the entire universe is teeming with intelligence. Every physical atom is a center of intellectual activity.

And every person who enters into harmony with this sea of intelligence will develop the most brilliant mentality and comprehend the greatest wisdom and the highest truth.

That spirit is real and matter unreal is another belief that the perfect understanding of truth will eliminate completely. Both are real, but we cannot discern the reality of either unless we view them on their own planes of existence. The mind that lives solely in physical consciousness cannot understand those elements and forces and states of being that are above physical consciousness. But every person can develop the consciousness that does understand what is above and beyond mere things.

To deny the reality of matter is to place one's self in that state of mind where it becomes impossible to understand the purpose of this present state of existence. However, we are here for a purpose, and if we do not fulfill that purpose now our present life will be for naught. But no one can go on toward the greater until he has finished the lesser.

It is necessary, therefore, to understand this tangible world if we wish to promote the purpose and the progress of life; but we cannot understand that which we believe to be unreal.

In like manner it is impossible to use and apply properly those powers that exist in nature so long as we affirm that there is neither power nor sensation in nature. If we continue in this belief we will pass through this sphere of existence in a sort of materialistic dream life, and our happiness will be limited, or it may seem to be an ecstasy resulting from an overwrought imagination. We may live in part because we understand in part, and the reason why we understand only in part is because we refused to recognize the whole. This method of living may give health and may satisfy some minds for a while, but it does not produce the greater, the larger and the richer life. And no one can really live who does not eternally press on toward higher, better and greater things.

Chapter 10

In Reality Everything is Good

When all things are reduced to their last analysis they culminate in what may be termed fundamental reality. And this reality is found to be good in every sense of the term. There is no evil in the fundamental state of things. And as the fundamental state is the origin of all expression there can, strictly speaking, be no evil in any form of expression. The effect cannot be evil in any of its phases if the cause be absolutely good. That is, the effect cannot be evil but it may contain conditions which can have an evil effect upon man. In other words, the expression of things must necessarily be good since the fundamental reality from which all things proceed is good But this expression may contain states or conditions that are not real, and that which is not real is not good, which means it has no actual existence.

Fundamental reality is complete in its fundamental state, but the expression of reality in any of its stages is never absolutely complete. All expression proceeds from the one state of completeness, and every expression is on the way to another state of completeness, but while on the way it is not absolutely complete. That which is being expressed is good in itself because it is real, and all that is real is good. But the expression is not real all the way through; that is, it is not filled to completeness all the way through. The expression itself does not have what may be termed fullness.

In other words, it does not contain all of the real that it can contain. An expression is fundamental fullness in a state of expansion, and therefore contains many vacuums, so to speak, or many empty states which are states of incompleteness.

What is Truth

While any state of being is filled with all the reality it can possibly contain it does not contain vacuums. It is absolutely full and complete in that particular state, but when that state begins to express itself it begins to expand. It seeks a larger sphere of existence, and until it has developed itself sufficiently to fill that larger state, its fullness will not be complete; that is, it will contain many empty states; and we shall find in all our study that this condition of emptiness that appears in every state of development, is the one cause of all such conditions as are called evil or undesirable.

Every expression contains undeveloped states, and these states are caused by the fact that every expression is in a state of development. To develop the capacity to fill a larger sphere of existence is the purpose of every expression and everything has this purpose. It is the natural tendency of the entire universe to advance. Therefore all reality either is in expression at any particular moment in time, or is about to seek that expression. This being true it is evident that there are undeveloped states, or states of incompleteness, in every field of action whatever the plane of that action may be.

Completeness exists only where action has not begun a new movement of expansion, or when that action has been finished, and thereby causes the new movement to have filled completely a new sphere of development. But every finished action will shortly be followed by another and a larger action, so that what we call completeness never continues for any length of time anywhere. Whenever a greater state of completeness has been reached preparations are made by the law of eternal progress, which acts everywhere, for the reaching of a still greater state, and this is natural.

All forms of life are seeking greater expression.

They are created for that purpose, and it is to their interest to promote that purpose. But every expression, being in a state of development, must necessarily contain states of incompleteness, and these states have been called evil because they are the direct or indirect causes of all those conditions that are not agreeable in the experience of man. However, these very states of incompleteness are necessary to continuous development.

There could be no advancement whatever if completeness were permanent everywhere; but since it is the purpose of all life to advance, these states of incompleteness are a necessary part of the great universal plan. These states therefore cannot, strictly speaking, be called evil. In fact, they are in a certain sense good, for without them we could not reach the greater good nor realize any change whatever. The truth is the entire universe would be at a standstill or absolutely dead if these states of incompleteness were eliminated, the reason being that all forms of development must have state of incompleteness through which and in which to develop. No development can take place where everything is already complete.

This being true, these states ought not to produce anything in the life of man that is not agreeable.

In other words, that which is necessary to his greater happiness should not produce unhappiness at any time; and that which is necessary to his realization of the greater good should not produce such conditions as do not appear to be good. From this conclusion we judge that there must be a definite reason why undesirable conditions come at all since the cause of those conditions is so highly beneficial.

And we also judge that man himself must be responsible. In brief, we naturally conclude that evil conditions do not come directly from states of incompleteness, but from man's ignorance of how to relate himself to those states.

It has been demonstrated conclusively that an incomplete state does not produce pain in its original condition of completeness, but that the pain comes when the state of incompleteness is unnecessarily prolonged.

To avoid pain, therefore, all that is necessary is to proceed at once to develop every state of incompleteness the very moment that state appears in consciousness. From this fact we realize that so long as every state of incompleteness is constantly advancing toward a higher degree of completeness it does not produce pain nor produce any undesirable condition whatever.

The fact is that the feeling of pain indicates that something is being retarded in its progress, and that we are holding ourselves back from something good that is in store. Pain therefore is a good friend and is in itself good. It comes with good intentions and aims to prompt us on toward greater good. It is a friend, however, that we would rather dispense with, and we can. It is possible for the purpose of pain to be carried out in every sense of the term and in every phase of life without anyone ever feeling pain.

The same is true concerning undesirable conditions in general. They simply indicate that something in the human system is being retarded in its progress. They are therefore good because they prompt us onward toward the greater good, the greater life and the greater joy. When we accept this view of things we shall not think of anything as evil. We shall think of all states of incompleteness as good because they are necessary to progress and actually are expressions of fundamental reality moving toward higher realizations of absolute reality. And in a certain sense all unpleasant conditions that come from retarding the progress of these states of incompleteness are also good because they tend to produce progress where progress has been retarded.

The purpose of pain is not only to prevent greater pain, but to teach man how to eliminate all pain.

The same is true of all conditions called evil. They tend not only to prevent greater evils, but also tend to arouse in man the desire to remove all evil in every shape and form. It is therefore scientific to state that everything is good because everything, that is at all, is an expression of fundamental reality, and fundamental reality is absolutely good.

When man begins to view all things in the light of this understanding he will realize the fact that all pain, all suffering, and all undesirable experiences come from retarded progress, and that he will need pain so long as he continues to retard his progress. But when he no longer retards his progress at any time he will no longer need pain to prompt him onward. He will live every moment for continuous advancement. And the more he lives in this manner the more desirable will his life become because he will constantly be rising toward a more perfect realization of a greater good and a higher truth.

Chapter 11

Causing the Best to Happen

A certain phase of modern optimism has fallen into the habit of saying that everything is for the best. Whatever comes or not, according to this idea, be it good or otherwise, the mind is consoled with the belief that it is all for the best. And although there is a pleasing side to this belief still the final result of it is not desirable. To live in the belief that anything is for the best is to get into the habit of becoming content with anything; and to become content with anything is to cease practically all efforts toward the attainment of the higher and the greater. Such an attitude will also cause the mind to admit everything that may enter its world, no matter how inferior it may be.

A great many people, however, think that if we live in the convictions that all is for the best, all things will work themselves out for the best, and there is some truth in this. But things will not work themselves out for the best unless we cause them to do their best; and before things will do their best we must do our best. But the doing of one's best requires more than a mere statement that all is for the best. No person is doing his best unless he is giving his entire life to the very highest goal that he can possibly imagine.

And no person can cause things to do their best unless his desire for the best is so immensely strong that all things are drawn into the irresistible life current of that desire. The mere passive belief about all being for the best is powerless in causing things to work for the best. And besides, to think that all is now for the best is to blind the mind so that it cannot see the better.

What is Truth

The rising mind sees greater things in the upper regions of the mental world, and must therefore realize that things as they are in the present are not the best, for they all can even now be made much better. The ideals of the present should be realized in the present; at least we should grow constantly in that realization; but the fact that we have failed to get what we want does not prove that it is best for us not to have it. It usually proves that we are incompetent, or that we have been negligent and indifferent, or that we have permitted ourselves to drift with the uncertainties of things. Had we lived more wisely in the past and taken advantage of the opportunities that the past presented, we should not have to wait now for opportunities to do now, what we think we should have the privilege to do. It is not for the best that any good thing should be deferred if we are ready to appreciate it in the present. It is not for the best that anyone who desires the greater should have to wait for opportunities to attain the greater. If he has to wait, his own past negligence is usually to blame. However, there must be no regrets. To weep over past failures is to waste those very energies that are required in the promotion of our present attainments.

If there is something that you want to do now do not think that it is for the best that circumstances are against you now. Instead, live in the faith that those circumstances must change, that it is for the best that they should change, and that you have the power to begin that change now. Circumstances did not make themselves. You have either made them yourself or you have accepted them ready made from someone else. But what you have made you can remake, and what you have accepted you can reject. Therefore, whatever may be the cause of your present circumstances you have the power to change those circumstances according to your own desire and need.

Circumstances, conditions and things have no particular object in view. Their function is to serve in the promotion of the objects that man may have in view. But when man has no definite object in view his circumstances will drift here and there as they are influenced by the circumstances of other and stronger minds. The man that has no definite purpose in life will invariably drift with the aimlessness of the conditions in which he may be placed.

If he does not control things he will drift with things, and he never controls things unless his desire to reach a certain goal is so strong that all things will be drawn into the immense force of that desire.

Here is the secret of controlling circumstances, conditions and things. Do not exercise any domineering force over things, but make the force of your own purpose so immensely strong that all things in your world will come and act in harmony with that purpose. The law is that every circumstance will conform itself to the strongest force that may pass through that circumstance. And the circumstance in question will give up all its power to work for the same purpose for which this strongest force is working. Therefore all things in your world will work for you when you make the force of your purpose in life a great deal stronger than any other force that may exist in your world. And this you can easily do by turning all the energies of your being into your one leading purpose.

Through this practice you will cause yourself to be your best now, and you will give your best to what you may be doing now. And when you are your best and do your best now all things will happen for the best in your life at present. The best does not happen to you in the present unless you are your best. And you are your best only when the best in

What is Truth

your nature is working for the best that you can find in your world.

When in the presence of confused circumstances do not become passive or inactive and do not let things take their natural course. Things can do nothing of value unless they are guided. Therefore to let them work themselves out is to let them scatter and work themselves into nothingness. The result will be, not the best that could come to you, but rather the worst. When in a place where you do not know where to turn do not give up and let matters take their course in the hope that everything will turn out all right. It will not turn out all right unless you take matters into your own hands and lead them into the right.

At such times be more determined than ever before; picture your higher goal more distinctly and have more faith than you ever had. Be your best and resolve to turn all things to the very best account. Thus the best will happen because you have made the best happen.

When you fail to get what you wanted never say that it must be best for you not to have it. You have a right to have what you want, and it is for the best that you should get it when you want it.

Your failure to get it comes because you fail to be all that you could be and do all that you could do.

So long as you continue to be the lesser, or be less than you can be, you will get the lesser, and the lesser is not best, for it could be better.

The belief that what is to be will be is also thoroughly wrong. Only that will be in the life of man that he himself will cause to be. And man has the power not only to change

What is Truth

causes but to create new and greater causes. True, he must follow the laws of life, but the capacities of those laws have no limit. Therefore there can be no end to the possibilities in him who applies those laws according to their largest possibility and measure.

There is no fixed time for life or death, and no events are preordained. Every life can be prolonged. Every event could have been different.

And everything that happens to man could have added far more to his life than it does. From this fact we judge that few things happen for the best because man himself is seldom at his best. Nearly everything could have been better; but if they are not now what they might be, if we had been what we could be, the wisest course is to turn them to the very best account, and in the future maintain the very highest standard that the mind can possibly construct. When every person takes his life into his own hands and lives that life so perfectly that the very best that can be done now is being done now, everything will happen for the best. And what is more, such a life will advance perpetually into the better.

To cause the best to happen at all times, the secret is to awaken the superior power within and to place the entire mind absolutely in the hands of that power. After this has been done all things will work together for good, the very best must positively come to pass and every seeming disappointment will be an open door to something better.

That better, however, will not be realized if we permit ourselves to be disappointed, because every depressed feeling takes the mind down away from the hands of superior power and will not be in a position therefore to appropriate those better things that this superior power is about to produce.

When the new way of living has been entered into and all of the energies of being have been directed to work together for the promotion of some great purpose, disappointments will hardly appear any more. But should they appear the fact must be faced with the conviction that our failure to realize what we try to secure, indicates positively that something of far greater worth is to be secured shortly instead. When this conviction is invariably adhered to, regardless of what appearances may indicate, the law will never fail to bring the greater good. However, to secure positive and continuous results from this law it is necessary to eliminate everything in life that is not in perfect accord with the real science of life. Those tendencies that retard progress must not be permitted to live and act after we have resolved to do that only which can produce the best The mind must live on the heights and the soul must live for that life that is revealed while the mind is on the heights. There must be no compromise with half truths or beliefs that are untrue, whatever experience may think.

Form your purpose clearly, definitely, and positively. Aim at the highest goal in view. Desire the very best and make that desire so immensely strong that all things in your life will be drawn irresistibly into the current of that desire. All things will thereby work for the best, and the best will always come to pass.

Chapter 12

The Truth About Right and Wrong

Everything that promotes the welfare, the advancement and the growth of the individual is right.

And everything that interferes with the welfare, the advancement and the growth of the individual is wrong. This is the only natural standard by which we can judge what is right and what is wrong. It is therefore the true standard, being based upon the nature, the principle and the purpose of life itself.

When we analyze life we find that all life is progressive. To live is to move forward, because the real living principle has but one ruling tendency, and that is the tendency to press on toward the higher, the larger and the greater.

We also find that all the laws of life are constructive. They are all created for the purpose of construction; therefore to be in harmony with the laws of life man must live, think and act constructively. When man does something that is not constructive he violates the laws of life, and this is wrong because the inherent purpose of life is interfered with.

Here we may ask why some of the laws of life appear to be destructive. We shall find upon closer examination that all such laws simply promote the process of reconstruction. And the lesser sometimes has to be removed or seemingly destroyed in order that the greater may be built up. Realizing this, we shall find that all the laws of life are, to all nature and purposes, purely constructive.

The average system of ethics defines wrong as violation of law, but as such systems do not find the inherent purpose of law their philosophies of conduct are always complex and frequently misleading. When we understand that the inherent purpose of every law is to build or promote advancement and progress we realize that the violation of the law consists simply in refusing to move forward; in consequence every act, physical or mental that in any way retards or prevents the steady growth of the individual is a wrong act. And conversely no act is wrong unless it retards or prevents the growth of the individual. Therefore if we wish to avoid that wrong and be absolutely right in every respect, we must determine which acts of mind or body are natural and constructive, and which ones are not. This, however, can be determined by a very simple method; that is, by a study of mental tendencies; and all tendencies spring from mental attitudes.

A mental tendency is the mind in definite concentrated motion; that is, the mind moving in a certain direction with a special object in view, although this object may be unconscious just as frequently as it is conscious. There are a number of mental tendencies that are in constant action without our being aware of their existence. So that in such cases, the objects in view have become subconscious though they were in the beginning wholly objective or conscious.

A mental attitude may be defined as the image of the mind facing that toward which it may wish to move. And here we must realize the great fact that the way we face life determines our attitude toward life; and also the way we face things or look upon things determines our attitude toward things. A mental attitude is the placing of the mind in a position ready to move, and the way the mind is placed determines where it is going to move.

When a mental attitude begins to move it becomes a tendency. And when the tendency reaches its climax it becomes an act. Therefore to know precisely the nature and inevitable result of the act we must know the exact position of the mental attitude from which it originally sprung.

There are a great many mental attitudes in existence, almost as many as there are views of life, and they divide themselves into two distinct divisions, the first division being right and the second wrong.

The reason why the attitudes of the second division are wrong is because the acts that proceed from those attitudes retard advancement and growth, and interfere with the welfare of man.

The first division of mental attitudes produces what may be called ascending tendencies, while the second division produces descending tendencies.

Ascending tendencies culminate in acts that are constructive. Descending tendencies culminate in acts that scatter force, waste energies, pervert mental states, retard progress and produce discord, confusion and disorder in general. Ascending tendencies promote construction because they follow the laws of life. Descending tendencies interfere with construction because they resist the laws of life, and the reason why is simple. The first division of mental attitudes produce ascending tendencies because those attitudes mentally face the higher and the larger. In other words, the mind looks up at the greater possibilities that are before us while those attitudes are in formation.

The second division of mental attitudes produces mental tendencies because those attitudes mentally face the lower and the smaller. In these attitudes the mind looks down and takes cognizance of the ordinary, the inferior and the mere surface of things. Growth is an upward process, a process of

What is Truth

expansion and enlargement. Therefore no tendency of mind can promote growth unless it is ascending, and moves upward into the larger and the greater.

From this brief analysis we conclude that the secret of being right is to mentally face the higher, the larger, the superior, the limitless and the absolute at all times. When all the attitudes of the mind are attitudes of an upward look all the tendencies of the mind will be ascending tendencies; thus the entire process of thinking will move constantly toward superiority, and every act will be in harmony with absolute law. This is simply understood because growth, advancement and ascension are the inherent purposes of all law. Therefore every act that is an act of advancement, or the result of advancement, must be in harmony with all natural law.

To violate law, to go against law, or to retard the purpose of law, is wrong; but to work with law and to promote the purpose of law is right. And since all laws are constructive, that is, tending toward the larger and the superior, we must, in order to be in harmony with every law cause every thought, every word and every act to have a tendency to move toward the larger and the superior.

Thoughts, words and acts are the results of tendencies and tendencies come from mental attitudes.

Therefore our effort should not be to determine what thoughts, words and acts are constructive, but what mental attitudes produce such thoughts, words and acts that are constructive. But here a multitude have made mistakes. They have tried to think right thoughts, but they have not tried to create those mental attitudes which naturally produce right thoughts. They have tried to express absolute truth in all their words and have expressed the letter of

What is Truth

truth, so to speak, but the spirit of truth has not been expressed. The fact is we cannot express the spirit of truth unless the mind feels truth, and it is only the mind that is ever ascending into more and more truth that actually feels the truth. This feeling of truth demands the ascending tendency, which in turn is the result of the upward look of mind. In consequence, the secret of giving expression to truth is to turn all the attitudes of mind toward the higher, the larger and the superior.

When we judge conduct we should always ask what the intention was that promoted the act, because if the intention was good the tendency back of the intention must of necessity have been an ascending tendency. Therefore something good will come from that act even though on the surface it may appear to be a mistake. There are many intentions, however, that are thought to be good when they are not, and whether they are or not we can determine by looking for the object the intention has in view. If the object is greater welfare, not only to self, but to everybody concerned, the intention must be good and good will come from it.

To formulate a system of conduct that will be right, the principle upon which to work is that of perpetual advancement along all lines. The central purpose should be to change the mind completely so that everything that pertains to the mind will face the greater possibilities of life. To this end all the eyes of the mind should be turned upon the most perfect mental image of complete character that we can possibly conceive of, and every act should be expressed with the positive intention of building toward that ideal image.

When all the attitudes of the mind are facing the greater possibilities of life everything that we do will carry us forward toward those greater things that we have in view. In brief, all things will work together in promoting this purpose to reach the greater things, and we will reach some of them every day. When the attitudes of the mind are turned toward the ideal, the perfect and the larger life, all things in life will turn the same way, because the mental attitudes determine how all other things in life are to be.

When everything in life is ascending toward the higher and the greater, everything will be right because to be right is to follow the laws of life, or to act as these laws act; that is, to promote the purpose that is inherent in every law. And that purpose is growth, advancement and ascension. In this study the great principle to be born in mind is, that so long as we are advancing along all lines we are obeying all the laws of life; we are not violating any of these laws and are therefore not doing anything wrong.

Another principle equally important is, that so long as all the attitudes of the mind are facing the greater possibilities of life, advancement along all lines will be promoted. The mind moves toward that part upon which its attention is directed.

Therefore when the attention of every part of the mind is directed toward the greater possibilities of life every part of the mind will move toward those greater possibilities, and that constitutes advancement along all lines. Here we have the great secret of all development, physical, mental, moral and spiritual. When all the teachers of the world, whether they appear in the pulpit, the schoolroom or other halls of learning, will recognize these principles and apply them, we shall soon find a decided improvement in the human race.

When we understand these principles we see the folly of hairsplitting arguments about what is right and what is wrong, and also the uselessness of trying to compel people to conform to artificial standards. Experience proves conclusively that those who are trying to live up to artificial standards of right and wrong are violating just as many laws as those who have no standards, but who simply are doing the best they know how. The cause for this is easily found. When a certain standard is fixed and you begin to pattern your life after such a standard your life will come to a standstill, and that in itself is a violation of all the laws of life. Even though the standard itself may be high, if your conception of that standard is fixed you will remain stationary by trying to live up to it. And the greatest wrong of all wrongs is to remain stationary; that is, to retard your own progress. We cannot obey the laws of life without moving forward, because as previously stated, the very principle of life itself is a perpetual forward movement; and so long as we move forward in all things and at all times we obey the laws of life without trying to do so. Therefore, instead of giving so much time trying to conform to all sorts of temporal laws we should give our time to the application of the principle of all law, which is growth, progress and ascension.

To obey consciously every law in our own sphere of existence is impossible. To simply enumerate them one after another would require an age. We realize therefore that in order to obey all the laws of life it is necessary to conform to the principle of all laws, which is advancement along all lines.

When we apply the principle of advancement to everything we do, we will be in harmony with all laws without ever thinking about them. And it is this state which has been described as being above the law, or a law unto one's self.

This fact gives us a new thought with respect to the problem of wrong in the world. Hitherto we have tried to prevent people from doing wrong by literally permeating society with rules and regulations. But experience proves that this method does not reach the ills we seek to cure, and a study of the principles under consideration explains why.

There is only one way to eliminate wrong in the world and that is to make it natural or second nature for man to do right. For so long as the tendencies of the mind are descending tendencies, wrong will be the result, and no number of regulations can prevent it. But make these tendencies ascending, and regulations will not be needed, because the inclinations of all minds will be to do right. We do not mean that manmade rules or laws should be done away with. Let society pass as many rules as desired, but there are two facts here that must be considered. One is, that the righteous man does not need the rules of man; and the other is, that the rules of man cannot reform the unrighteous. All that manmade laws can do is to protect society in a measure from the actions of the wrongdoer, but the wrongs themselves will continue as before.

Our object, however, is not simply to protect society, but to remove the cause of wrong in the human race; and to do this something else is needed besides the rules and regulations of society. The fact is that as soon as any mind begins real growth and progress all tendencies and desires to do wrong will disappear. This is perfectly natural because since growth is the normal purpose of every law you will by promoting your own growth naturally enter into perfect harmony with every law; and since there is absolutely no desire to violate law while we are in perfect harmony with law, all desire to do wrong will thereby disappear.

The man who advances along all lines naturally conforms with all laws, and he actually desires to conform with all laws because he has found that every law in life is a path to greater things. No manmade law therefore is necessary to prevent him from doing wrong. So long as he is advancing along all lines he cannot possibly have any desire to do wrong. Therefore if we would help mankind to do the right, and the right only, the secret is to teach every individual mind to promote the perpetual growth of his entire being, body, mind and soul.

Chapter 13

The Truth About Freedom

Freedom is largely a state of mind. It does not consist of the privilege to do as one pleases, nor does it mean deliverance from certain persons, environments or conditions. On the contrary, it is the consciousness of the fact that you have applied the truth as you understand it, and have lived according to your highest conception of eternal law.

When you know that you have done right or have done your best you create a state of mind which to you, fulfills all the essentials of freedom, and in reality constitutes real freedom.

You are free when you are able to do what your present circumstances may require, and when you are able at the same time to rejoice in the privilege of such doing. The free man feels equal to all occasions and never dislikes what he is called upon to do, the reason being that freedom means not only emancipation from limitations, but also emancipation from any feeling of dislike toward anything whatever.

That person who believes freedom to mean the liberty to do as he pleases is in almost complete bondage, because when he is called upon to do what does not please, he either rebels or proceeds unwillingly, and there is no freedom in such a state of existence. Nothing, however, displeases the free man. He feels able to do everything with joy, and that is one reason why he is free.

The man who does what he pleases, or who tries to do what he pleases is on the down grade. He is following the desires of his physical nature, and those desires when left uncontrolled invariably lead to trouble and pain. But to be free we should follow the leadings of the soul and the desires of our higher and finer nature. The soul never asks to be pleased, but finds its greatest pleasure in constantly searching for opportunities to please others. The soul is constructed in this manner; therefore it is only by following the soul that we can find real freedom. The happiest and the freest man in the world is the one who never thinks of satisfying self, but who lives, thinks and acts according to the law of truth, and for the benefit of every living creature.

When you live simply to please yourself your consciousness becomes absorbed in the personal ego, and is therefore separated more and more from everything and everybody. The result is that your life is not only isolated from its higher source, but also becomes smaller and smaller until finally it does not seem to be worth living. When you follow the laws of life regardless of present personal desires you place yourself in harmony with the source of everything that is necessary to the welfare of the person. So that by a seeming personal sacrifice at first you enter into a larger life and come into possession of all that body, mind and soul may now require.

The world believes that the greatest joy comes from satisfying the desires of the person, and that freedom means to be so situated that one can always fulfill the wants of the present without being interfered with. But on this subject the world is wholly wrong. To follow the desires of the person is to enter hopeless confusion and ceaseless trouble and pain, the reason being that the person was made to serve and not to lead or rule. When the mind follows the soul and does what the soul may desire to have done, then it is that the larger, fuller life begins, and this life continues to grow and develop until the limitless is attained.

Here it must be remembered that whatever comes into one's life the person will receive, and also that the person has nothing to give, but is created to serve only as a receiving instrument. We realize therefore that if we continue to depend exclusively upon the person we finally come to a place where we depend upon nothing, and in consequence receive nothing. On the other hand, when the person is trained to give free and full expression to the life that is unfolded from within, and the mind is trained to enlarge its scope constantly so as to gain possession of a larger and a larger measure of life from within, the superior mind within is not only developed, but all the true desires of the person will be supplied.

We all realize that real personal satisfaction must inevitably follow the continuous expression of higher and superior states of being. But such expressions cannot take place until we follow absolutely the desires of our higher and finer nature, that is, the soul. The soul is the master, being the real individual you. The mind is the creator of the soul's ideals; and the function of the person is to receive and express in practical life what the mind creates. This is the law of life, and to live in harmony with this law is to attain perfect freedom.

There are thousands in the world today who can say that they have enjoyed perfect personal satisfaction for months or even years by following constantly the leadings and desires of the soul. These people did not do what they pleased to do in a personal sense, they did rather what the finer life within them sought to have done. And they found that in this way the higher pleasures were given to the person, while to mind and soul came visions of the endless paths and realizations of the life that goes upward and onward forever.

What is Truth

In our study of freedom it is highly important to understand that freedom never comes through a forceful separation from what we may call undesirable persons or environments. Freedom comes when we discover that these persons and things have a better side, and when we enter into conscious mental and spiritual unity with that better side. So long as you have the desire in your heart to separate yourself from anything, you are in bondage. The very fact that you desire separation from a person, an environment or a condition proves that you believe there is something evil in those things, and no one can be free so long as he recognizes evil or rebels against evil. Besides, the very fact you desire to separate yourself from anything that you consider undesirable proves that you are not above those things; and it is only the man who realizes he is above all conditions or things that is really free.

When you seek to unite more closely with the better side of what you previously disliked, the desire for separation will disappear, and the feeling of bondage will vanish. What is more, when you feel absolutely free, it is then that you are naturally and orderly separated from that which does not belong to you, and are thus transferred into the company of what is truly your own. When we do what is right and best because we want to, then we are free; but when we do not want to, we are in bondage to our own feelings or inclinations; that is, we are in bondage to ourselves. And he who is not free from himself is not free from anything. Briefly stated we enter that state of mind that we call freedom, when we can do properly and with pleasure what the present moment requires.

Order is heaven's first law. There is a time and place for everything, and everything is good when in its time and place. What we call evil is after all simply a misplacing of things. We produce evil when we do now what should have

What is Truth

been done at another time or place. To use what is not ripe for use, or to neglect to use things before they are too ripe is to act at the wrong time and place. And such actions will produce adverse conditions.

Neither the green apple nor the decayed apple are intended for the human system, but we partake of both when we try to live in the past or the future instead of exclusively in the present. In like manner, when we use certain faculties or expressions where the law of order never intended that those things should be used, we misplace things. The result is confusion, and confusion always leads to bondage. To be in bondage is to have something in your way and when things are confused there are always some things in the way.

Freedom is a state wherein everything is in its true place and performing its true function; that is, a state wherein absolute order and perfect harmony of action prevails. However, the only way to have order is to follow the absolute law of life which is continuous advancement, or to live according to the truth and to do things as they ought to be done.

But how are we to know these things? The person does not and cannot know; in fact, the average person is in a state of more or less confusion, and confusion is liable at any time to misdirect or misplace.

Therefore it is not possible to learn to do these things properly by doing what the person pleases to have done. We all know too well that the guidance of mere personal desire leads to darkness, disorder and pain, the reason being that the person was not created to dictate to the mind. In consequence, whoever permits the person to rule or to lead, and who blindly follows the desires of the person, will invariably go wrong.

What is Truth

We shall know how to establish order and how to do things as they ought to be done when we know the truth, understand the principles of life, and follow the light of the soul at all times — never asking what we would like to do, but what is the best thing to do, because what is best we shall like the best when we find what it really is. And most important of all we should do with joy whatever the present moment may require. When we begin to follow the soul and begin to work toward higher and greater things we shall find that ever3rthing coming into life comes for a purpose, and also that the superior state of existence always follows when such purposes are fulfilled. Knowing this, we shall count it a privilege to do whatever comes our way.

We free ourselves from the disagreeable in life by placing ourselves in harmony with the better side of all things. And there is no better way to find the truer side of things than to meet all things in the spirit of a lofty rejoicing. To dislike anything that comes to us to be done is one of the greatest obstacles to freedom, because what we dislike we resist, and what we resist we place in our own way.

What comes to us to be done we should work out.

We cannot afford to shirk anything because what we neglect to do now we shall have to do later. In this connection we must realize that the only way to attain the higher is to work out of the lower; and this is a pleasure when done in harmony with the eternal order of things. However, if we wish to work out of present limitations into superior states we must follow the soul; that is, seek higher and higher realizations of the truth as viewed from the superior viewpoints of the soul, and do what the soul desires to have done.

What is Truth

To follow the person is to place ourselves in greater bondage to the limited than we ever were before because the person has nothing of its own.

The person is only what we bring forth from within, and is large or small depending upon how much we express from our larger interior nature. But when we follow the soul and try to do what the soul may desire, we shall never fail to ascend into superior states of life because the soul is already in touch with the superior and the limitless. In like manner, absolute freedom must positively come when we follow the soul, because the soul lives and moves and has its being in that higher state of consciousness where absolute freedom is continuous, being the normal condition of that higher consciousness.

Chapter 14

The Royal Path to Freedom

There are many when taken to task for not doing what propriety declares ought to be done, usually reply that they may do as they please with their own. They emphasize the statement, "What is ours, is ours," and we believe no one has the right to tell us what we should or should not do with our own.

This form of logic may appear sound on the surface, or rather it may look good at a distance, but it changes completely upon closer acquaintance.

The fact is that the idea, "We may do as we please with our own," is contrary to all true propriety, all principle, all science and all law. And whoever lives in the belief that he may do as he pleases will finally come to a place where he will not have the privilege to please to do anything. He will be in complete bondage to adverse circumstances which he himself has created, and absolutely at the mercy of a fate for which he alone is responsible.

When a person does as he pleases he usually follows the whims of fancy or obeys the commands of a per verse nature. He therefore disregards the real law of his being, and to disregard this law is to produce those very conditions that we do not want, and which do not please under any circumstance.

To do as you please in the general sense of that term is to produce that which does not please, while to act in accordance with natural law is to produce a perpetual increase of everything that is good and desirable. To do as you please with physical functions is to produce disease, because such actions will follow abnormal desire instead of natural law. To follow natural law, however, is not to go contrary to desire because normal desire and natural law are always in harmony. When the person is normal in all his tastes, appetites and tendencies every desire will desire to act according to natural law, and such desires when in action will not only promote construction and advancement, but will give the person far greater pleasure than the average person has ever known.

To do as you please with your mental powers is to weaken those powers, and to do as you please with your external possessions is to begin the downgrade to failure; because you will, when you do as you please, act contrary to the laws of accumulation and gain. In fact, no person can ever gain anything from any source so long as he uses things as he may please to use them. There is only one way to use anything, and that is according to law, because everything is subject to law; that is, natural law.

To disregard law in the use of anything is to step out of the world of law. And there is only one world that exists outside of the world of law, and that is the world of chaos. But to act in the world of chaos is to misdirect everything. In consequence we get only that which we do not desire or that which cannot possibly please in any sense of the term. When we act as we please we invariably follow the inclinations of the external person. But it is not the function of the external person to govern. The personality is but an instrument and was created to serve. It is the individuality that constitutes the real man; therefore it is the individuality that alone has the right to govern.

The normal attitude of the individuality, however, is not to do at any time what may seem to please the person at that particular time, but to act always in harmony with natural law, because it is such action that will in the long run please everything in the being of man. When the mind begins to do as it pleases it begins to drift, but so long as it follows natural law absolutely, it will advance toward greater power, greater wisdom and greater joy. It will gain ground constantly, and it will invariably reach the greater goal in view.

A fact of extreme importance in this connection is that the person who does as he pleases usually ignores the welfare of others and therefore tries consciously or unconsciously to live to himself, or to act to himself, which is not possible. To ignore the welfare of others is to place ourselves out of harmony with human life. And we can gain nothing of value from life when we are at variance with human life, because we are all dependent upon each other for what we receive in this world.

The man who ignores the welfare of the world will be ignored by the world because every action produces a reaction and the "select positions" he sought and gained will finally become a prison. To cut loose from the world in any manner or form is to create for ourselves a state of existence that can receive nothing of worth from the world. We will then not only be in a prison, so to speak, but that prison will be empty.

What man does to himself he does to the race.

And what he fails to do to the race, the race will fail to do to him. Therefore no person can live to himself or act to himself. The part is invariably sustained by the whole, and is in consequence responsible to the whole. This is the law, but it is not a hard law. It is a law that governs every channel of supply or increase; therefore every individual who complies with this law will be supplied with everything that his life may require or need.

To violate this law constantly is to receive less and less until one receives practically nothing; and every person who does as he pleases invariably does violate this law. To live in harmony with this law is to receive more and more until one receives everything, and this is the destiny of him who does not do as he pleases, but rather pleases to do what his larger and finer nature has the power to do.

This conception of life does not in any way antagonize the principle of freedom because freedom is also based upon the same law. And it is a fact that there is no similarity whatever between the life of real freedom and the doing as one pleases.

The man who does as he pleases is in bondage to his own misdirected nature, while that man alone is free who wants to do what his true nature declares he was created to do.

The purpose of life is to advance perpetually into the larger life, the greater life, the more beautiful life. And he alone is absolutely free whose whole life is devoted to the fullest possible promotion of that purpose. You are not free to do as you please, but you are free to become more and more and achieve more and more. And when you have learned to become and achieve more and more you shall find that it is such a mode of living alone that really does please.

To be free is not to have the privilege to follow any inclination that may happen along, because such actions lead to bondage, and we are not free to place ourselves in prison. For when the effect is bondage, the cause cannot be freedom. To be free is to have the power and the desire to follow the ascending, expanding, growing, developing, transcending tendency; that is, to break bounds continually and to rise perpetually in the scale of being, power and life. In brief, the free mind turns neither to the left nor to the right, but moves upward and onward eternally. The one purpose of such a mind is progress, and its ruling desire is to be all that is possible for a limitless mind to be.

To be free is not to have the privilege to anything you like regardless of whether those likes be normal or abnormal. To be free is to have the privilege to do that which leads to greater things; and than this there is nothing that could please us more. The man who does what he pleases will never be pleased with anything he has done, while the man who never pleases his personal self, but who gives his entire attention to his superior self, will be pleased with everything he has done. He will give a magic touch of high worth to every thought and to every act because he is living in the mental world of high worth. Besides, he is daily rising in the scale and will in consequence be more and more pleased with everything he may do or undertake.

There is no pleasure that is greater, no satisfaction that is more thorough, and no attainment that penetrates the soul more deeply than that which comes when we realize that we are steadily gaining ground. But to gain ground steadily we must transcend the present. We must grow out of the limited, we must live to be all that we can be. And it is such living that constitutes freedom. To gain freedom is to outgrow the present. To gain more freedom is to enter larger and larger mental domains, for the attitude of freedom is always a rising attitude. And when we learn this great fact we shall have found the royal path to freedom.

Chapter 15

The Truth Beyond Truth

There is something more in life besides that which appeals to the physical senses; there are other forces in the human personality besides those that are employed in muscular or chemical action; and there are faculties in the mind that far transcend the ones we usually employ in objective thought and reason. And since our purpose is to make the fullest and best use of everything that we may now possess, or later develop, nothing can be more important than to know what to do with those things that lie just beyond the limitations of the present, or to understand such truths as may be found beyond the truth we now understand.

The many are in the habit of declaring "one world at a time," meaning that they purpose to consider only what they are normally conscious of in the present. They refuse therefore to recognize what the senses do not seem to fully comprehend now.

But in this connection we must remember that no step forward was ever taken without trying to transcend the ordinary and to picture the unknown.

The very moment we resolve to consider only one world at a time, that is, only as much as present limitations can appreciate, we settle down in those limitations, and all advancement is brought to a standstill. Even in practical everyday life no progress is possible unless we try to go beyond the ordinary of the present; because in all things the greater lies before us and above us.

What is Truth

The truth we are now conscious of is only a small fraction of the whole truth. An infinite sea of truth lies beyond our present consciousness, and it is our privilege to become conscious of more and more of this immensity as we advance in life. Therefore our purpose must be to try again and again to go beyond what we are conscious of now. All will admit that it is necessary in a certain sense to go out upon the seeming void in order to find the greater and the superior in reality. But the majority have placed an obstacle in their way as far as such an effort is concerned, though this obstacle exists wholly in their own minds.

That which lies beyond present ordinary mental action is frequently looked upon as supernatural or even abnormal. And it is simple to understand that no mind can gain control or possession of that which he looks upon as supernatural. And herein we find the obstacle to which we refer. To think of anything as supernatural is to place that particular thing so far beyond normal action that it cannot be attained through normal action. In other words we always place our own normal actions so far below those things that we think of as supernatural that an immense mental gulf is placed between the two. True, this gulf exists wholly in our own minds and is purely artificial, nevertheless, it tends to separate the normal actions of our minds from those higher things that we must of necessity realize and understand if we are to gain possession of a greater measure of truth than we now possess.

The fact is that when we think of anything as supernatural we tend to so belittle our present normal actions that the greater cannot be reached nor comprehended by the normal actions of the mind.

Frequently the greater cannot even be discerned since we have pushed it so far off, so to speak, into the supernormal.

To state that the known is normal and the unknown supernormal or supernatural is to produce the same artificial gulf between the known and the unknown. And frequently this gulf is so wide that the unknown on the other side of consciousness continues to remain but a cloudy mist. In the meantime the normal mind continues to remain in the limitations of present ordinary knowledge.

Consciousness does not expand, the mental faculties do not develop and the mentality itself does not transcend that sphere of consciousness in which we function at the present time.

Those who think of the unknown as supernatural must remember that all things have in their day been unknown, and even the most usual of all things in our environments are still unknown to millions. But nothing can be normal or natural and supernatural at the same time; and what is more, that which can be comprehended by the natural cannot be supernatural; in fact, it must have been natural all the time.

There was a time when classical music was unknown, but that does not prove that the classical is supernatural. There are thousands today who cannot appreciate classical music. It is beyond their reach. And though it is beyond the normal functioning of their minds, this fact does not prove that the music itself is supernormal or supernatural.

Many have found classical music to be perfectly natural so that the power to appreciate such music is inherent in all minds; and therefore what some can appreciate in this connection all would appreciate sooner or later.

Nearly everything that is known today was at one time unknown and was looked upon by many as supernatural.

But we have found all of these things to be perfectly natural, and we are fully justified in thinking that all things are normal and natural. To think of certain parts of life as supernatural is to form a wrong mental conception of those things, which will interfere with our better understanding of them, because men cannot gain a normal understanding of that which he thinks of as supernormal.

To state that all things are normal is simply to reaffirm the great statement that all things come from the same source, or that all parts are of one stupendous whole., And this is something we all believe now. There is not a person living that has not had, and that does not have experiences that are more or less beyond the ordinary. And a great deal of practical good might be obtained from such experiences if the qualities through which they are produced were more fully developed. But those faculties cannot be developed so long as they think of them as being out of the ordinary, as being special faculties, or as being supernatural functions of the mind.

To the average mind the supernatural means something that is beyond the present, something that the present cannot control, or something that is caused to transpire in the life of the person by some outside power or agency acting upon the person. But we cannot develop in ourselves that which we believe to exist outside or separate from ourselves. Nor can we learn to exercise a power which we think we do not possess. In the development of any faculty the first essential is to realize that that faculty is our own. And before any power can be mastered we must realize that that power exists in us and not apart from us. True, there are many minds who have extraordinary experiences even though they believe that those experiences come from supernatural sources, but it can easily be demonstrated that those very persons are highly developed along certain lines, and that they receive what they do because that development has taken place.

Those people, however, have no control over the faculties through which those experiences come.

They cannot get what they want when it is wanted in this way, and they are more frequently misled than wisely guided by those things that are supposed to come in this helter-skelter fashion from higher sources. The reason for this is that no faculty, no matter how active it may be or how well developed it may seem to be, can serve us properly unless it is placed under our control. But to control a faculty we must know that it is our own.

When an impression comes to your mind that you ought to act thus or so and you obey that impression with profit, it is probable that you are informed by some outside agency since you were not conscious of exercising any special faculty yourself.

Though it is also likely that that information came to you from your own subconscious mind. But if that information had been given to you by an outside agency you could not have received it if you had not developed that faculty through which it was received.

The gaining of that information therefore was wholly dependent upon your own mental development. We shall find that everything we gain, be it ordinary or extraordinary, comes through faculties of our own, no matter what the original source may be. And we must admit that we could receive a great deal more if those same faculties were highly developed. But we cannot develop those things that we look upon as supernatural, as being beyond us, or as being separated from us. Therefore to promote growth, development or attainment in any direction we must think of all things as natural and normal and as having the one Supreme Source. In like manner we must think of all truth as being expressions of the whole truth, and that higher truth is just as natural and intelligible as the truth we now understand. In brief, we must realize that that truth which may be beyond what we now know to be truth, is just as natural as the truth we now possess, and may be gained in the same way as we have gained such truth as we realize in the present.

There is a certain faculty usually termed interior insight that has become highly active in thousands of minds at the present time, and many of those who have it think that they are especially favored.

They are sometimes warned from danger through mysterious premonitions and are frequently led into circumstances through which much good is gained.

But in the last analysis can we say that a person who has a very active interior insight is favored to a greater degree than a person who has a good normal eyesight? Is not the one as wonderful as the other? Is not the one as natural as the other; and if it is true that mysterious warnings in the time of danger are supernatural, the ability to see the delicate colorings of the rainbow must also be supernatural. Though on the other hand if the latter is natural, as we know it to be, the former must also be natural, which fact proves that the sphere of the natural is infinitely more immense than we ever believed before.

To have a premonition of coming danger is wonderful, but to be able to see a broken plank in the sidewalk at a distance of one hundred feet is just as wonderful. Nevertheless, we have been in the habit of calling the one natural and the other supernatural. And for this reason we have pushed the former so far beyond us that we are hardly ever able to develop it further.

In this connection it is well to emphasize the fact that if we make it a practice to think of all extraordinary experiences as perfectly natural, we shall find it an easy matter to develop to a greater degree those faculties through which such experiences come. In consequence our minds would be enlarged along many new and interesting lines. Seeing and hearing and feeling have become so commonplace that we do not think of them as wonderful any more, and yet to be able to see or hear or feel is just as marvelous as the most astonishing miracle that we ever heard of. In fact, to be able to predict events for a thousand years to come is no more wonderful than to be able to see physical objects a thousand feet in the distance.

This is something that we must realize if we wish to develop the mind along those higher lines through which greater truth may be discerned; because so long as we look upon certain things as extraordinary or supernatural we shall not be able to widen the mind into that consciousness through which such things may be realized or gained at will.

All things that are possible are wonderful— even extraordinary. Therefore if we should say that anyone of them is caused by outside powers or agencies, or powers that are beyond us, we would have to say that they are all produced by such superior powers. Though if this were true man would be a mere automaton. To realize, however, on the contrary, that all these things, no matter how wonderful they may be, are being produced through faculties that belong to man, and that still more wonderful things can be produced through higher faculties already latent in man — this is to make man what he really is — a marvel of creative power.

What is Truth

To admit that some of these remarkable things take place through the actions of human faculties is to admit that more and greater things can take place through the further development of those same faculties and we know that this is true.

Therefore we must conclude that every faculty is a marvelous faculty. For the same reason we must conclude that physical sight is just as wonderful and just as sacred as spiritual discernment; and also that the latter is just as natural and just as I normal as the former.

If some things were sacred and some were not there would be two antagonistic causes in the universe, which is impossible, because a mind divided against itself cannot stand. The universe, however, has continued for ages and its laws and forces are still working together in harmony, invariably producing the same effects from the same causes, proving thereby that all things come from the one supreme source, and are governed by the one fundamental law.

Therefore if anything is natural, all things are natural since all things are produced by the one power. Also for the same reason all things must be sacred and good in their own place of action.

And if one faculty in man belongs to man himself all faculties or powers that act in man must belong to man himself. The so-called higher faculties are parts of the human mind. They are not produced by special actions or by special powers outside of ourselves, but are caused to act by the same law that operates through all our faculties.

These faculties can be developed to higher and higher degrees just as every faculty in mind can be developed. However, to develop any faculty we must become conscious of the greater life and the greater possibilities that lie back of and above that faculty. But if we think of the greater life as being supernatural we at once imagine that it is beyond us. In consequence, the normal mind being lowered, cannot go up within reach of this greater life, but will hold itself back, so to speak, and thus be unable to promote the development desired along those lines.

But when we think of the greater life as being united with the lesser life, just as the inlet is united with the sea, we place the mind in that position where it can draw upon the greater life and thus increase constantly the power of every faculty. In like manner when we think of the limitless sea of infinite truth as being united with what truth we possess now, we place the mind in that position where it can gradually and steadily enter into the understanding of truth that is beyond what is understood now. And it is in this way that the mind goes into the realization of higher and greater truth along all lines, thereby fulfilling the one purpose of every mind in search of truth; that is, to become conscious of a wider and a higher world of truth every day. When we know that the higher faculties may be developed by the same power through which any development is promoted, that power will enter such higher faculties as we may wish to develop. The result will be that everything that now seems supernatural will be placed under the full normal control of the mind. And the dawn of the limitless life, as well as the understanding of infinite truth, will be at hand.

Chapter 16

Discernment of Absolute Truth

It is impossible to define absolute truth, as that which is absolute is beyond definition, containing within itself the elements of all definitions that might be formulated with regard to the truth. But for practical purposes we can say that absolute truth is the real or the whole truth in its changeless condition without any colorings or modifications whatever from the mind of man. Therefore to discern absolute truth the human mind must transcend all relative and isolated viewpoints of truth, and look upon the whole truth as it is in its fundamental and unmodified state.

This, however, is not possible so long as the ordinary senses are depended upon exclusively, because the senses invariably take special or isolated viewpoints, not being able to see anything from all points of view. For this reason the senses do not see things as they are in themselves all around, so to speak, but see things only as they appear from certain viewpoints. What is discerned from these viewpoints, however, is true as far as it goes, but it is not the whole truth. It is not the pure light, but simply a certain shade or color of the light.

But the absolute truth is the pure light — all the rays of light and all the colors of those rays blended in the one complete light. And it is such light that we must search for when trying to discern absolute truth. For the term "absolute truth" means practically the same as the pure white light of the whole truth. However, as the external senses and the usual actions of the mind approach the truth from certain viewpoints only we shall not be able to discern absolute truth, the pure white light of truth, unless there is some faculty or sense in the human mind that is in possession of this particular power.

But there is such a sense — well termed the metaphysical sense — a finer sense in the human mind through which the absolute truth may be discerned.

It is the advent of modern metaphysics that has demonstrated the existence of a metaphysical sense, or rather a special mental faculty through which the whole truth about things, and the perfect soul of things, may be discerned. And it is through this discovery of the metaphysical sense that practically all misunderstandings concerning the study of metaphysics may be thoroughly cleared up.

An instance of such misunderstanding is found in the fact that a number of minds find the principle of metaphysics very simple; in brief, so simple that no mental effort whatever is required to understand them. While on the other hand a large number are unable to see anything of worth in those principles.

When we compare the intelligence of those who appreciate metaphysics and those who do not we usually find very little difference. There are many brilliant minds in both classes, and any number of lesser minds in both classes.

It is very evident that the principles of metaphysics are not discerned through the channels of ordinary objective intelligence. Neither does the understanding of metaphysics necessarily follow the higher development of character, because some of the best characters in the world are wholly unable to appreciate metaphysics, while there are a number who do appreciate such thought whose characters are by no means strong. And so marked is this difference between the two classes in this regard, that those who understand metaphysics are extremely surprised to find so many intelligent people seemingly unable to understand it. On the other hand, those who do not appreciate metaphysics are surprised to find so many believing in what to them appears to be nothing but illusions. Thus each party feels sorry for the lack of intelligence in the other, neither party knowing the cause of this particular difference.

The fact is, that those who appreciate metaphysics do so not on account of any superiority in character or intelligence, but because they have the metaphysical sense developed to a considerable degree. On the other hand, those who do not fully appreciate metaphysics fail, not on account of any inferiority in character or intelligence, but because the metaphysical sense in them has not been developed.

They may be very superior both in character and intellect, but if they have no development of the metaphysical sense, metaphysical principles will not be clear to them.

And here let us remember that metaphysics, properly defined, means the interior understanding of absolute truth. In brief, if you can discern what is usually spoken of as pure metaphysics you have the metaphysical sense, and have the power to discern, at least to some extent, the pure white light of absolute truth.

To criticize those who do not understand metaphysics, therefore, is not wisdom, for it is not their fault. Neither do we necessarily deserve any special credit for being able to understand metaphysical principles. Usually we are born with the metaphysical sense, and that is why metaphysical ideas are so simple to us. Why some are born with that sense and others not is a different question, however — a question that can readily be answered; but the answer has no direct bearing upon the subject under consideration.

The fact that the metaphysical sense is developed in some and not in others explains why some can appreciate metaphysics while others cannot. And the fact that the understanding of metaphysical principles is of extraordinary value leads us to enquire if the metaphysical sense can be developed in anybody here and now. The result of such inquiry and investigation proves that this sense can be developed. For the fact is that anything in the being of man can be developed. We all have the same powers and faculties latent within us, and the elements of growth are present in every faculty and power, so that it is only necessary to apply the law of development to that which we wish to develop and such development will invariably be secured.

The development of the metaphysical sense is important for many reasons, though there are two reasons that occupy the first place. The first reason is, that it is only through this sense that we can discern absolute truth, or pure truth, or the whole truth, in connection with anything in existence.

And second, it is only through this sense that the mind can discern the causes of things. And here it is well to emphasize the fact that the world of cause exists entirely within the world of absolute truth. If man desires to master himself, take his life into his own hands and create his own destiny, he must understand the causes of the many effects in his life. And as causes can be discerned only through the metaphysical sense we realize its exceptional importance in this connection.

When man knows the cause of everything that takes place in his body, mind or character, and learns how to produce that cause he can produce practically any effect in his system that he may desire. If man knew the cause of health and knew how to produce that cause he could banish sickness from his life for all time. If he knew the cause of peace, harmony, wisdom and power he could in the same way produce those faculties or conditions in his life to any measure desired. The same would be true with regard to any other faculty or power that may exist in the being of man.

It is evident that when the metaphysical sense is highly developed we shall be able to know instantaneously the exact cause of everything that transpires in the human system. And this is perfectly natural, because if the physical sense can discern effects it is evident that the metaphysical sense can discern causes, functioning as it does in the world of cause. There are already thousands of people in the world who know that the causes of things can be discerned through the metaphysical sense, and who have had remarkable experiences in this connection, even though the development of this sense is as yet in its infancy.

We ourselves produce the causes of everything that happens in our own personalities or in our own world, though all such causes are as a rule produced ignorantly. The way we think and live will determine what is to happen to us. But the average person does not know what kind of thinking and living is necessary to produce the things desired.

He knows desirable effects when he sees them, but he does not know what causes will produce those effects. And his ignorance in this regard is due to the fact that his metaphysical sense is not developed.

When the metaphysical sense is developed we shall be able to know the exact cause of every effect, and will therefore know what to do and what not to do in order to secure the results desired. The advantage of having a highly developed metaphysical sense therefore is extraordinary, to say the least, though its most important function will be found in connection with the discernment of absolute truth.

To develop this sense the principal essential is to train consciousness to go back of things, back of effects and into the world of underlying principles; that is, every mental effort should have cause in view, and every mental action should be animated with the realization that the principle that underlies every cause is not only ideal, but real; and that the real is perfect and complete, existing fundamentally in absolute truth.

To realize the completeness, the perfection and the wholeness of life, and the power that is back of things and within things, is also extremely important, because what we become conscious of in the interior life, that we shall invariably express in the exterior life. Through the metaphysical sense we discern the ideal, we realize the perfect, the greater and the complete. We become conscious of those elements in life that have superior quality and worth; and according to the law just stated we will thereby bring forth into tangible life the greater, the superior, the perfect and the ideal. Our ideals will thus be realized, and the remarkable possibilities that are latent within us will steadily unfold themselves into practical life.

To dwell mentally in the consciousness of the ideal, as far as that consciousness has been awakened, and to give constant attention to the discernment of the pure white light of absolute truth, is to aid remarkably in the development of the metaphysical sense. Here we must remember an important law; that is, that we tend to develop the power to discern and understand those things that we think of the most. Therefore, if we think a great deal of the pure white light of absolute truth, and try to enter into that light as far as possible, and as frequently as possible, the metaphysical sense will steadily develop.

Every action of consciousness that tries to feel the soul of things will produce the same effect; that is, tend to develop the mind toward the realization of the soul of reality, or absolute truth, and especially so if we think of the soul of things as being perfect and complete in every sense of the term; for the soul of things contains the whole truth that is in things and upon which the true existence of things is based. The workings of this law of consciousness, and the expression of what we become conscious of, is well illustrated in the fact that when the metaphysical sense discerns that the soul of things has perfect health, we thereby cause the mind to become conscious of perfect health. Perfect health, therefore, according to the law will become an active power in mind, which means that the power of health will fill the entire body. And this is true because the ruling power of the mind always becomes the ruling power of the body.

The metaphysical sense can also discern all other desirable qualities in the being of man. And since we always bring forth into expression whatever we become conscious of, a high development of the metaphysical sense will enable us to unfold and develop almost anything that we may desire, especially the full understanding of absolute truth. In addition, we shall know the cause of things, which means that we can determine the effect of all things in our world, thereby placing conditions, circumstances and destiny in our own hands. And this must be the inevitable result where the understanding of absolute truth is attained. For to know the truth is to be free, and to be free is to be able to make our own life and our own nature what we wish it to be. In brief, we are absolutely free when we have gained power to become and attain according to our deepest desires and highest ideals. And we approach absolute freedom as we grow in that power. The path of freedom is the path that leads upward and onward. And the further we advance in this path the more we discern and understand of the pure white light of absolute truth.

Your Forces and How to Use Them

Your Forces and How to Use Them

Table of Contents

Foreword	276
Chapter 1 - The Ruling Principle in Man	280
Chapter 2 - How We Govern the Forces We Possess	288
Chapter 3 - The Use of Mind in Practical Action	298
Chapter 4 - The Forces of the Subconscious	314
Chapter 5 - Training the Subconscious for Special Results	324
Chapter 6 - The Power of Subjective Thought	332
Chapter 7 - How Man Becomes What He Thinks	350
Chapter 8 - The Art of Changing for the Better	360
Chapter 9 - He Can Who Thinks He Can	369
Chapter 10 - How We Secure What We Persistently Desire	375
Chapter 11 - Concentration and the Power Back of Suggestion	386
Chapter 12 - The Development of the Will	396
Chapter 13 - The Building of a Great Mind	412
Chapter 14 - How Character Determines Constructive Action	423
Chapter 15 - The Art of Building Character	432
Chapter 16 - The Creative Forces in Man	445
Chapter 17 - The Building Power of Constructive Speech	462
Chapter 18 - Imagination and the Master Mind	475
Chapter 19 - The Higher Forces in Man	486
Chapter 20 - The Greatest Power in Man	507
The Optimist Creed	512

Foreword

"There are a million energies in man. What may we not become when we learn to use them all." This is the declaration of the poet; and though poetry is usually inspired by transcendental visions, and therefore more or less impressed with apparent exaggerations, nevertheless there is in this poetic expression far more actual, practical truth than we may at first believe.

How many energies there are in man, no one knows; but there are so many that even the keenest observers of human activity have found it impossible to count them all. And as most of these energies are remarkable, to say the least, and some of them so remarkable as to appear both limitless in power and numberless in possibilities, we may well wonder what man will become when he learns to use them all.

When we look upon human nature in general we may fail to see much improvement in power and worth as compared with what we believe the race has been in the past; and therefore we conclude that humanity will continue to remain about the same upon this planet until the end of time. But when we investigate the lives of such individuals as have recently tried to apply more intelligently the greater powers within them, we come to a different conclusion. We then discover that there is evidence in thousands of human lives of a new and superior race of people -- a race that will apply a much larger measure of the wonders and possibilities that exist within them.

It is only a few years, not more than a quarter of a century, since modern psychology began to proclaim the new science of human thought and action, so that we have had but a short time to demonstrate what a more intelligent application of our energies and forces can accomplish. But already the evidence is coming in from all sources, revealing results that frequently border upon the extraordinary. Man can do far more with himself and his life than he has been doing in the past; he can call into action, and successfully apply, far more ability, energy and worth than his forefathers ever dreamed of. So much has been proven during this brief introductory period of the new-age. Then what greater things may we not reasonably expect when we have had fifty or a hundred years more in which to develop and apply those larger possibilities which we now know to be inherent in us all.

It is the purpose of the following pages, not only to discuss these greater powers and possibilities in man, but also to present practical methods through which they may be applied. We have been aware of the fact for centuries that there is more in man than what appears on the surface, but it is only in recent years that a systematic effort has been made to understand the nature and practical use of this "more," as well as to work out better methods for the thorough and effective application of those things on the surface which we have always employed. In dealing with a subject that is so large and so new, however, it is necessary to make many statements that may, at first sight, appear to be unfounded, or at least exaggerations. But if the reader will thoroughly investigate the basis of such statements as he goes along, he will not only find that there are no unfounded statements or exaggerations in the book, but will wish that every strong statement made had been made many times as strong.

When we go beneath the surface of human life and learn what greater things are hidden beneath the ordinary layers of mental substance and vital energy, we find man to be so wonderfully made that language is wholly inadequate to describe even a fraction of his larger and richer life. We may try to give expression to our thoughts, at such times, by employing the strongest statements and the most forceful adjectives that we can think of; but even these prove little better than nothing; so therefore we may conclude that no statement that attempts to describe the "more" in man can possibly be too strong. Even the strongest fails to say one thousandth of what we would say should we speak the whole truth. We shall all admit this, and accordingly shall find it advisable not to pass judgment upon strong statements but to learn to understand and apply those greater powers within ourselves that are infinitely stronger than the strongest statement that could possibly be made.

Those minds who may believe that the human race is to continue weak and imperfect as usual, should consider what remarkable steps in advance have recently been taken in nearly all fields of human activity. And then they should remember that the greater powers in man, as well as a scientific study of the use of his lesser powers, have been almost wholly neglected. The question then that will naturally arise is, what man might make of himself if he would apply the same painstaking science to his own development and advancement as he now applies in other fields. If he did, would we not, in another generation or two, witness unmistakable evidence of the coming of a new and superior race, and would not strong men and women become far more numerous than ever before in the history of the world?

Each individual will want to answer these questions according to his own point of view, but whatever his answer may be, we all must agree that man can be, become and achieve far more than even the most sanguine indications of the present may predict. And it is the purpose of the following pages to encourage as many people as possible to study and apply these greater powers within them so that they may not only become greater and richer and more worthy as individuals, but may also become the forerunners of that higher and more wonderful race of which we all have so fondly dreamed.

Chapter 1

The Ruling Principle of Man

The purpose of the following pages will be to work out the subject chosen in the most thorough and practical manner; in brief, to analyze the whole nature of man, find all the forces in his possession, whether they be apparent or hidden, active or dormant, and to present methods through which all those forces can be applied in making the life of each individual richer, greater and better. To make every phase of this work as useful as possible to the greatest number possible, not a single statement will be made that all cannot understand, and not a single idea will be presented that anyone cannot apply to everyday life.

We all want to know what we actually possess both in the physical, the mental and the spiritual, and we want to know how the elements and forces within us can be applied in the most successful manner. It is results in practical life that we want, and we are not true to ourselves or the race until we learn to use the powers within us so effectively, that the greatest results possible within the possibilities of human nature are secured.

When we proceed with a scientific study of the subject, we find that the problem before us is to know what is in us and how to use what is in us. After much study of the powers in man, both conscious and subconscious, we have come to the conclusion that if we only knew how to use these powers, we could accomplish practically anything that we may have in view, and not only realize our wants to the fullest degree, but also reach even our highest goal. Though this may seem to be a strong statement, nevertheless when we examine the whole nature of man, we are compelled to admit that it is true even in its fullest sense, and that therefore, not a single individual can fail to realize his wants and reach his goal, after he has learned how to use the powers that are in him. This is not mere speculation, nor is it simply a beautiful dream. The more we study the lives of people who have achieved, and the more we study our own experience every day, the more convinced we become that there is no reason whatever why any individual should not realize all his ambitions and much more.

The basis of this study will naturally be found in the understanding of the whole nature of man, as we must know what we are, before we can know and use what we in inherently possess. In analyzing human nature a number of methods have been employed, but there are only three in particular that are of actual value for our present purpose. The first of these declares that man is composed of ego, consciousness and form, and though this analysis is the most complete, yet it is also the most abstract, and is therefore not easily understood. The second analysis, which is simpler, and which is employed almost exclusively by the majority, declares that man is body, mind and soul; but as much as this idea is thought of and spoken of there are very few who actually understand it. In fact, the usual conception of man as body, mind and soul will have to be completely reversed in order to become absolutely true. The third analysis, which is the simplest and the most serviceable, declares that man is composed of individuality and personality, and it is this conception of human nature that will constitute the phases of our study in this work.

Before we pass to the more practical side of the subject, we shall find it profitable to examine briefly these various ideas concerning the nature of man; in fact, every part of our human analysis that refers to the ego, simply must be understood if we are to learn how to use the forces we possess, and the reason for this is found in the fact that the ego is the "I AM," the ruling principle in man, the centre and source of individuality, the originator of everything that takes place in man, and that primary something to which all other things in human nature are secondary.

When the average person employs the term "ego," he thinks that he is dealing with something that is hidden so deeply in the abstract that it can make but little difference whether we understand it or not. This, however, does not happen to be true, because it is the ego that must act before any action can take place anywhere in the human system, and it is the ego that must originate the new before any step in advance can be taken. And in addition, it is extremely important to realize that the power of will to control the forces we possess, depends directly upon how fully conscious we are of the ego as the ruling principle within us. We understand therefore, that it is absolutely necessary to associate all thought, all, feeling and all actions of mind or personality with the ego, or what we shall hereafter speak of as the " I AM."

The first step to be taken in this connection, is to recognize the "I AM" in everything you do, and to think always of the "I AM," as being you, the supreme you. Whenever you think, realize that it is the "I AM" that originated the thought. Whenever you act, realize that it is the " I AM" that gives initiative to that action, and whenever you think of yourself or try to be conscious of yourself, realize that the "I AM" occupies the throne of your entire field of consciousness.

Another important essential is to affirm silently in your own mind that you are the "I AM," and as you affirm this statement or as you simply declare positively, "I AM" think of the "I AM" as being the ruling principle in your whole world, as being distinct and above and superior to all else in your being, and as being you, yourself, in the highest, largest, and most comprehensive sense. You thus lift yourself up, so to speak, to the mountain top of masterful individuality; you enthrone yourself; you become true to yourself; you place yourself where you belong.

Through this practice you not only discover yourself to be the master of your whole life, but you elevate all your conscious actions to that lofty state in your consciousness that we may describe as the throne of your being, or as that centre of action within which the ruling "I AM " lives and moves and has its being. If you wish to control and direct the forces you possess, you must act from the throne of your being, so to speak or in other words, from that conscious point in your mental world wherein all power of control, direction and initiative proceeds; and this point of action is the centre of the " I AM." You must act, not as a body, not as a personality, not as a, mind, but as the "I AM," and the more fully you recognize the lofty position of the "I AM," the greater becomes your power to control and direct all other things that you may possess. In brief, whenever you think or act, you should feel that you stand with the "I AM," at the apex of mentality on the very heights of your existence, and you should at the same time, realize that this "I AM" is you the supreme you. The more you practice these methods, the more you lift yourself up above the limitations of mind and body, into the realization of your own true position as a masterful individuality; in fact, you place yourself where you belong, over and above everything in your organized existence.

When we examine the mind of the average person, we find that they usually identify themselves with mind or body. They either think that they are body or that they are mind, and therefore they can control neither mind nor body. The "I AM" in their nature is submerged in a bundle of ideas, some of which are true and some of which are not, and their thought is usually controlled by those ideas without receiving any direction whatever from that principle within them that alone was intended to give direction. Such a one lives in the lower story of human existence but as we can control life only when we give directions from the upper story, we discover just why the average person neither understands their forces nor has the power to use them.

They must first elevate themselves to the upper story of the human structure, and the first and most important step to be taken in this direction is to recognize the "I AM" as the ruling principle and that the "I AM" is you.

Another method that will be found highly important in this connection is to take a few moments every day and try to feel that you the "I AM" are not only above mind and body, but in a certain sense, distinct from mind and body; in fact, try to isolate the "I AM" for a few moments every day from the rest of your organized being. This practice will give you what may be termed a perfect consciousness of your own individual "I AM," and as you gain that consciousness you will always think of the supreme "I AM" whenever you think of yourself. Accordingly, all your mental actions will, from that time on, come directly from the "I AM"; and if you will continue to stand above all such actions at all times, you will be able to control them and direct them completely.

To examine consciousness and form in this connection is hardly necessary, except to define briefly their general nature, so that we may have a clear idea of what we are dealing with in the conscious field as well as in the field of expression. The "I AM" is fundamentally conscious: that is, the "I AM" knows what exists in the human field or in the human sphere and what is taking place in the human sphere; and that constitutes consciousness. In brief, you are conscious when you know that you exist and have some definite idea as to what is taking place in your sphere of existence. What we speak of as form, is everything in the organized personality that has shape and that serves in any manner to give expression to the forces within us.

In the exercise of consciousness, we find that the "I AM" employs three fundamental actions. When the "I AM" looks out upon life we have simple consciousness. When the "I AM" looks upon its own position in life we have self consciousness, and when the "I AM" looks up into the vastness of real life we have cosmic consciousness.

In simple consciousness, you are only aware of those things that exist externally to yourself, but when you begin to become conscious of yourself as a distinct entity, you begin to develop self consciousness. When you begin to turn your attention to the great within and begin to look up into the real source of all things, you become conscious of that world that seemingly exists within all worlds, and when you enter upon this experience, you are on the borderland of cosmic consciousness, the most fascinating subject that has ever been known.

When we come to define body, mind and soul, we must, as previously stated, reverse the usual definition. In the past, we have constantly used the expression, "I have a soul," which naturally implies the belief that "I AM a body"; and so deeply has this idea become fixed in the average mind that nearly everybody thinks of the body whenever the term "me" or "myself " is employed. But in this attitude of mind the individual is not above the physical states of thought and feeling; in fact, he is more or less submerged in what may be called a bundle of physical facts and ideas, of which he has very little control. You cannot control anything in your life, however, until you are above it. You cannot control what is in your body until you realize that you are above your body. You cannot control what is in your mind until you realize that you are above your mind, and therefore no one can use the forces within them to any extent so long as they think of themselves as being the body, or as being localized exclusively in the body.

When we examine the whole nature of man, we find that the soul is the man himself, and that the ego is the central principle of the soul; or to use another expression, the soul, including the "I AM," constitutes the individuality, and that visible something through which individuality finds expression, constitutes the personality.

If you wish to understand your forces, and gain that masterful attitude necessary to the control of your forces, train yourself to think that you are a soul, but do not think of the soul as something vague or mysterious. Think of the soul as being the individual you and all that that expression can possibly imply. Train yourself to think that you are master of mind and body, because you are above mind and body, and possess the power to use everything that is in mind and body.

Man is ever in search of strength. It is the strong man that wins. It is the man with power that scales the heights. To be strong is to be great; and it is the privilege of greatness to satisfy every desire, every aspiration, every need. But strength is not for the few alone; it is for all, and the way to strength is simple. Proceed this very moment to the mountain tops of the strength you now possess, and whatever may happen do not come down. Do not weaken under adversity. Resolve to remain as strong, as determined and as highly enthused during the darkest night of adversity as you are during the sunniest day of prosperity. Do not feel disappointed when things seem disappointing. Keep the eye single upon the same brilliant future regardless of circumstances, conditions or events. Do not lose heart when things go wrong. Continue undisturbed in your original resolve to make all things go right. To be overcome by adversity and threatening failure is to lose strength; to always remain in the same lofty, determined mood is to constantly grow in strength. The man who never weakens when things are against him will grow stronger and stronger until all things will delight to be for him. He will finally have all the strength he may desire or need. Be always strong and you will always be stronger

Chapter 2

How We Govern the Forces We Possess

Whenever you think or whenever you feel, whenever you speak, whenever you act, or whatever may be taking place in your life, your supreme idea should be that you are above it all, superior to it all, and have control of it all. You simply must take this higher ground in all action, thought and consciousness before you can control yourself and direct, for practical purposes, the forces you possess. Therefore, what has been said in connection with the "I AM," the soul and the individuality as being one, and as standing at the apex of human existence, is just as important as anything that may be said hereafter in connection with the application of the forces in man to practical action. And though this phase of the subject may appear to be somewhat abstract, we shall find no difficulty in understanding it more fully as we apply the ideas evolved. In fact, when we learn to realize that we, by nature, occupy a position that is above mind and body, this part of the subject will be found more interesting than anything else, and its application more profitable.

We can define individuality more fully by stating that it is the invisible man and that everything in man that is invisible belongs to his individuality. It is the individuality that initiates, that controls or directs. Therefore to control and use a force in your own system, you must understand and develop individuality. Your individuality must be made distinct, determined and positive. You must constantly know what you are and what you want, and you must constantly be determined to secure what you want. It is individuality that makes you different from all other organized entities, and it is a highly developed individuality that gives you the power to stand out distinct above the mass, and it is the degree of individuality that you possess that determines largely what position you are to occupy in the world.

Whenever you see a man or woman who is different, who seems to stand out distinct, and who has something vital about them that no one else seems to possess, you have someone whose individuality is highly developed, and you also have someone who is going to make their mark in the world. Take two people of equal power, ability and efficiency, but with this difference. In the one individuality is highly developed, while in the other it is not. You know at once which one of these two is going to reach the highest places in the world of achievement; and the reason is that the one who possesses individuality lives above mind and body, thereby being able to control and direct the forces and powers of mind and body. The man or woman, however, whose individuality is weak, lives more or less down in mind and body, and instead of controlling mind and body, is constantly being influenced by everything from the outside that may enter their consciousness.

Whenever you find a man or a woman who is doing something worthwhile, who is creating an impression upon the race, who is moving forward towards greater and better things, you find the individuality strong, positive and highly developed. It is therefore absolutely necessary that you give your best attention to the development of a strong, positive individuality if you wish to succeed in the world and make the best use of the forces in your possession. A negative or weak individuality drifts with the stream of environment, and usually receives only what others choose to give, but a firm, strong, positive, well-developed individuality, actually controls the ship of their life and destiny, and sooner or later will gain possession of what they originally set out to secure. A positive individuality has the power to take hold of things and turn them to good account. This is one reason why such an individuality always succeeds. Another reason is that the more fully your individuality is developed, the more you are admired by everybody with whom you may come in contact. The human race loves power, and counts it a privilege to give lofty positions to those who have power, and every man or woman whose individuality is highly developed, does possess power usually exceptional power.

To develop individuality, the first essential is to give the "I AM" its true and lofty position in your mind. The "I AM" is the very centre of individuality, and the more fully conscious you become of the "I AM" the more of the power that is in the "I AM" you arouse, and it is the arousing of this power that makes individuality positive and strong. Another essential is to practice the idea of feeling or conceiving yourself as occupying the masterful attitude. Whenever you think of yourself, think of yourself as being and living and acting in the masterful attitude. Then in addition, make every desire positive, make every feeling positive, make every thought positive, and make every action of mind positive. To make your wants distinct and positive, that is, to actually and fully know what you want and then proceed to want what you want with all the power that is in you, will also tend to give strength and positiveness to your individuality; and the reason is that such actions of mind will tend to place in positive, constructive action every force that is in your system.

A most valuable method is to picture in your mind your own best idea of what a strong, well-developed individuality would necessarily be, and then think of yourself as becoming more and more like that picture. In this connection it is well to remember that we gradually grow into the likeness of that which we think of the most. Therefore, if you have a very clear idea of a highly developed individuality, and think a great deal of that individuality with a strong, positive desire to develop such an individuality, you will gradually and surely move towards that lofty ideal. Another valuable method is to give conscious recognition to what may be called the bigger man on the inside. Few people think of this greater man that is within them, but we cannot afford to neglect this interior entity for a moment. This greater or larger man is not something that is separate and distinct from ourselves. It is simply the sum total of the greater powers and possibilities that are within us. We should recognize these, think of them a great deal, and desire with all the power of heart and mind and soul to arouse and express more and more of these inner powers. Thus we shall find that the interior man, our real individuality, will become stronger and more active, and our power to apply our greater possibilities will increase accordingly. The value of individuality is so great that it cannot possibly be overestimated. Every known method that will develop individuality, therefore, should be applied faithfully, thoroughly and constantly. In fact, no one other thing we can do will bring greater returns.

The personality is the visible man. Everything that is visible in the human entity belongs to the personality, but it is more than the body. To say that someone has a fine personality may and may not mean that that personality is beautiful, in the ordinary sense of the term. There might be no physical beauty and yet the personality might be highly developed. There might be nothing striking about such a personality, and yet there would be something extremely attractive, something to greatly admire. On the other hand, when the personality is not well developed, there is nothing in the visible man that you can see, besides ordinary human clay. Everything existing in such a personality is crude and even gross; but there is no excuse for any personality being crude, unrefined or undeveloped. There is not a single personality that cannot be so refined and perfected as to become strikingly attractive, and there are scores of reasons why such development should be sought.

The most important reason is that all the forces of man act through the personality, and the finer the personality, the more easily can we direct and express the forces we possess. When the personality is crude, we find it difficult to apply in practical life the finer elements that are within us, and here we find one reason why talent or ability so frequently fails to be its best. In such cases the personality has been neglected, and is not a fit instrument through which finer things and greater things can find expression. The personality is related to the individual as the piano is to the musician. If the piano is out of tune the musician will fail no matter how much of a musician they may be; and likewise, if the piano or instrument is crude in construction, the finest music cannot be expressed through it as a channel. To develop the personality, the principal essential is to learn how to transmute all the creative energies that are generated in the human system, a subject that will be given thorough attention in another chapter.

When we proceed to apply the forces within us, we find three fields of action. The first is the conscious field, the field in which the mind acts when we are awake. The second field is the subconscious, that field in which the mind acts when it goes beneath consciousness. It is also the field in which we act when asleep. The term, "falling asleep," is therefore literally true, as when we go to sleep, the ego goes down, so to speak, into another world a world so vast, that only portions of it have thus far been explored. The third field is the superconscious, the field in which the mind acts when it touches the upper realm, and it is when acting in this field that we gain real power and real inspiration; in fact, when we touch the superconscious, we frequently feel as if we have become more than mere man. To know how to act in the superconscious field, is therefore highly important, even though the idea may at first sight seem to be vague and somewhat mystical.

We are constantly in touch, however, with the superconscious whether we know it or not. We frequently enter the superconscious when we listen to inspiring music, when we read some book that touches the finer intellect, when we listen to someone who speaks from what may be termed the inner throne of authority, when we witness some soul-stirring scene in nature. We also touch the superconscious when we are carried away with some tremendous ambition, and herein we find practical value in a great measure. When men of tremendous ambition are carried away, so to speak, with the power of that ambition, they almost invariably reach the higher and finer state of mind a state where they not only feel more power and determination than they ever felt before, but a state in which the mind becomes so extremely active that it almost invariably gains the necessary brilliancy to work out those plans or ideas that are required in order that the ambition may be realized.

It can readily be demonstrated that we get our best ideas from this lofty realm, and it is a well-known fact that no one ever accomplishes great or wonderful things in the world, without touching frequently this sublime inspiring state. When we train the mind to touch the superconscious at frequent intervals, we always find the ideas we want. We always succeed in providing the ways and means required. No matter what the difficulties may be, we invariably discover something by which we may overcome and conquer completely.

Whenever you find yourself in what may be termed a difficult position, proceed at once to work your mind up into higher and higher attitudes, until you touch the superconscious, and when you touch that lofty state you will soon receive the ideas or the methods that you need. But this is not the only value connected with the superconscious. The highest forces in man are the most powerful, but we cannot use those higher forces without acting through the superconscious field. Therefore, if you want to understand and apply all the forces you possess, you must train the mind to act through the superconscious as well as the conscious and the subconscious.

However, we must not permit ourselves to live exclusively in this lofty state; though it is the source of the higher forces in man, those forces that are indispensable to the doing of great and important things; nevertheless, those forces cannot be applied unless they are brought down to earth, so to speak, and united with practical action. He who lives exclusively in the superconscious, will dream wonderful dreams, but if he does not unite the forces of the superconscious with practical action, he will do nothing else but dream dreams, and those dreams will not come true. It is when we combine mental action in the conscious, subconscious and superconscious, that we get the results we desire. In brief, it is the full use of all the forces in mind through all the channels of expression that leads to the highest attainment and the greatest achievements.

When we proceed with the practical application of any particular force, we shall not find it necessary to cause that force to act through what may be termed the psychological field, and the reason is that the psychological field in man is the real field of action. It is the field through which the undercurrents flow, and we all understand that it is these undercurrents that determine, not only the direction of action, but the results that follow action. This idea is well illustrated in the following lines:

"Straws upon the surface flow; He who would seek for pearls must dive below."

The term "below" as applied to the life and consciousness of man, is synonymous with the psychological field, or the field of the undercurrents. Ordinary minds skim over the surface. Great minds invariably sound these deeper depths, and act in and through the psychological field. Their minds dive below into the rich vastness of what may be termed the gold mines of the mind, and the diamond fields of the soul.

When we enter the psychological field of any force, which simply means the inner and finer field of action of that force, we act through the undercurrents, and thereby proceed to control those currents. It is in the field of the undercurrents that we find both the origin and the action of cause, whether physical or mental. It is these currents, when acted upon intelligently, that remove what we do not want and produce those changes that we do want. They invariably produce effects, both physical and mental, according to the action that we give to them, and all those things that pertain to the personality will respond only to the actions of those currents; that is, you cannot produce any effect in any part of the mind or body unless you first direct the undercurrents of the system to produce those effects. To act through the undercurrents therefore is absolutely necessary, no matter what we may wish to do, or what forces we may wish to control, direct or apply; and we act upon those undercurrents only when we enter the psychological field.

In like manner, we can turn to good account all things in practical everyday life only when we understand the psychology of those things. The reason is, that when we understand the psychology of anything, we understand the power that is back of that particular thing, and that controls it and gives it definite action. In consequence, when we understand the psychology of anything in our own field of action or in our own environment, we will know how to deal with it so as to secure whatever results that particular thing has the power to produce. But this law is especially important in dealing with forces whether those forces act through the mind or through anyone of the faculties, through the personality or through the conscious, subconscious or superconscious fields. In brief, whatever we do in trying to control and direct the powers we possess, we must enter the deeper life of those powers, so that we can get full control of the undercurrents. It is the way those undercurrents flow that determines results, and as we can direct those currents in any way that we desire, we naturally conclude that we can secure whatever results we desire.

Man lives to move forward, To move forward is to live more. To live more is to be more and do more; and it is being and doing that constitutes the path to happiness. The more you are the more you do, the richer your life, the greater your joy. But being and doing must always live together as one. To try to be much and not try to do much is to find life a barren waste. To try to do much and not try to be much is to find life a burden too heavy and wearisome to bear. The being of much gives the necessary inspiration and the necessary power to the doing of much. The doing of much gives the necessary expression to the being of much. And it is the bringing forth of being through the act of doing that produces happiness that is happiness. Being much gives capacity for doing much. Doing much gives expression to the richest and the best that is within us. And the more we increase the richness of that which is within us, the more we increase our happiness, provided we increase, in the same proportion, the expression of that greater richness. The first essential is provided for by the being of much; the second, by the doing of much; and the secret of both may be found by him who lives to move forward.

Chapter 3

The Use of Mind in Practical Action

In the present age, it is the power of mind that rules the world, and therefore it is evident that he who has acquired the best use of the power of mind, will realize the greatest success, and reach the highest places that attainment and achievement hold in store. The man who wins is the man who can apply in practical life every part of his mental ability, and who can make every action of his mind tell.

We sometimes wonder why there are so many capable men and admirable women who do not reach those places in life that they seem to deserve, but the answer is simple. They do not apply the power of mind as they should. Their abilities and qualities are either misdirected or applied only in part. These people, however, should not permit themselves to become dissatisfied with fate, but should remember that every individuality who learns to make full use of the power of their mind will reach their goal; they will realize their desire and will positively win.

There are several reasons why, though the principle reason is found in the fact that when the power of the mind is used correctly in working out what we wish to accomplish, the other forces we possess are readily applied for the same purpose, and this fact becomes evident when we realize that the power of mind is not only the ruling power in the world, but is also the ruling power in man himself. All other faculties in man are ruled by the power of his mind. It is the action of his mind that determines the action of all the other forces in his possession. Therefore, to secure the results desired, he must give his first thought to the scientific and constructive application of mental action.

In a preceding chapter, it was stated that the "I AM" is the ruling principle in man, and from that statement the conclusion may be drawn that the "I AM" is the ruling power as well, but this is not strictly correct. There is a difference between principle and power, though for practical purposes it is not necessary to consider the abstract phase of this difference. All that is necessary is to realize that the "I AM" directs the mind, and that the power of the mind directs and controls everything else in the human system. It is the mind that occupies the throne but the "I AM" is the power behind the throne.

This being true, it becomes highly important to understand how the power of the mind should be used, but before we can understand the use of this power, we must learn what this power actually is. Generally speaking, we may say that the power of mind is the sum total of all the forces of the mental world, including those forces that are employed in the process of thinking. The power of mind includes the power of the will, the power of desire, the power of feeling, and the power of thought. It includes conscious action in all its phases and subconscious action in all its phases; in fact, it includes anything and everything that is placed in action through the mind, by the mind or in the mind.

To use the power of the mind, the first essential is to direct every mental action toward the goal in view, and this direction must not be occasional, but constant. Most minds, however, do not apply this law. They think about a certain thing one moment, and about something else the next moment. At a certain hour their mental actions work along a certain line, and at the next hour those actions work along a different line. Sometimes the goal in view is one thing, and sometimes another, so the actions of the mind do not move constantly toward a certain definite goal, but are mostly scattered. We know, however, that every individual who is actually working themselves steadily and surely toward the goal they have in view, invariably directs all the power of their thought upon that goal. In their mind not a single mental action is thrown away, not a single mental force wasted. All the power that is in them is being directed to work for what they wish to accomplish, and the reason that every power responds in this way is because they are not thinking of one thing now and something else the next moment. They are thinking all the time of what they wish to attain and achieve. The full power of mind is turned upon that object, and as mind is the ruling power, the full power of all their other forces will tend to work for the same object.

In using the power of mind as well as all the other forces we possess, the first question to answer is what we really want, or what we really want to accomplish; and when this question is answered, the one thing that is wanted should be fixed so clearly in thought that it can be seen by the mind's eye every minute. But the majority do not know what they really want. They may have some vague desire, but they have not determined clearly, definitely and positively what they really want, and this is one of the principal causes of failure. So long as we do not know definitely what we want, our forces will be scattered, and so long as our forces are scattered, we will accomplish but little, or fail entirely. When we know what we want, however, and proceed to work for it with all the power and ability that is in us, we may rest assured that we will get it. When we direct the power of thinking, the power of will, the power of mental action, the power of desire, the power of ambition, in fact, all the power we possess on the one thing we want, on the one goal we desire to reach, it is not difficult to understand why success in a greater and greater measure must be realized.

To illustrate this subject further, we will suppose that you have a certain ambition and continue to concentrate your thought and the power of your mind upon that ambition every minute for an indefinite period, with no cessation whatever. The result will be that you will gradually and surely train all the forces within you to work for the realization of that ambition, and in the course of time, the full capacity of your entire mental system will be applied in working for that particular thing.

On the other hand, suppose you do as most people do under average circumstances. Suppose, after you have given your ambition a certain amount of thought, you come to the conclusion that possibly you might succeed better along another line. Then you begin to direct the power of your mind along that other line. Later on, you come to the conclusion that there is still another channel through which you might succeed, and you proceed accordingly to direct your mind upon this third ambition. Then what will happen? Simply this: You will make three good beginnings, but in every case you will stop before you have accomplished anything. There are thousands of capable men and women, however, who make this mistake every year of their lives. The full force of their mental system is directed upon a certain ambition only for a short time; then it is directed elsewhere. They never continue long enough along any particular line to secure results from their efforts, and therefore results are never secured.

Then there are other minds who give most of their attention to a certain ambition and succeed fairly well, but give the rest of their attention to a number of minor ambitions that have no particular importance. Thus they are using only a fraction of their power in a way that will tell. The rest of it is thrown away along a number of lines through which nothing is gained. But in this age efficiency is demanded everywhere in world's work, and anyone who wants to occupy a place that will satisfy their ambition and desire, cannot afford to waste even a small part of the power they may possess. They need it all along the line of their leading ambition, and therefore should not permit counter attractions to occupy their mind for a moment.

If you have a certain ambition or a certain desire, think about that ambition at all times. Keep that ambition before your mind constantly, and do not hesitate to make your ambition as high as possible. The higher you aim, the greater will be your achievements, though that does not necessarily mean that you will realize your highest aims as fully as you have pictured them in your mind; but the fact is that those who have low aims, usually realize what is even below their aims, while those who have high aims usually realize very nearly, if not fully, what their original ambition calls for. The principle is to direct the power of mind upon the very highest, the very largest and the very greatest mental conception of that which we intend to achieve. The first essential therefore, is to direct the full power of mind and thought upon the goal in view, and to continue to direct the mind in that manner every minute, regardless of circumstances or conditions.

The second essential is to make every mental action positive. When we desire certain things or when we think of certain things we wish to attain or achieve, the question should be if our mental attitudes at the time are positive or negative. To answer this we only have to remember that every positive action always goes toward that which receives its attention, while a negative action always retreats. A positive action is an action that you feel when you realize that every force in your entire system is pushed forward, so to speak, and that it is passing through what may be termed an expanding and enlarging state of feeling or consciousness.

The positive attitude of mind is also indicated by the feeling of a firm, determined fullness throughout the nervous system. When every nerve feels full, strong and determined, you are in the positive attitude, and whatever you may do at the time will produce results along the line of your desire or your ambition. When you are in a positive state of mind you are never nervous or disturbed, you are never agitated or strenuous; in fact, the more positive you are the deeper your calmness and the better your control over your entire system.

The positive man is not one who rushes helter-skelter here and there regardless of judgment or constructive action, but one who is absolutely calm and controlled under every circumstance, and yet so thoroughly full of energy that every atom in his being is ready, under every circumstance, to accomplish and achieve. This energy is not permitted to act, however, until the proper time arrives, and then its action goes directly to the goal in view.

The positive mind is always in harmony with itself, while the negative mind is always out of harmony, and thereby loses the greater part of its power. Positiveness always means strength stored up, power held in the system under perfect control, until the time of action; and during the time of action directed constructively under the same perfect control. In the positive mind, all the actions of the mental system are working in harmony and are being fully directed toward the object in view, while in the negative mind, those same actions are scattered, restless, nervous, disturbed, moving here and there, sometimes under direction, but most of the time not. That the one should invariably succeed is therefore just as evident as that the other should invariably fail. Scattered energy cannot do otherwise but fail, while positively directed energy simply must succeed. A positive mind is like a powerful stream of water that is gathering volume and force from hundreds of tributaries all along its course. The further on it goes the greater its power, until when it reaches its goal, that power is simply immense. A negative mind, however, would be something like a stream, that the further it flows the more divisions it makes, until, when it reaches its goal, instead of being one powerful stream, it has become a hundred small, weak, shallow streams.

To develop positiveness it is necessary to cultivate those qualities that constitute positiveness. Make it a point to give your whole attention to what you want to accomplish, and give that attention firmness, calmness and determination. Try to give depth to every desire until you feel as if all the powers of your system were acting, not on the surface, but from the greater world within. As this attitude is cultivated, positiveness will become more and more distinct, until you can actually feel yourself gaining power and prestige. And the effect will not only be noticed in your own ability to better direct and apply your talents, but others will discover the change. Accordingly, those who are looking for people of power, people who can do things, will look to you as the one to occupy the position that has to be filled. Positiveness therefore, not only gives you the ability to make a far better use of the forces you possess, but it also gives you personality, that much admired something that will most surely cause you to be selected where people of power are needed. The world does not care for negative personalities. Such personalities look weak and empty, and are usually ignored, but everybody is attracted to a positive personality; and it is the positive personality that is always given the preference. Nor is this otherwise but right, because the positive personality has better use of their power, and therefore is able to act with greater efficiency wherever they are called upon to act.

The third essential in the right use of the mind is to make every mental action constructive, and a constructive mental action is one that is based upon a deep seated desire to develop, to increase, to achieve, to attain in brief, to become larger and greater, and to do something of far greater worth than has been done before. If you will cause every mental action you entertain to have that feeling, constructiveness will soon became second nature to your entire mental system; that is, all the forces of your mind will begin to become building forces, and will continue to build you up along any line through which you may desire to act.

Inspire your mind constantly with a building desire, and make this desire so strong that very part of your system will constantly feel that it wants to become greater, more capable and more efficient. An excellent practice in this connection is to try to enlarge upon all your ideas of things whenever you have spare moments for real thought. This practice will tend to produce a growing tendency in every process of your thinking. Another good practice is to inspire every mental action with more ambition. We cannot have too much ambition. We may have too much aimless ambition, but we cannot have too much real constructive ambition. If your ambition is very strong, and is directed toward something definite, every action of your mind, every action of your personality, and every action of your faculties will become constructive; that is, all those actions will be inspired by the tremendous force of your ambition to work for the realization of that ambition.

Never permit restless ambition. Whenever you feel the force of ambition, direct your mind at once in a calm, determined manner upon that which you really want to accomplish in life. Make this a daily practice, and you will steadily train all your faculties and powers not only to work for the realization of that ambition, but become more and more efficient in that direction. Before long your forces and faculties will be sufficiently competent to accomplish what you want.

In the proper use of the mind therefore, these three essentials should be applied constantly and thoroughly. First, direct all the powers of mind, all the powers of thought, and all your thinking upon the goal you have in view. Second, train every mental action to be deeply and calmly positive. Third, train every mental action to be constructive, to be filled with a building spirit, to be inspired with a ceaseless desire to develop the greater, to achieve the greater, to attain the greater. When you have acquired these three, you will begin to use your forces in such a way that results must follow. You will begin to move forward steadily and surely, and you will be constantly gaining ground. Your mind will have become like the stream mentioned above. It will gather volume and force as it moves on and on, until finally that volume will be great enough to remove any obstacle in its way, and that force powerful enough to do anything you may have in view.

In order to apply these three essentials in the most effective manner, there are several misuses of the mind that must be avoided. Avoid the forceful, the aggressive, and the domineering attitudes, and do not permit your mind to become intense, unless it is under perfect control. Never attempt to control or influence others in any way whatever. You will seldom succeed in that manner, and when you do, the success will be temporary; besides, such a practice always weakens your mind.

Do not turn the power of your mind upon others, but turn it upon yourself in such a way that it will make you stronger, more positive, more capable, and more efficient, and as you develop in this manner, success must come of itself. There is only one way by which you can influence others legitimately and that is through the giving of instruction, but in that case, there is no desire to influence. You desire simply to impart knowledge and information, and you exercise a most desirable influence without desiring to do so.

A great many men and women, after discovering the immense power of mind, have come to the conclusion that they might change circumstances by exercising mental power upon those circumstances in some mysterious manner, but such a practice means nothing but a waste of energy. The way to control circumstances is to control the forces within yourself to make a greater human being of yourself, and as you become greater and more competent, you will naturally gravitate into better circumstances. In this connection, we should remember that like attracts like. If you want that which is better, make yourself better. If you want to realize the ideal, make yourself more ideal. If you want better friends, make yourself a better friend. If you want to associate with people of worth, make yourself more worthy. If you want to meet that which is agreeable, make yourself more agreeable. If you want to enter conditions and circumstances that are more pleasing, make yourself more pleasing. In brief, whatever you want, produce that something in yourself, and you will positively gravitate towards the corresponding conditions in the external world. But to improve yourself along those lines, it is necessary to apply for that purpose, all the power you possess. You cannot afford to waste any of it, and every misuse of the mind will waste power.

Avoid all destructive attitudes of the mind, such an anger, hatred, malice, envy, jealousy, revenge, depression, discouragement, disappointment, worry, fear, and so on. Never antagonize, never resist what is wrong, and never try to get even. Make the best use of your own talent and the best that is in store for you will positively come your way. When others seem to take advantage of you, do not retaliate by trying to take advantage of them. Use your power in improving yourself, so that you can do better and better work. That is how you are going to win in the race. Later on, those who tried to take advantage of you will be left in the rear. Remember, those who are dealing unjustly with you or with anybody are misusing their mind. They are therefore losing their power, and will, in the course of time, begin to lose ground; but if you, in the mean time, are turning the full power of your mind to good account, you will not only gain more power, but you will soon begin to gain ground. You will gain and continue to gain in the long run, while others who have been misusing their minds will lose mostly everything in the long run. That is how you are going to win, and win splendidly regardless of ill treatment or opposition.

A great many people imagine that they can promote their own success by trying to prevent the success of other, but it is one of the greatest delusions in the world. If you want to promote your own success as thoroughly as your capacity will permit, take an active interest in the success of everybody, because this will not only keep your mind in the success attitude and cause you to think success all along the line, but it will enlarge your mind so as to give you a greater and better grasp upon the fields of success. If you are trying to prevent the success of others, you are acting in the destructive attitude, which sooner or later will react on others, but if you are taking an active interest in the success of everybody, you are entertaining only constructive attitudes, and these will sooner or later accumulate in your own mind to add volume and power to the forces of success that you are building up in yourself.

In this connection, we may well ask why those succeed who do succeed, why so many succeed only in part, and why so many fail utterly. These are questions that occupy the minds of most people, and hundreds of answers have been given, but there is only one answer that goes to rock bottom. Those people who fail, and who continue to fail all along the line, fail because the power of their minds is either in a habitual negative state, or is always misdirected. If the power of mind is not working positively and constructively for a certain goal, you are not going to succeed. If your mind is not positive, it is negative, and negative minds float with the stream. We must remember that we are in the midst of all kinds of circumstances, some of which are for us and some of which are against us, and we will either have to make our own way or drift, and if we drift we go wherever the stream goes. But most of the streams of human life are found to float in the world of the ordinary and the inferior. Therefore, if you drift, you will drift with the inferior, and your goal will be failure.

When we analyze the minds of people who have failed, we invariably find that they are either negative, non-constructive or aimless. Their forces are scattered, and what is in them is seldom applied constructively. There is an emptiness about their personality that indicates negativeness. There is an uncertainty in their facial expression that indicates the absence of definite ambition. There is nothing of a positive, determined nature going on in their mental world. They have not taken definite action along any line. They are dependent upon fate and circumstances. They are drifting with some stream, and that they should accomplish little if anything is inevitable. This does not mean, however, that their mental world is necessarily unproductive; in fact, those very minds are in many instances immensely rich with possibilities. The trouble is, those possibilities continue to be dormant, and what is in them is not being brought forth and trained for definite action or actual results.

What these people should do, is to proceed at once to comply with the three essentials mentioned above, and before many months there will be a turn in the lane. They will soon cease to drift, and will then begin to make their own life, their own circumstances, and their own future.

In this connection, it is well to remember that negative people and non-constructive minds never attract that which is helpful in their circumstances. The more you drift, the more people you meet who also drift, while on the other hand, when you begin to make your own life and become positive, you begin to meet more positive people and more constructive circumstances. This explains why "God helps them that help themselves." When you begin to help yourself, which means to make the best of what is in yourself, you begin to attract to yourself more and more of those helpful things that may exist all about you. In other words, constructive forces attract constructive forces; positive forces attract positive forces. A growing mind attracts elements and forces that help to promote growth, and people who are determined to make more and more of themselves, are drawn more and more into circumstances through which they will find the opportunity to make more of themselves. And this law works not only in connection with the external world, but also the internal world. When you begin to make a positive determined use of those powers in yourself that are already in Positive action, you draw forth into action powers within you that have been dormant, and as this process continues, you will find that you will accumulate volume, capacity and power in your mental world, until you finally become a mental giant.

As you begin to grow and become more capable, you will find that you will meet better and better opportunities, not only opportunities for promoting external success, but opportunities for further building yourself up along the lines of ability, capacity and talent. You thus demonstrate the law that "Nothing succeeds like success," and "To him that hath shall be given." And here it is well to remember that it is not necessary to possess external things in the beginning to be counted among them "that hath.." It is only necessary in the beginning to possess the interior riches; that is, to take control of what is in you, and proceed to use it positively with a definite goal in view. He who has control of his own mind has already great riches. He has sufficient wealth to be placed among those who have. He is already successful, and if he continues as he has begun, his success will soon appear in the external world. Thus the wealth that existed at first in the internal only will take shape and form in the external. This is a law that is unfailing, and there is not a man or woman on the face of the earth that cannot apply it with the most satisfying results.

The reason why so many fail is thus found in the fact that they do not fully and constructively apply the forces and powers they possess, and the reason why so many succeed only to a slight degree is found in the fact that only a small fraction of their power is applied properly. But anyone can learn the full and proper use of all that is in them by applying faithfully the three essentials mentioned above. The reason why those succeed who do succeed is found in the fact that a large measure of their forces and powers is applied according to those three essentials, and as those essentials can be applied by anyone, even to the most perfect degree, there is no reason why all should not succeed.

Sometimes we meet people who have only ordinary ability, but who are very successful. Then we meet others who have great ability but who are not successful, or who succeed only to a slight degree. At first we see no explanation, but when we understand the cause of success as well as the cause of failure, the desired explanation is easily found. The man or woman with ordinary ability, if they comply with the three essentials necessary to the right use of mind, will naturally succeed, though if they had greater ability, their success would of course become greater in proportion. But the individual who has great ability, yet does not apply the three essentials necessary to the right use of mind, cannot succeed.

The positive and constructive use of the power of mind, with a definite goal in view will invariably result in advancement, attainment and achievement, but if we wish to use that power in its full capacity, the action of the mind must be deep. In addition to the right use of the mind, we must also learn the full use of mind, and as the full use implies the use of the whole mind, the deeper mental fields and forces, as well as the usual mental fields and forces, it is necessary to understand the subconscious as well as the conscious.

When you think of yourself do not think of that part of yourself that appears on the surface. That part is the smaller part and the lesser should not be pictured in mind. Think of your larger self, the immense subconscious self that is limitless both in power and in possibility.

Believe in yourself but not simply in a part of yourself. Give constant recognition to all that is in you, and, in that all have full faith and confidence.

Give the bigger being on the inside full right of way. Believe thoroughly in your greater interior self. Know that you have something within you that is greater than any obstacle, circumstance or difficulty that you can possibly meet. Then in the full faith in this greater something, proceed with your work.

Chapter 4

The Forces of the Subconscious

In using the power of the mind, the deeper the action of thought, will and desire, the greater the result. Accordingly, all mental action to be strong and effective, must be subconscious; that is, it must act in the field of the mental undercurrent as it is in this field that things are actually done. Those forces that play upon the surface of mind may be changed and turned from their course by almost any outside influence, and their purpose thus averted. But this is never true of the undercurrents. Anything that gets into the mental undercurrents will be seen through to a finish, regardless of external circumstances or conditions; and it is with difficulty that the course of these currents is changed when once they have been placed in full positive action. It is highly important therefore that we permit nothing to take action in these undercurrents that we do not wish to encourage and promote; and for the same reason, it is equally important that we cause everything to take action in these currents that we do wish to encourage and promote.

These undercurrents, however, act only through the subconscious, and are controlled by the subconscious. In consequence, it is the subconscious which we must understand and act upon if we want the power of mind to work with full capacity and produce the greatest measure possible of the results desired.

In defining the subconscious mind, it is first necessary to state that it is not a separate mind. There are not two minds. There is only one mind in man, but it has two phases the conscious and the subconscious. We may define the conscious as the upper side of the mentality, and the subconscious as the underside. The subconscious may also be defined as a vast mental field permeating the entire objective personality, thereby filling every atom of the personality through and through. We shall come nearer the truth, however, if we think of the subconscious as a finer mental force, having distinct powers, functions and possibilities, or as a great mental sea of life, energy and power, the force and capacity of which has never been measured.

The conscious mind is on the surface, and therefore we act through the conscious mind whenever mental action moves through the surface of thought, will or desire, but whenever we enter into deeper mental action and sound the vast depths of this underlying mental life, we touch the subconscious, though we must remember that we do not become oblivious to the conscious every time we touch the subconscious, as the two are inseparably united.

That the two phases of the mind are related can be well illustrated by comparing the conscious mind with a sponge, and the subconscious with the water permeating the sponge. We know that every fiber of the sponge is in touch with the water, and in the same manner, every part of the conscious mind, as well as every atom in the personality, is in touch with the subconscious, and completely filled, through and through, with the life and the force of the subconscious.

It has frequently been stated that the subconscious mind occupies the Fourth. Dimension of space, and though this is a matter that cannot be exactly demonstrated, nevertheless, the more we study the nature of the subconscious, as well as the Fourth Dimension, the more convinced we become that the former occupies the field of the latter. This, however, is simply a matter that holds interest in philosophical investigation. Whether the subconscious occupies the Fourth

Dimension or some other dimension of space will make no difference as to its practical value.

In order to understand the subconscious, it is well at the outset to familiarize ourselves with its natural functions, as this will convince ourselves of the fact that we are not dealing with something that is beyond normal mental action. The subconscious mind controls all the natural functions of the body, such as the circulation, respiration, digestion, assimilation, physical repair, etc. It also controls all the involuntary actions of the body, and all those actions of mind and body that continue their natural movements without direction from the will. The subconscious perpetuates characteristics, traits, and qualities that are peculiar to individuals, species and races. What is called heredity therefore is altogether a subconscious process. The same is true of what is called second nature. Whenever anything has been repeated a sufficient number of times to have become habitual, it becomes second nature, or rather a subconscious action. It frequently happens, however, that a conscious action may become a subconscious action without repetition, and thus becomes second nature almost at once.

When we examine the nature of the subconscious, we find that it responds to almost anything the conscious mind may desire or direct, though it is usually necessary for the conscious mind to express its desire upon the subconscious for some time before the desired response is secured. The subconscious is a most willing servant, and is so competent that thus far we have failed to find a single thing along mental lines that it will not or cannot do. It submits readily to almost any kind of training, and will do practically anything that it is directed to do, whether the thing is to our advantage or not.

In this connection, it is interesting to learn that there are a number of things in the human system usually looked upon as natural, and inevitable, that are simply the results of misdirected subconscious training in the past. We frequently speak of human weaknesses as natural, but weakness is never natural. Although it may appear, it is invariably the result of imperfect subconscious training. It is never natural to go wrong, but it is natural to go right, and the reason why is simple. Every right action is in harmony with natural law, while every wrong action is a violation of natural law.

It has also been stated that the aging process is natural, but modern science has demonstrated that it is not natural for a person to age at sixty, seventy, or eighty years. The fact that the average person does manifest nearly all the conditions of old age at those periods of time, or earlier, simply proves that the subconscious mind has been trained through many generations to produce old age at sixty, seventy, eighty or ninety, as the case may be, and the subconscious always does what it has been trained to do. It can just as readily be trained, however, to produce greater physical strength and greater mental capacity at ninety than we possess at thirty or forty. It can also be trained to possess the same virile youth at one hundred as the healthiest man or woman of twenty may possess. In fact, practically every condition that appears in the mind, the character and the personality of the human race, is the result of what the subconscious mind has been directed to do during past generations. It is therefore evident that as the subconscious is directed to produce different conditions in mind, character, and personality conditions that are in perfect harmony with the natural law of human development, such conditions will invariably appear in the race. Thus we understand how a new race or a superior race may appear upon this planet.

There are a great many people who are disturbed over the fact that they have inherited certain characteristics or ailments from their parents, but what they have inherited is simply subconscious tendencies in that direction, and those tendencies can be changed absolutely. What we inherit from our parents can be eliminated so completely that no one would ever know it had been there. In like manner, we can improve so decidedly upon the good qualities that we have inherited from our parents that any similarity between parent and child in those respects would disappear completely. The subconscious mind is always ready, willing and competent to make any change for the better in our physical or mental makeup that we may desire, though it does not work in some miraculous manner, nor does it usually produce results instantaneously. In most instances its actions are gradual, but they invariably produce the results intended if the proper training continues.

The subconscious mind will respond to the directions of the conscious mind so long as those directions do not interfere with the absolute laws of nature. The subconscious never moves against natural law, but it has the power to so use natural law that improvement along any line can be secured. It will reproduce in mind and body any condition that is thoroughly impressed and deeply felt by the conscious mind. It will bring forth undesirable conditions when directed to produce such conditions, and it will bring forth health, strength, youth and added power when so directed. If you continue to desire a strong physical body, and fully expect the subconscious to build for you a stronger body, you will find that this will gradually or finally be done. You will steadily grow in physical strength. If you continue to desire greater ability along a certain line and expect the subconscious to produce greater mental power along that line, your ability will increase as expected, but it is necessary in this connection to be persistent and persevering. To become enthusiastic about these things for a few days is not sufficient. It is when we apply these laws persistently for weeks, months and years that we find the results to be, not only what we expected, but frequently far greater.

Everything has a tendency to grow in the subconscious. Whenever an impression or desire is placed in the subconscious, it has a tendency to become larger and therefore the bad becomes worse when it enters the subconscious, while the good becomes better. We have the power, however, to exclude the bad from the subconscious and cause only the good to enter that immense field. Whenever you say that you are tired and permit that feeling to sink into the subconscious, you will almost at once feel more tired. Whenever you feel sick and permit that feeling to enter the subconscious, you always feel worse. The same is true when you are weak, sad, disappointed or depressed. If you let those feelings sink into your subconscious, they will become worse. On the other hand, when we feel happy, strong, persistent and determined, and permit those feelings to enter the subconscious, we always feel better. It is therefore highly important that we positively refuse to give in to any undesirable feeling. Whenever we give in to any feeling, it becomes subconscious, and if that feeling is bad, it becomes worse; but so long as we keep undesirable feelings on the outside, so to speak, we will hold them at bay, until nature can readjust itself or gather reserve force and thus put them out of the way altogether.

We should never give in to sickness, though that does not mean that we should continue to work as hard as usual when not feeling well, or cause mind and body to continue in their usual activities. When we find it necessary, we should give ourselves a complete rest, but we should never give in to the feeling of sickness. The rest that may be taken will help the body to recuperate, and when it does the threatening ailment will disappear. When you feel tired or depressed, do not admit it, but turn your attention at once upon something that is extremely interesting something that will completely turn your mind towards the pleasing, the more desirable or the ideal. Persist in feeling the way you want to feel, and permit only wholesome feelings to enter the subconscious. Thus wholesome feelings will live and grow, and after awhile your power to feel good at all times will have become so strong that you can put out of the way any adverse feeling that may threaten at any time.

In this connection, we may mention something that holds more than usual interest. It has been stated by those who are in a position to know, that no one dies until they give up; that is, gives in to those adverse conditions that are at work in their system, tending to produce physical death. So long as he or she refuses to give in to those conditions, they continue to live. How long a person could refuse to give in even under the most adverse circumstances is a question, but one thing is certain, that thousands and thousands of deaths could be prevented every year if the patient in each case refused to give in. In many instances, the forces of life and death are almost equally balanced.

Which one is going to win depends upon the mental attitude of the patient. If he or she gives over the mind and will to the side of the forces of life, those forces are most likely to win, but if they permit the mind to act with death, the forces of death are most certain to win. So long as one continues to persist in living, refusing absolutely to give into death, they are throwing the full power of mind, thought and will on the side of life. They thereby increase the power of life, and may increase that power sufficiently to overcome death. Again we say that it is a question how many times a person could overcome death by this method, but the fact remains that this method alone can save life repeatedly in the majority of cases; and all will admit after further thought on this subject that the majority will be very large.

This is a method, therefore, that deserves the best of attention in every sickroom. No person should be permitted to die until all available methods for prolonging life have been exhausted, and this last mentioned method is one that will accomplish far more than most of us may expect; and its secret is found in the fact that whenever we give in to any condition or action, it becomes stronger, due to the tendency of the subconscious to enlarge, increase and magnify whatever it receives. Give in to the forces of death, and the subconscious mind will increase the powers of that force. Give in to the forces of life, and the subconscious mind will increase the power of your life and you will continue to live.

Concerning the general possibilities of the subconscious, we should remember that every faculty has a subconscious side, and that it becomes larger and more competent as this subconscious side is developed. This being true, it is evident that ability and genius might be developed in any mind even to a remarkable degree, as no limit has been found to the subconscious in any of its forces. In like manner, every cell in the body has a subconscious side, and therefore, if the subconscious side of the personality were developed, we can realize what improvement would become possible in that field.

There is a subconscious side to all the faculties in human nature, and if these were developed, we understand how man could become ideal, even far beyond our present dreams of a new race. It is not well however to give the major portion of our attention to future possibilities. It is what is possible now that we should aim to develop and apply, and present possibilities indicate that improvement along any line, whether it be in working capacity, ability, health, happiness and character can be secured without fail if the subconscious is properly directed.

To direct the subconscious along any line, it is only necessary to desire what you want and to make those desires so deep and so persistent that they become positive forces in the subconscious field. When you feel that you want a certain thing, give in to that feeling and also make that feeling positive. Give in to your ambitions in the same manner, and also to every desire that you wish to realize. Let your thought of all those things that you wish to increase in any line get into your system, because whatever gets into your system, the subconscious will proceed to develop, work out and express.

In using the subconscious, we should remember that we are not using something that is separated from normal life. The difference between the individual who makes scientific use of the subconscious and the one who does not, is simply this; the latter employs only a small part of their mind, while the former employs the whole of their mind. And this explains why those who employ the subconscious intelligently have greater working capacity, greater ability and greater endurance. In consequence they sometimes do the work of two or three people, and do excellent work in addition. To train the subconscious for practical action is therefore a matter of common sense. It is a matter of refusing to cultivate only a small corner of your mental field when you can cultivate the entire field.

The Path to Greater Things

Dream constantly of the ideal; work ceaselessly to perfect the real.

Believe in yourself; believe in everybody; believe in all that has existence.

Give the body added strength; give the mind added brilliancy; give the soul added inspiration.

Do your best under every circumstance, and believe that every circumstance will give its best to you.

Live for the realization of more life and for the more efficient use of everything that proceeds from life.

Desire eternally what you want; and act always as if every expectation were coming true.

Chapter 5

Training the Subconscious for Special Results

When we proceed to train the subconscious along any line, or for special results, we must always comply with the following law: The subconscious responds to the impressions, the suggestions, the desires, the expectations and the directions of the conscious mind, provided that the conscious touches the subconscious at the time. The secret therefore is found in the two phases of the mind touching each other as directions are being made; and to cause the conscious to touch the subconscious, it is necessary to feel conscious action penetrating your entire interior system; that is, you should feel at the time that you are living not simply on the surface, but through and through. At such times, the mind should be calm and in perfect poise, and should be conscious of that finer, greater something within you that has greater depth than mere surface existence.

When you wish to direct the subconscious to produce physical health, first picture in your mind a clear idea of perfect health. Try to see this idea with the mind's eye, and then try to feel the meaning of this idea with consciousness, and while you are in the attitude of that feeling, permit your thought and your attention to pass into that deep quiet, serene state of being wherein you can feel the mental idea of wholeness and health entering into the very life of every atom in your system. In brief, try to feel perfectly healthy in your mind and then let that feeling sink into your entire physical system.

Whenever you feel illness coming on, you can nip it in the bud by this simple method, because if the subconscious is directed to produce more health, added forces of health will soon begin to come forth from within, and put out of the way, so to speak, any disorder or ailment that may be on the verge of getting a foothold in the body. Always remember that whatever is impressed on the subconscious will after a while be expressed from the subconscious into the personality; and where the physical conditions that you wish to remove are only slight, enough subconscious power can be aroused to restore immediate order, harmony and wholeness. When the condition you wish to remove has continued for some time, however, repeated efforts may be required to cause the subconscious to act in the matter. But one thing is certain, that if you continue to direct the subconscious to remove that condition, it positively will be removed.

The subconscious does not simply posses the power to remove undesirable conditions from the physical or mental state. It can also produce those better conditions that we may want, and develop further those desirable conditions that we already possess. To apply the law for this purpose, deeply desire those conditions that you do want, and have a very clear idea in your mind as to what you want those conditions to be. In giving the subconscious directions for anything desired in our physical or mental makeup, we should always have improvement in mind, as the subconscious always does the best work when we are thoroughly filled with the desire to do better. If we want health, we should direct the subconscious to produce more and more health.

If we want power, we should direct the subconscious not simply to give us a great deal or a certain amount of power, but to give us more and more power. In this manner, we shall secure results from the very beginning. If we try to train the subconscious to produce a certain amount, it might be some time before that amount can be developed. In the meantime, we should meet disappointment and delay, but if our desire is for steady increase along all lines from where we stand now, we shall be able to secure, first, a slight improvement and then added improvement to be followed with still greater improvement until we finally reach the highest goal we have in view. No effort should be made to destroy those qualities that we may not desire.

Whatever we think about deeply or intensely, the subconscious will take up and develop further. Therefore, if we think about our failings, shortcomings or bad habits, the subconscious will take them up and give them more life and activity than they ever had before. If there is anything in our nature therefore that we wish to change, we should simply proceed to build up what we want and forget completely what we wish to eliminate. When the good develops, the bad disappears. When the greater is built up, the lesser will either be removed or completely transformed and combined with the greater.

That the subconscious can increase your ability and your capacity is a fact that is readily demonstrated. Whenever the subconscious mind is aroused, mental power and working capacity are invariably increased sometimes to such an extent that the individual seems to be possessed with a super human power. We all know of instances where great things were accomplished simply through the fact that the individual was carried on and on by an immense power within them that seemed to be distinct from themselves and greater than themselves; but it was simply the greater powers of the subconscious that were aroused and placed in positive, determined action. These instances, however, need not be exceptions. Any individual, under any circumstances, can so increase the power of their mind, their thought and their will as to be actually carried away with the same tremendous force; that is, the power within them becomes so strong that they are actually pushed through to the goal they have in view regardless of circumstances, conditions or obstacles.

This being true, we should arouse the subconscious no matter what it is we have to do. No day is complete unless we begin that day by making alive everything that we possess in our whole mind, conscious and subconscious. Whenever you have work to do at some future time, direct the subconscious to increase your ability and capacity at the time specified, and fully expect the desired increase to be secured. If you want new ideas on certain studies or new plans in your work, direct the subconscious to produce them and you will get them without fail. The moment the direction is given, the subconscious will go to work along that line; and in this connection, we should remember that though we may fail to get the idea desired through the conscious mind alone, it is quite natural that we should get it when we also enlist the subconscious, because the whole mind is much greater, far more capable and far more resourceful than just a small part of the mind.

When demands are urgent, the subconscious responds more readily, especially when feelings at the time are also very deep. When you need certain results, say that you must have them, and put your whole energy into the "must." Whatever you make up your mind that you must do, you will in some manner get the power to do. There are a number of instances on record where people were carried through certain events by what seemed to be a miraculous power, but the cause of it all was simply this that they had to do it, and whatever you have to do, the subconscious mind will invariably give you the power to do. The reason for this is found in the fact that when you feel that you must do a thing and that you have to do it, your desires are so strong and so deep that they go into the very depths of the subconscious and thus call to action the full power of that vast interior realm.

If you have some great ambition that you wish to realize, direct the subconscious several times each day and each night before you go to sleep, to work out the necessary ways and means; and if you are determined, those ways and means will be forthcoming. But here it is necessary to remember that we must concentrate on the one thing wanted. If your mind scatters, sometimes giving attention to one ambition and sometimes to another, you will confuse the subconscious and the ways and means desired will not be secured. Make your ambition a vital part of your life, and try to feel the force of that ambition every single moment of your existence. If you do this, your ambition will certainly be realized. It may take a year, it may take five years, it may take ten years or more, but your ambition will be realized. This being true, no one need feel disturbed about the future, because if they actually know what they want to accomplish, and train the subconscious to produce the idea, the methods, the necessary ability and the required capacity, all these things will be secured.

If there is any condition from which you desire to secure emancipation, direct the subconscious to give you that information through which you may find a way out. The subconscious can. We all remember the saying, "Where there is a will there is a way," and it is true, because when you actually will to do a certain thing, the power of the mind becomes so deep and so strong along that line, that the entire subconscious mind is put to work on the case, so to speak; and under such circumstances, the way will always be found. When you put your whole mind, conscious and subconscious, to work on any problem, you will find the solution. If there is any talent that you wish to develop further, direct the subconscious every day, and as frequently as possible, to enlarge the inner life of that talent and to increase its brilliancy and power.

When you are about to undertake anything new, do not proceed until you have submitted the proposition to the subconscious, and here we find the real value of "sleeping over" new plans before we finally decide. When we go to sleep, we go more completely into the subconscious, and those ideas that we take with us when we go to sleep, especially those that engage our serious attention at the time, are completely turned over, so to speak, during the period of sleep, and examined from all points of view. Sometimes it is necessary to take those ideas into the subconscious a number of times when we go to sleep, as well as to submit the matter to the subconscious many times in the day during the waking state, but if we persevere, the right answer will finally be secured.

The whole mind, conscious and subconscious, does possess the power to solve any problem that may come up, or provide the necessary ways and means through which we can carry out or finish anything we have undertaken. Here, as elsewhere, practice makes perfect. The more you train the subconscious to work with you, the easier it becomes to get the subconscious to respond to your directions, and therefore the subconscious mind should be called into action, no matter what comes up; in other words make it a practice to use your whole mind, conscious and subconscious, at all times, not only in large matters, but in all matters.

Begin by recognizing the subconscious in all thought and in all action. Think that it can do what you have been told it can do, and eliminate doubt absolutely. Take several moments every day and suggest to the subconscious what you want to have done. Be thoroughly sincere in this matter;

be determined; have unbounded faith, and you can expect results; but do not permit the mind to become wrought up when giving directions. Always be calm and deeply poised when thinking out or suggesting to the subconscious, and it is especially important that you be deeply calm before you go to sleep.

Do not permit any idea, suggestion or expectation to enter the subconscious unless it is something that you actually want developed or worked out, and here we should remember that every idea, desire or state of mind that is deeply felt will enter the subconscious. When there are no results, do not lose faith. You know that the cause of the failure was the failure of the conscious to properly touch the subconscious at the time the directions were given, so therefore try again, giving your thought a deeper life and a more persistent desire.

Always be prepared to give these methods sufficient time. Some have remarkable results at once, while others secure no results for months; but whether you secure results as soon as you wish or not, continue to give your directions every day, fully expecting results. Be determined in every effort you may make in this direction, but do not be overanxious. Make it a point to give special directions to the subconscious every day for the steady improvement of mind, character and personality along all lines. You cannot give the subconscious too much to do because its power is immense, and as far as we know, its capacity limitless. Every effort you may make to direct or train the subconscious, will bring its natural results in due time, provided you are always calm, well balanced, persistent, deeply poised and harmonious in all your thoughts and actions.

When you have made up your mind what you want to do, say to yourself a thousand times a day that you will do it. The best way will soon open. You will have the opportunity you desire.

If you would be greater in the future than you are now, be all that you can be now. He who is his best develops the power to be better. He who lives his ideals is creating a life that actually is ideal.

There is nothing in your life that you cannot modify, change or improve when you learn to regulate your thought.

Our destiny is not mapped out for us by some exterior power; we map it out for ourselves. What we think and do in the present determines what shall happen to us in the future.

Chapter 6

The Power of Subjective Thought

The first important factor to consider in connection with the study of thought is that every thought does not possess power. In modern times, when thinking has been studied so closely, a great many have come to the conclusion that every thought is itself a force and that it invariably produces certain definite results; but this is not true, and it is well, for if every thought had power we could not last very long as the larger part of ordinary human thinking is chaotic and destructive.

When we proceed to determine what kinds of thought have power and what kinds have not, we find two distinct forms. The one we call objective, the other subjective. Objective thought is the result of general thinking, such as reasoning, intellectual research, analysis, study, the process of recollection, mind-picturing where there is no feeling, and the usual activities of the intellect. In brief, any mental process that calls forth only the activities of the intellect is objective, and such thinking does not affect the conditions of mind and body to any extent; that is, it does not produce direct results corresponding to its own nature upon the system. It does not immediately affect your health, your happiness, your physical condition nor your mental condition. It may, however, affect these things in the long run, and for that reason must not be ignored.

Subjective thinking is any form of thinking or mind-picturing that has depth of feeling, that goes beneath the surface in its action, that moves through the undercurrents, that acts in and through the psychological field. Subjective thought is synonymous with the thought of the heart, and it is subjective thought that is referred to in the statement, "As a man thinketh in his heart so is he." Subjective thought proceeds from the very heart of mental existence; that is, it is always in contact with everything that is vital in life. It is always alive with feeling, and originates, so to speak, in the heart of the mind. The term "heart" in this connection has nothing to do with the physical organ by that name. The term "heart" is here used in its metaphysical sense. We speak of the heart of a great city, meaning thereby, the principal part of the city, or that part of the city where its most vital activities are taking place; likewise, the heart of the mind is the most vital realm of the mind, or the centre of the mind, or the deeper activities of the mind as distinguished from the surface of the mind.

Subjective thinking being in the heart of the mind is therefore necessarily the product of the deepest mental life, and for this reason every subjective thought is a force. It will either work for you or against you, and has the power to produce direct effects upon mind or body, corresponding exactly with its own nature. But all thinking is liable to become subjective at times. All thoughts may sink into the deeper or vital realms of mind and thus become direct forces for good or ill. Therefore, all thinking should be scientific; that is, designed or produced with a definite object in view. All thought should be produced according to the laws of right thinking or constructive thinking. Though objective thinking usually produces no results whatever, nevertheless there are many objective thoughts that become subjective and it is the objective mind that invariably determines the nature of subjective thinking. Every thought therefore should have the right tendency, so that it may produce desirable results in case it becomes subjective, or may act in harmony with the objective mind whenever it is being employed in giving directions to the subjective.

In this connection, it is well to remember that subjective thinking invariably takes place in the subconscious mind, as the terms subjective and subconscious mean practically the same; though in speaking of thought, the term subjective is more appropriate in defining that form of thought that is deep, vital and alive, or that acts through the mental undercurrents.

To define scientific thinking, it may be stated that your thinking is scientific when your thought has a direct tendency to produce what you want, or when all the forces of your mind are working together for the purpose you desire to fulfill. Your thinking is unscientific when your thought has a tendency to produce what is detrimental, or when your mental forces are working against you.

To think scientifically, the first essential is to think only such thoughts and permit only such mental attitudes as you know to be in your favor; and the second essential is to make only such thoughts subjective. In other words, every thought should be right and every thought should be a force. When every thought is scientific, it will be right, and when every thought is subjective it will be a force.

Positively refuse to think of what you do not wish to retain or experience. Think only of what you desire, and expect only what you desire, even when the very contrary seems to be coming into your life. Make it a point to have definite results in mind at all times. Permit no thinking to be aimless. Every aimless thought is time and energy wasted, while every thought that is inspired with a definite aim will help to realize that aim, and if all your thoughts are inspired with a definite aim, the whole power of your mind will be for you and will work with you in realizing what you have in view.

That you should succeed is therefore assured, because there is enough power in your mind to realize your ambitions, provided all of that power is used in working for your ambitions. And in scientific thinking all the power of mind and thought is being caused to work directly and constantly for what you wish to attain and achieve.

To explain further the nature of scientific thinking, as well as unscientific thinking, it is well to take several well-known illustrations from real life. When things go wrong, people usually say, "That's always the way"; and though this may seem to be a harmless expression, nevertheless, the more you use that expression the more deeply you convince your mind that things naturally go wrong most of the time. When you train your mind to think that it is usual for things to go wrong, the forces of your mind will follow that trend of thinking, and will also go wrong; and for that reason it is perfectly natural that things in your life should go wrong more and more, because as the forces of your mind are going wrong, you will go wrong, and when you go wrong, those things that pertain to your life cannot possibly go right.

A great many people are constantly looking for the worst. They usually expect the worst to happen; though they may be cheerful on the surface, deep down in their heart they are constantly looking for trouble. The result is that their deeper mental currents will tend to produce trouble. If you are always looking for the worst, the forces of your mind will be turned in that direction, and therefore will become destructive. Those forces will tend to produce the very thing that you expect. At first they will simply confuse your mind and produce troubled conditions in your mental world; but this will in turn confuse your faculties, your reason and your judgment, so that you will make many mistakes; and he who is constantly making mistakes will certainly find the worst on many or all occasions.

When things go wrong, do not expect the wrong to appear again. Look upon it as an exception. Call it past and forget it. To be scientific under these circumstances, always look for the best. By constantly expecting the best, you will turn the different forces of your mind and thought to work for the best. Every power that is in you will have a higher and finer ideal upon which to turn its attention, and accordingly, results will be better, which is perfectly natural when your whole system is moving towards the better.

A number of people have a habit of saying, "Something is always wrong"; but why should we not say instead, "Something is always right"? We would thereby express more of the truth and give our minds a more wholesome tendency. It is not true that something is always wrong. When we compare the wrong with the right, the wrong is always in the minority. However, it is the effect of such thinking upon the mind that we wish to avoid, whether the wrong be in our midst or not. When you think that there is always something wrong, your mind is more or less concentrated on the wrong, and will therefore create the wrong in your own mentality; but when you train yourself to think there is always something right, your mind will concentrate upon the right, and accordingly will create the right.

And when the mind is trained to create the right it will not only produce right conditions within itself, but all thinking will tend to become right; and right thinking invariably leads to health, happiness, power and plenty. The average person is in the habit of saying, "The older I get"; and they thereby call the attention of the mind to the idea that they are getting older. In brief, they compel their mind to believe that they are getting older and older, and thereby direct the mind to produce more and more age. The true expression in this connection is, "The longer I live." This expression calls the mind's attention to the length of life, which will, in turn, tend to increase the power of that process in you that can prolong life. When people reach the age of sixty or seventy, they usually speak of "the rest of my days," thus implying the idea that there are only a few more days remaining. The mind is thereby directed to finish life in a short period of time, and accordingly, all the forces of the mind will proceed to work for the speedy termination of personal existence. The correct expression is "from now on," as that leads thought into the future indefinitely without impressing the mind with any end whatever.

We frequently hear the expression, "I can never do anything right," and it is quite simple to understand that such a mode of thought would train the mind to act below its true ability and capacity. If you are fully convinced that you can never do anything right, it will become practically impossible for you to do anything right at any time, but on the other hand, if you continue to think, "I AM going to do everything better and better," it is quite natural that your entire mental system should be inspired and trained to do things better and better. Hundreds of similar expressions could be mentioned, but we are all familiar with them, and from the comments made above, anyone will realize that such expressions are obstacles in our way, no matter what we may do.

In right thinking the purpose should be never to use any expression that conveys to your mind what you do not want, or what is detrimental or unwholesome in any manner whatever. Think only what you wish to produce or realize. If trouble is brewing, think about the greater success that you have in mind. If anything adverse is about to take place, do not think of what that adversity may bring, but think of the greater good that you are determined to realize in your life. When trouble is brewing, the average person usually thinks of nothing else. Their mind is filled with fear, and not a single faculty in their possession can do justice to itself. And as trouble is usually brewing in most places, more or less, people have what may be called a chronic expectation for trouble; and as they usually get more or less of what they expect, they imagine they are fully justified in entertaining such expectations.

But here it is absolutely necessary to change the mind completely. Whatever our present circumstances may be, we should refuse absolutely to expect anything but the best that we can think of. The whole mind, with all its powers and faculties, should be thrown, so to speak, into line with the optimistic tendency, and whatever comes or not, we should think only of the greater things that we expect to realize. In brief, we should concentrate the mind absolutely upon whatever goal we may have in view, and I should look neither to the left nor to the right.

When we concentrate absolutely upon the greater things we expect to attain or achieve, we gradually train all the forces of the mind and all the powers of thought to work for those greater things. We shall thereby begin in earnest to build for ourselves a greater destiny; and sooner or later we shall find ourselves gaining ground in many directions. Later on, if we proceed, we shall begin to move more rapidly, and if we pay no attention to the various troubles that may be brewing in our environment, those troubles will never affect us nor disturb us in the least.

The mental law involved in the process of scientific thinking may be stated as follows: The more you think of what is right, the more you tend to make every action in your mind right. The more you think of the goal you have in view, the more life and power you will call into action in working for that goal. The more you think of your ambition, the more power you will give to those faculties that can make your ambitions come true. The more you think of harmony, of health, of success, of happiness, of things that are desirable, of things that are beautiful, of things that have true worth, the more the mind will tend to build all those things in yourself, provided, of course, that all such thinking is subjective.

To think scientifically, therefore, is to train your every thought and your every mental action to focus the whole of attention upon that which you wish to realize, to gain, to achieve or attain in your life. In training the mind along the lines of scientific thinking begin by trying to hold the mind upon the right, regardless of the presence of the wrong, and here we should remember that the term "right" does not simply refer to moral actions, but to all actions. When the wrong is coming your way, persist in thinking of the right; persist in expecting only the right. And there is a scientific reason for this attitude, besides what has been mentioned above.

We know that the most important of all is to keep the mind right or moving along right lines, and if we persistently expect the right, regardless of circumstances, the mind will be kept in the lines of right action. But there is another result that frequently comes from this same practice. It sometimes happens that the wrong which is brewing in your environment, has such a weak foundation that only a slight increase in the force of the right would be necessary to overthrow that wrong completely; in fact, we shall find that most wrongs that threaten can be overcome in a very short time, if we continue to work for the right in a positive, constructive, determined manner.

It is when the individual goes all to pieces, so to speak, that adversity gets the best of them; but no individual will go to pieces unless their thinking is chaotic, destructive, scattered, confused and detrimental. Continue to possess your whole mind and you will master the situation, no matter what it may be, and it is scientific thinking that will enable you to perform this great feat. To make thinking scientific, there are three leading essentials to be observed. The first is to cultivate constructive mental attitudes, and all mental attitudes are constructive when mind, thought, feeling, desire and will constantly face the greater and the better.

A positive and determined optimism has the same effect, and the same is true of the practice of keeping the mental eye single on the highest goal in view. To make every mental attitude constructive the mind must never look down, and mental depression must be avoided completely. Every thought and every feeling must have an upward look, and every desire must desire to inspire the same rising tendency in every action of mind. The second essential is constructive mental imagery. Use the imagination to picture only what is good, what is beautiful, what is beneficial, what is ideal, and what you wish to realize. Mentally see yourself receiving what you deeply desire to receive. What you imagine, you will think, and what you think, you will become. Therefore, if you imagine only those things that are in harmony with what you wish to obtain or achieve, all your thinking will soon tend to produce what you want to attain or achieve.

The third essential is constructive mental action. Every action of the mind should have something desirable in view and should have a definite, positive aim. Train yourself to face the sunshine of life regardless of circumstances. When you face the sunshine, everything looks right, and when everything looks right, you will think right. It matters not whether there is any sunshine in life just now or not. We must think of sunshine just the same. If we do not see any silver lining, we must create one in our own mental vision.

However dark the dark side may seem to be, we cannot afford to see anything but the bright side, and no matter how small or insignificant the bright side may be, we must continue to focus attention on that side alone.

Be optimistic, not in the usual sense of that term, but in the real sense of that term. The true optimist not only expects the best to happen, but goes to work to make the best happen. The true optimist not only looks upon the bright side, but trains every force that is in them to produce more and more brightness in their life, and therefore complies with the three essentials just mentioned. Their mental attitudes are constructive because they are always facing greater things. Their imagination is constructive because it is always picturing the better and the ideal, and their mental actions are constructive because they are training the whole of their life to produce those greater and better things that their optimism has inspired them to desire and expect.

In this connection, we must remember that there is a group of mental forces at work in every mental attitude, and therefore if that attitude is downcast, those forces will become detrimental; that is, they will work for the lesser and the inferior. On the other hand, if every mental attitude is lifted up or directed towards the heights of the great and the true and the ideal, those forces will become constructive, and will work for the greater things in view.

In the perusal of this study, we shall find it profitable to examine our mental attitudes closely, so as to determine what our minds are actually facing the greater part of the time. If we find that we are mentally facing things and conditions that are beneath our expectations, or find that our imaginations are concerned too much about possible failure, possible mistakes, possible trouble, possible adversity, etc., our thinking is unscientific, and no time should be lost in making amends. When you are looking into the future, do not worry about troubles that might come to pass. Do not mentally see yourself as having a hard time of it.

Do not imagine yourself in this hostile condition or that adverse circumstance. Do not wonder what you would do if you should lose everything, or if this or that calamity should befall. Such thinking is decidedly unscientific and most detrimental. If you entertain such thoughts you are causing the ship of your life to move directly towards the worst precipice that may exist in your vicinity. Besides, you are so weakening this ship through wrong treatment, that it will someday spring a leak and go down.

Think of the future whenever it is unnecessary for you to give your attention to the present, but let your thought of the future be wholesome, constructive, optimistic and ideal. Mentally see yourself gaining the best that life has to give, and you will meet more and more of the best. Think of yourself as gaining ground along all lines, as finding better and better circumstances, as increasing in power and ability, and as becoming more healthful in body, more vigorous and brilliant in mind, more perfect in character, and more powerful in soul. In brief, associate your future with the best that you can think of along all lines.

Fear nothing for the days that are to be, but expect everything that is good, desirable, enjoyable and ideal. This practice will not only make your present happier, but it will tend to strengthen your mind and your life along wholesome constructive lines to such a degree that you will actually gain the power to realize, in a large measure, those beautiful and greater things that you have constantly expected in your optimistic dreams.

In living and building for a larger future, we should remember that our mind and thoughts invariably follow the leadership of the most prominent mental picture. The man or woman who clearly and distinctly pictures for themselves a brilliant future will inspire the powers of their entire mental world to work for such a future; in fact, all the forces of thought, mind, life, personality, character and soul will move in that direction.

They may not realize as brilliant a future as they have pictured, but their future is certainly going to be brilliant, and it is quite possible, as is frequently the case, that it may become even more brilliant than they dreamed of in the beginning. When the average mind thinks of the future, they usually picture a variety of conflicting events and conditions. They have nothing definite in mind. There is no actual leadership therefore in their mind, and nothing of great worth can be accomplished.

When we look into the lives of men and women who have reached high places, we always find that they were inspired with some great idea. That idea was pictured again and again in their mental vision, and they refused to let it go. They clung tenaciously to that idea, and thereby actually compelled every force and element within them to enlist in the working out of that idea. It is therefore simple enough that they should realize every aim and reach the highest places that achievement has in store. Such men and women possibly did not understand the science or the process, but they were nevertheless thinking scientifically to a most perfect degree. Their ambition pictured only that lofty goal which they wanted to reach. All their mental attitudes were constantly facing that lofty goal, and thereby became constructive; and all the actions of mind were directed toward the same goal. Accordingly, everything within them was trained to work for the realization of their dream, and that is what we mean by scientific thinking; that is what we mean by thinking for results. And anyone who will train themselves to think for results in this manner, will positively secure results; though in this connection it is well to remember that persistence and determination are indispensable every step of the way.

When we do not secure results at once, we sometimes become discouraged, and conclude that it is no use to try. At such times, friends will usually tell us that we are simply dreaming, and they will advise us to go to work at something practical, something that we really can accomplish; but if we ignore the advice of our friends, and continue to be true to the great idea that we have resolved to work out, we shall finally reach our goal, and when we do, those very same friends will tell us that we took the proper course.

So long as the man with ambition is a failure, the world will tell him to let go of his ideal; but when his ambition is realized, the world will praise him for the persistence and the determination that he manifested during his dark hours, and everybody will point to his life as an example for coming generations. This is invariably the rule. Therefore pay no attention to what the world says when you are down. Be determined to get up, to reach the highest goal you have in view, and you will.

There are a great many ambitious men and women, who imagine that they will succeed provided their determination is strong and their persistence continuous, regardless of the fact that their thinking may be unscientific; but the sooner we dispel this illusion, the better. Unscientific thinking, even in minor matters, weakens the will. It turns valuable thought power astray, and we need the full power of thought, positively directed along the line of our work if we are going to achieve, and achieve greatly. The majority of the mental forces in the average person are working against them, because they are constantly entertaining depressed mental states or detrimental habits of thought; and even though they may be ambitious, that ambition has not sufficient power to work itself out, because most of the forces of their mind are thrown away.

We therefore see the necessity of becoming scientific in all thinking, and in making every mental habit wholesome and beneficial in the largest sense of those terms. But scientific thinking not only tends to turn the power of thought in the right direction; it also tends to increase mental power, to promote efficiency and to build up every faculty that we may employ.

To illustrate the effect of right thinking upon the faculties, we will suppose that you have musical talent, and are trying to perfect that talent. Then, we will suppose that you are constantly expressing dissatisfaction with the power of that talent. What will be the result? Your mental action upon that faculty will tend to lower its efficiency, because you are depressing its action instead of inspiring those actions. On the other hand, if you encourage this talent, you will tend to expand its life, and thereby increase its capacity for results.

In this respect, talents are similar to people. Take two people of equal ability and place them in circumstances that are direct opposites. We will suppose that the one is mistreated every day by those with whom he is associated. He is constantly being criticized and constantly being told that he will never amount to anything; he is blamed for everything that is wrong, and is in every manner discouraged and kept down. What would happen to the ability and efficiency of that man if he continued under such treatment year after year? He simply could not advance unless he should happen to be a mental giant, and even then, his advancement would be very slow; but if he was not a mental giant, just an average man, he would steadily lose ambition, self-confidence, initiative, judgment, reasoning power, and in fact, everything that goes to make up ability and capacity.

We will suppose the other man is encouraged continually. He is praised for everything, he is given every possible opportunity to show and apply what ability he may possess; he is surrounded by an optimistic atmosphere, and is expected by everybody to advance and improve continually. What will happen to this man? The best will be brought out in his power and ability. He will be pushed to the fore constantly and he will climb steadily and surely until he reaches the top.

Treat your talents in the same way, and you have the same results in every case. To state it briefly, make it a point to encourage your talents, your faculties and your powers. Give every element and force within you encouragement and inspiration. Expect them all to do their best, and train yourself to think and feel that they positively will. Train yourself to think of your whole system as all right. Deal with your mental faculties in this manner, under all circumstances, and deal with your physical organs in the same way.

Most people among those who do not have perfect health, have a habit of speaking of their stomachs as bad, their livers as always out of order, their eyes as weak, their nerves as all upset, and the different parts of their systems as generally wrong. But what are they doing to their physical organs through this practice? The very same as was done to the unfortunate man just mentioned, and we shall find, in this connection, one reason why so many people continue to be sick. They are keeping their physical organs down, so to speak, by depressing the entire system with unwholesome thinking; but if they would change their tactics and begin to encourage their physical organs, praise them and expect them to do better, and to treat them right from the mental as well as a physical standpoint, they would soon be restored to perfect health.

In training the mind in scientific thinking, the larger part of attention should be given to that of controlling our feelings. It is not difficult to think scientifically along intellectual lines, but to make our feelings move along wholesome, constructive, optimistic lines requires persistent training. Intellectual thought can be changed almost at anytime with little effort, but feeling usually becomes stronger and stronger the longer it moves along a certain line, and thus becomes more difficult to change.

When we feel discouraged, it is so easy to feel more discouraged; when we feel dissatisfied, it is only a step to that condition that is practically intolerable. It is therefore necessary to stop all detrimental feeling in the beginning. Do not permit a single adverse feeling to continue for a second. Change the mind at once by turning your attention upon something that will make you feel better. Resolve to feel the way you want to feel under all circumstances, and you will gradually develop the power to do so. Depressed mental feelings are burdens, and we waste a great deal of energy by carrying them around on our mental shoulders. Besides, such feelings tend to direct the power of thought towards the lower and the inferior.

Whenever you permit yourself to feel bad, you will cause the power of mind and thought to go wrong. Therefore, persist in feeling right and good. Persist in feeling joyous. Persist in feeling cheerful, hopeful, optimistic and strong. Place yourself on the bright side and the strong side of everything that transpires in your life, and you will constantly gain power, power that will invariably be in your favor.

Life is growth and the object of right thinking is to promote that growth.

Give less time trying to change the opinions of others, and more time trying to improve your own life.

Life becomes the way it is lived; and man may live the way he wants to live when he learns to think what he wants to think.

Create your own thought and you become what you want to become because your thought creates you.

We all know that man is as he thinks. Then we must think only such thoughts as tend to make us what we wish to be.

The secret of right thinking is found in always keeping the mind's eye stayed upon the greater and the better in all things.

Chapter 7

How Man Becomes What He Thinks

Scientific research in the metaphysical field has demonstrated the fact that man is as he thinks, that he becomes what he thinks, and that what he thinks in the present, determines what he is to become in the future; and also that since he can change his thought for the better along any line, he can therefore completely change himself along any line. But the majority who try to apply this law do not succeed to a great degree, the reason being that instead of working entirely upon the principle that man is as he thinks, they proceed in the belief that man is what he thinks he is.

At first sight there may seem to be no difference between the principle that man is as he thinks and the belief that man is as he thinks he is, but close study will reveal the fact that the latter is absolutely untrue. Man is not what he thinks he is, because personality, mentality and character are not determined by personal opinions. It is the thought of the heart, that is, the mental expression from the subconscious that makes the personal man what he is; but the subconscious is effected only by what man actually thinks in the real field of creative thought, and not by what he may think of himself in the field of mere personal opinion.

It is subjective thought that makes you what you are; but to think that you are thus or so, will not necessarily make you thus or so. To create subjective thought you must act directly upon the subconscious, but it is not possible to impress the subconscious while you are forming opinions about your personal self. A mere statement about yourself will not affect or change the subconscious, and so long as the subconscious remains unchanged, you will remain unchanged. While you are thinking simply about your external or personal self you are acting upon the objective, but to change yourself you must act upon the subjective.

Man may think that he is great, but so long as he continues to think small thoughts, he will continue to be small. No matter how high an opinion he may have of himself, while he is living in the superficial, his thoughts will be empty, and empty thoughts are not conducive to high attainments and great achievements. Man becomes great when he thinks great thoughts, and to think great thoughts he must transcend the limitations and circumscribed conditions of the person, and mentally enter into the world of the great and the superior. He must seek to gain a larger and a larger consciousness of the world of real quality, real worth and real superiority, and must dwell upon the loftiest mountain peaks of mind that he can possibly reach. He must live in the life of greatness, breathe the spirit of greatness, and feel the very soul of greatness. Then, and only then, will he think great thoughts; and the mind that continues to think great thoughts will continue to grow in greatness.

It is not what you state in your thought but what you give to your thought that determines results. The thought that is merely stated may be empty, but it is the thought with something in it that alone can exercise real power in personal life. And what is to be in your thought will depend upon what you think into your thought. What you give to your thought, your thought will give to you, and you will be and become accordingly, no matter what you may think that you are. The cause that you originate in the within will produce its effect in the without, regardless of what your opinions may be. Your personal life will consequently be the result of what you think, but it will not necessarily be what you think it is.

Having discovered the fact that the physical body is completely renewed every eight or ten months, you will naturally think that you are young, but to simply think you are young will not cause the body to look as young as it really is. To retain your youth you must remove those subconscious tendencies and conditions that produce old age, and you must eliminate worry. So long as you worry you will cause your personality to grow older and older in appearance, no matter how persistently you may think that you are young. To simply think that you are young will not avail. You must think thoughts that produce, retain and perpetuate youth. If you wish to look young, your mind must feel young, but you will not feel young until the whole of your mind produces the feeling of youth. To develop the feeling of youth in the whole mind, you must become fully conscious of the fact that youth is naturally produced in your entire system every minute, and you must train the mind to take cognizance only of the eternal now.

So long as we feel that we are passing with time, we will imagine that we feel the weight of more and more years, and this feeling will invariably cause the body to show the mark of years, growing older and older in appearance as more years are added to the imaginary burden of age. You will look young when you feel young, but to simply feel that you are young will not always cause you to feel young. The real feeling of youth comes when we actually think in the consciousness of youth and give the realization of the now to every thought.

You may think that you are well, but you will not secure health until you think thoughts that produce health. You may persistently affirm that you are well, but so long as you live in discord, confusion, worry, fear and other wrong states of mind, you will be sick; that is, you will be as you think and not what you think you are. You may state health in your thought, but if you give worry, fear and discord to that thought, your thinking will produce discord.

It is not what we state in our thoughts, but what we give to our thoughts that determine results. To produce health, thought itself must be healthful and wholesome. It must contain the quality of health, and the very life of health. This, however, is not possible unless the mind is conscious of health at the time when such thought is being produced. Therefore, to think thoughts that can produce health, the mind must enter into the realization of the being of health, and not simply dwell in the objective belief about health.

Again, to produce health, all the laws of life must be observed; that is, the mind must be in that understanding of law, and in that harmony with law where the guiding thought will naturally observe law. To simply think that you are well will not teach the mind to understand the laws of life and health, nor will that thinking place you in harmony with those laws. That thinking that does understand the laws of life will not come from the mere belief that you are well, but from the effort to enter into the understanding of all law, the spirit of all law, the very life of health, and into the very soul of all truth.

You may think that your mind is brilliant and may undertake most difficult tasks in the belief that you are equal to the occasion, but the question is if your conception of brilliancy is great or small. If your conception of brilliancy is small, you may be right to that degree in thinking you are brilliant; that is, you may be brilliant as far as your understanding of brilliancy goes. Whether that is sufficient or not to carry out the task that is before you is another question. Your opinion of your mental capacity may be great, but if your idea of intelligence is crude, your intelligence producing thought will also be crude, and can produce only crude intelligence. It is therefore evident that to simply think that you are brilliant will not produce brilliancy, unless your understanding of brilliancy is made larger, higher and finer.

What you understand and mentally feel concerning intelligence, mental capacity and brilliancy, is what you actually think on those subjects, and it is this understanding or feeling or realization that will determine how much intelligence you will give to your thought. Your thought will be as brilliant as the brilliancy you think into your thought, and how much brilliancy you will think into your thought will depend upon how high your realization of brilliancy happens to be at the time.

When your thinking is brilliant, you will be brilliant, but if your thinking is not brilliant you will not be brilliant, no matter how brilliant you may think you are. To make your thinking more brilliant, try to enter into the consciousness of finer intelligence, larger mental capacity, and the highest order of mental brilliancy that you can possibly realize. Do not call yourself brilliant at any time, or do not think of yourself as lacking in brilliancy. Simply fix the mental eye upon absolute brilliancy, and desire with all the power of mind and soul to go on and on into higher steps of that brilliancy.

When all the elements and forces of your system are working in such a way that beauty will naturally be produced, you will be beautiful, whether you think you are beautiful or not, and it is the actions of the subconscious that determine how the elements and forces of the system are to work. Therefore, the beautiful person is beautiful because her real interior thinking is conducive to the creation of the beautiful. That person, however, who is not beautiful, does not necessarily think ugly thoughts, but her interior mental actions have not been brought together in such a way as to produce the expression of beauty; that is the subconscious actions have not been arranged according to the most perfect pattern.

But these actions can be arranged in that manner, not by thinking that one is beautiful. but by thinking thoughts that are beautiful. When you think that you are beautiful, you are liable to think that you are more beautiful than others, and such a thought is not a beautiful thought. To recognize or criticize ugliness and inferiority in others is to create the inferior and the ugly in yourself, and what you create in yourself will sooner or later be expressed through your mind and personality.

So long as you worry, hate or fear, your thought will make you disagreeable in mind and character, and later on in the person as well; and no amount of affirming or thinking that you are beautiful will overcome those ugly states of mind that you have created. You will thus be as you think worried, hateful and ugly, and not beautiful as you may try to think you are.

The personal man is the result, not of beliefs or opinions, but of the quality of all the mental actions that are at work throughout the whole mind. Man is as he thinks in every thought, and not what he thinks he is in one or more isolated parts of his personal self. You may think that you are good, but your idea of goodness may be wrong. Your thought therefore will not be conducive to goodness. On the contrary, the more you praise yourself for being good, the less goodness you will express in your nature. In addition, to think of yourself as good will have a tendency to produce a feeling of self-righteousness. This feeling will cause the mind to look down upon the less fortunate, and a mind that looks down will soon begin to go down, and you will be no better than those whom you criticized before.

You are only as good as the sum total of all your good thoughts, and these can be increased in number indefinitely by training the mind to perpetually grow in the consciousness of absolute goodness. To grow in the consciousness of goodness, keep the mental eye upon the highest conception of absolute goodness. Try to enlarge, elevate and define this conception or understanding of goodness perpetually. Pattern your whole life, all your thoughts and all your actions after the likeness of this highest understanding.

Then never look back nor try to measure the goodness that you may think you now possess. Press on eternally to the higher and larger realization of absolute goodness, and leave results to the law. More and more real goodness will naturally appear in all your thoughts and actions. You will therefore become good, not by thinking that you are good, but by thinking thoughts that are created in the image and likeness of that which is good.

From the foregoing it is evident that man is as he thinks, and not necessarily what he thinks he is. But there is still more evidence. That your personal self is the result of your thought has been demonstrated, but what thought? To make yourself thus or so, the necessary thought must first be created but to think that you are thus or so, will not create the thought that can make you thus or so. The reason is because it is subconscious thought alone that can produce effects in your nature, physical or mental, and you cannot enter the subconscious while you are thinking exclusively of your personal self. What you think about yourself is always objective thought, and mere objective thought is powerless to effect or change anything in your nature.

To think thoughts that can give you more life, you must enter into the consciousness of absolute life, but you cannot enter the absolute while you are defining or measuring the personal. If you wish to possess more quality, you must give your thoughts more quality and worth, you must forget the lesser worth of the personal and enter into the consciousness of the greater worth of absolute worth itself. So long as you think that you are thus or so in the personal sense, your thought will be on the surface. You will mentally live among effects. You will not create new causes, therefore will not produce any changes in yourself. You will continue to be as you are thinking deep down in the subconscious where hereditary tendencies, habits, race thoughts and other mental forces continue their usual work, regardless of your personal opinion or empty thoughts on the surface.

To change yourself you must go to that depth of mind where the causes of your personal condition exist. But your mind will not enter the depth of the within so long as your thought is on the surface and your thought will be on the surface so long as you are thinking exclusively about your personal self.

The secret therefore is not to form opinions about yourself or to think about yourself as being thus or so, but to form larger conceptions of principles and qualities. Enter the richness of real life and you will think richer thoughts. Forget the limitations, the weaknesses and the shortcomings of your personal self as well as your superficial opinions of your personal self, and enter mentally into the greatness, the grandeur, the sublimity and the splendor of all things. Seek to gain a larger and a larger understanding of the majesty and marvelousness of all life, and aspire to think the thoughts of the Infinite. This is the secret of thinking great thoughts, and he will positively become great whose thoughts are always great.

In like manner, he who thinks wholesome thoughts, and wholesome thoughts only, will become healthful and wholesome. Such thoughts will have the power to produce health, and thoughts never fail to do what they have the power to do. Place in action the necessary subconscious thought and the expected results will invariably follow. Man therefore is not what he thinks he is because such thinking is personal, and consequently superficial and powerless. The thought that determines his personality, his character, his mentality and his destiny is his subjective thought, the thought that is produced in the subconscious during those moments when he forgets his personal opinions about himself and permits his mind to act with deep feeling and subjective conviction. But those thoughts that enter the subconscious are not always good thoughts.

Man's subjective thinking is not always conducive to the true, the wholesome and the best, as his thinking is not always right. For this reason, man himself is not always good, nor his life as beautiful as he might wish to be. His thinking is in his own hands, however. He can learn to think what he wants to think, and as he is and becomes as he thinks, we naturally conclude that he may, in the course of time, become what he wants to become.

The greatest remedy in the world is change; and change implies the passing from the old to the new. It is also the only path that leads from the lesser to the greater, from the dream to the reality, from the wish to the heart's desire fulfilled. It is change that brings us everything we want. It is the opposite of change that holds us back from that which we want. But change is not always external. Real change, or rather the cause of all change, is always internal. It is the change in the within that first produces the change in the without. To go from place to place is not a change unless it produces a change of mind a renewal of mind. It is the change of mind that is the change desired. It is the renewal of mind that produces better health, more happiness, greater power, the increase of life, and the consequent increase of all that is good in life. And the constant renewal of mind the daily change of mind is possible regardless of times, circumstances or places. He who can change his mind every day and think the new about everything every day, will always be well; he will always have happiness; he will always be free; his life will always be interesting; he will constantly move forward into the larger, the richer and the better; and whatever is needed for his welfare today, of that he shall surely have abundance.

Chapter 8

The Art of Changing for the Better

Personal man gradually but surely grows into the likeness of that which he thinks of the most, and man thinks the most of what he loves the best. This is the law through which man has become what he is, and it is through the intelligent use of this law that man may change for the better and improve in any way desired. The thought you think not only effects your character, your mind and your body, but also produces the original cause of every characteristic, every habit, every tendency, every desire, every mental quality and every physical condition that appears in your system.

Thought is the one original cause of the conditions, characteristics and peculiarities of the human personality, and everything that appears in the personality is the direct or indirect effect of the various actions of thought. It is therefore evident that man naturally grows into the likeness of the thought he thinks, and it is also evident that the nature of his thought would be determined by that which he thinks of the most.

The understanding of this fact will reveal to all minds the basic law of change, and though it is basic, its intelligent use may become simplicity itself. Through the indiscriminate use of this law, man has constantly been changing, sometimes for the better, sometimes not, but by the conscious, intelligent, use of this law he may change only for the better and as rapidly as the sum total of his present ability will permit.

The fact that mental conditions and dispositions may be changed through the power of thought, will readily be accepted by every mind, but that mental qualities, abilities, personal appearances and physical conditions may be changed in the same way all minds may not be ready to accept. Nevertheless, that thought can change anything in the human system, even to a remarkable degree, is now a demonstrated fact. We have all seen faces change for the worse under the influence of grief, worry and misfortune, and we have observed that all people grow old who expect to do so, regardless of the fact that the body of the octogenarian is not a day older than the body of a little child. We have unlimited evidence to prove that ability will improve or deteriorate according to the use that is made of the mind.

A man's face reveals his thought, and we can invariably detect the predominating states of the mind that lives in a groove. When a person changes their mental states at frequent intervals, no one state has the opportunity to produce an individual, clear-cut expression, and therefore cannot be so readily detected, but where one predominating state is continued in action for weeks or months or years, anyone can say what that state is, by looking at the face of the one who has it. Thus we can detect different kinds of disposition, different grades of mind, different degrees of character and different modes of living, and convince ourselves at the same time, that man in general, looks, acts and lives the way he thinks.

The fact that every mental state will express its nature in body, mind and character, proves that we can, through the intelligent use of mental action, cause the body to become more beautiful, the mind more brilliant, character more powerful and the soul life more ideal. To accomplish these things, however, it is necessary to apply the law continuously in that direction where we desire to secure results.

When a person thinks of the ordinary for a few weeks, they invariably begin to look ordinary. Then when something impels them to think for a while of the ideal, the true and the beautiful, they begin to look like a new creature; but if reverses threaten, they will feel worried, dejected and afraid, and everybody observes that they look bad. Then if the tide turns in their favor, they will begin to look content, and if something should suggest to their mind the thought of the wholesome, the sound and the harmonious, they will begin to look remarkably well. In this manner they are daily using the law of change, but never intelligently.

They do not take the law into their own hands, but use the law only as suggestions from their environment may direct. They advance one day and fall back the next. One week their physical mansion is painted with colors of health and beauty; the next week only the conditions of age and disease are in evidence. They plant a flower seed today, and tomorrow they hoe it up to plant a weed in its place.

Thus the average person continues to live, and every change comes from the unconscious, indiscriminate use of the power of their thought. This power, however, can be employed more wisely, and when the many begin to do so, the progress of the race will be remarkable indeed. The basic law of change must be taken into our own hands, and must be employed directly for producing the change we have in view; and to accomplish this the love nature must be so trained that we shall love only what we want to love, only what is greater and better than that which we have realized up to the present time.

In this respect strong, highly developed souls will have no difficulty, because they have the power to see the great, the beautiful and the ideal in all things, but those who have not as yet acquired that power, must train their feelings with care, lest love frequently turns thought upon the low, the common or the ordinary.

What you admire in others will develop in yourself. Therefore, to love the ordinary in anyone is to become ordinary, while to love the noble and the lofty in all minds is to grow into the likeness of that which is noble and lofty. When we love the person of someone who is in the earth earthy, we tend to keep ourselves down in the same place. We may give our kindness and our sympathies to all, but we must not love anything in anyone that is not ideal. It is a misdirection of love to love exclusively the visible person. It is the ideal, the true and the beautiful in every person that should be loved, and as all persons have these qualities, we can love everybody with a whole heart in this more sublime manner.

In this connection a great problem presents itself to many men and women who aspire to a life of great quality. These people feel that they cannot give their personal love to husbands, wives, relatives or friends that persist in living in the mere animal world; but the problem is easily solved. We must not love what is ordinary in anyone; in fact, the ordinary must not be recognized, but we can love the real life in everyone, and if we will employ our finer perceptions we will find that this real life is ideal in every living creature in the world. We need not love the perversions of a person, but we can love the greater possibilities and the superior qualities that are inherent in the individual.

It is not the imperfections or appearances that should be loved, but the greatness that is within; and what we love in others we not only awaken in others, but we develop those very things more or less in ourselves. To promote the best welfare of individuals under all sorts of circumstances, personal loves should be exchanged only by persons who live in the same world. When the woman has found the superior world, the man must not expect her personal love unless he also goes up to live in the same world. It is simply fair that he should do so. The woman who lives in a small world must not expect the love of a man who lives in a great world. He would lose much of his greatness if he should give his personal love to such a woman.

The tendency of all life is onward and upward. Therefore, to ask anything to come down is to violate the very purpose of existence. If we wish to be with the higher, the greater and the superior, we must change ourselves and become higher, greater and superior; and this we all can do. In the application of the basic law of change, no factor is more important than that of pleasure. We are controlled to a great extent by the pleasures we enjoy, ofttimes so much so that they may even determine our destiny.

The reason why is found in the fact that we deeply love what we thoroughly enjoy, and since we think the most of what we love the best, we naturally become like the pleasures we thoroughly enjoy, because man gradually grows into the likeness of his predominating thought. It is therefore unwise to permit ourselves to enjoy anything that is beneath our most perfect conception of the ideal, and it is likewise unwise to associate personally with people who care only for the ordinary and the common. What we enjoy becomes a part of ourselves, and for the good of everybody, we cannot afford to go down; but when we love only those pleasures that are as high as our own ideal of joy, then we are truly on the great ascending path.

To overlook the wrongs, the defects and the perversions of life, and to look only for that beautiful something in every soul that we simply want to love, even without trying, is one of the greatest things that we can do; but we must not permit our conception of the beautiful within to become a mere, cold abstraction. It is most important that we be as emotional as we possibly can without permitting ourselves to be controlled by our emotions. The heart should be most tender and warm, and every feeling constantly on fire; but if all such feelings are turned into the secret realms of soul life, we shall find that the forces of love are drawn insistently towards the highest, the truest, and most noble and the most beautiful that our inspired moments have revealed. When this is done we can readily love with the whole heart any noble quality, or high art, or great work upon which we may direct our attention, and what we can love at will, that we can think of as deeply and as long as we may desire.

When we have formulated in our minds what changes we wish to make, the course to pursue is to love the ideal that corresponds to those changes. This love must be deep and strong, and must be continued until the desired change has actually taken place. Know what better qualities you want; then love those qualities with all your mind and heart and soul. To love the higher and the greater qualities of life is to cause the creative qualities of mind to produce those same qualities in our own nature; and in consequence, we steadily grow into the likeness of that which we constantly love. This is the great law the law that governs all change for the better. But to use this law intelligently the power of love must cease to respond to every whim or notion that the suggestibility of environment may present to the mind.

The power of love is the greatest power in the world, but it can cause persons or nations to fall to the lowest state, as well as rise to the highest state. Every fall in the history of the race has been caused largely by the misdirection of love, while every step in advance has been prompted largely by the power of love turned upon better things. To misdirect love is to love that which is beneath our present stage in advancement; it is turning the forces of life backward, and retrogression must inevitably follow. In the average person, love is directed almost exclusively upon the personal side of life. In consequence, the love nature becomes so personal, so limited and so superficial, that materialism follows. In many other minds, it is mere appearances that attract the power of admiration, and the finer things in mind, soul and character, are wholly ignored. The result is that the finer qualities of such people gradually disappear, and grossness, both in thought and in appearance naturally follow.

But we must not conclude in this connection that it is wrong to admire the beautiful wherever it may be seen in the external world. We should love the beautiful everywhere, no matter where it may be found; we should admire the richness of life, both in the external and in the internal; and by living a complete life, we shall enjoy more and more of the richness and the beautiful in life, in the within as well as in the without. But the power of love must direct the greater part of its attention upon that which is rich and beautiful in mind and soul. It is that which is finer than the finest of external things that must be loved if man is to grow into the likeness of the great, the superior and the ideal, because man is as he thinks, and he thinks the most of what he loves the best.

When any individual begins to love the finer qualities in life, and gives all the power of mind and soul to that love, they have taken the first step in the changing of their destiny. They are laying the foundation for a great and a better future, and if they continue as they have begun, they will positively reach the loftiest goal that they may have in view.

There are many laws to apply in the beginning of a great life, but the law that lies at the foundation of them all is the law of love. It is love that determines what we are to think, what we are to work for, where we are to go, and what we are to accomplish. Therefore, among all great essentials, the principal one is to know how to love. To apply this essential for all practical purposes, the secret is to love the great, the beautiful, and the ideal in everybody and in everything; and to love with such a strong, passionate love that its ascending power becomes irresistible. The whole of life will thus change and go up with the power of love into the great, the superior and the ideal; everything, both in the being of man and in his environment will advance and change accordingly, and the dreams of the soul will come true. The ideal will become real, the desires of the heart will be granted, and what man has hoped to make his own will be absent no more.

When failure comes be more determined than ever to succeed.

The more feeling there is in your thought the greater its power.

You steadily and surely become in the real what you constantly and clearly think that you are in the ideal.

The more you believe in yourself the more of your latent powers and possibilities you place in action. And the more you believe in your purpose the more of your power you apply in promoting that purpose.

Depend only upon yourself but work in harmony with all things. Thus you call forth the best that is in yourself and secure the best that external sources have to give.

Chapter 9

He Can Who Thinks He Can

The discovery of the fact that man is as he thinks, has originated a number of strange ideas concerning the power of thought. One of the principal of these is the belief that thought is a domineering force to be used in controlling things and in compelling fate to come our way. But that this belief is unscientific in every sense of the term has been demonstrated any number of times.

Those who have accepted this belief, and who have tried to use thought as a compelling force, have seemingly succeeded in the beginning, but later on have utterly failed, and the reason is that the very moment we proceed to apply thought in this manner, we place ourselves out of harmony with everything, both within ourselves and in our environment. The seeming success that such people have had in the beginning, or for a season, is due to the fact that a strong compelling force can cause the various elements of life to respond for a while, but the force that compels, weakens itself through the very act of compelling, and finally loses its power completely; and then, whatever has been gathered begins to slip away.

This explains why thousands of ardent students of metaphysics have failed to secure the results desired, or have succeeded only in spurts. They have taken the wrong view of the power of thought, and therefore have caused their power to work against them during the greater part of the time. The power of thought is not a compelling force. It is a building force, and it is only when used in the latter sense that desirable results can be produced. The building capacity of thought, however, is practically unlimited. Therefore there is actually no end to what might be accomplished, so long as this power is employed intelligently.

To apply the full building power of thought, we should proceed upon the principle that he can who thinks he can, and we should act in the full conviction that whatever man thinks he can do, he can do, because there is no limit to the power that such thinking can bring forth. The majority among intelligent minds admit that there is some truth in the statement that he can who thinks he can, but they do not, as a rule, believe it to be a very large truth. They admit that we gain more confidence in ourselves when we think that we can do what we have undertaken to do, and also that we become more determined, but aside from that, they see no further value in that particular attitude of mind. They do not realize that he who thinks he can, develops the power that can; but this is the truth, and it is one of the most important of all truths in the vast metaphysical domain.

The law that governs this idea, and its process while in action, is absolutely unlimited in its possibilities, and therefore is in a position to promise almost anything to one who is faithful. When a person begins to think that they can do certain things that they desire to do, their mind will naturally proceed to act on those faculties that are required in the working out of their purpose; and so long as the mind acts upon a certain faculty, more and more life, nourishment and energy will accumulate in that faculty. In consequence, that faculty will steadily develop. It will become larger, stronger and more efficient, until it finally is competent to do what we originally wanted done. Thus we understand how he who thinks he can develops the power that can.

When someone begins to think that they can apply the power of invention, their mind will begin to act upon the faculty of invention. The latent powers of this faculty will be aroused. These powers will accordingly be exercised more and more, and development will be promoted. This, however, is not all. Whenever the mind concentrates its attention upon a certain faculty, additional energy will be drawn into that faculty; thus power will be added to power, much will gather more, and as this may continue indefinitely there need be no end to the capacity and the ability that can be developed in that faculty.

In the course of time, be it in a few months or in a few years, that person will actually have developed the power of invention to such a degree that they can invent successfully; and through the application of the same law, can further develop this same faculty, year after year, until they may finally become an inventive genius.

When an individual has some inventive power in the beginning, they will secure, through the application of this law, more remarkable results and in less time than if there were originally no indications of that faculty; but even if there were no original indications of individual power, that power can be developed to a high degree through the faithful application of the great law he can who thinks he can, or to state it differently one who thinks they can develops the power that can.

There is no faculty that we all do not possess, either in the active or in the latent state. Every faculty that naturally belongs to the human mind is latent in every mind, and it can be awakened and developed, provided the proper laws are faithfully applied. It should be our object, however, to accomplish as much as possible in the present. It is therefore advisable to proceed in the beginning to work through, and develop, those faculties that already indicate considerable power. The mind that has some talent for invention should proceed to think that they can invent. Thus they will accumulate more and more inventive ability or genius. The mind that has some talent for music, should proceed to think that they can master the art of music.

They will thereby cause the creative energies of their mentality to accumulate more and more in the faculty of music, until that faculty will be developed to a greater and greater degree. The mind that has some talent for art should apply the same law upon that talent. The mind that has literary ability should proceed to think that they can write what they want to write, and they will finally secure that literary ability or genius with which they can write what they want to write. The mind that has ability in any line of business should proceed to think that they can conduct that business in the most successful manner. Should they enter that business and continue to think that they can, combining such thought with good work, enterprise and the full use of their personal ability, their success will continue to grow indefinitely.

Whatever man or woman may think that they can do, let them proceed to carry out that undertaking, constantly thinking that they can. They will succeed from the beginning, and their advancement will be continuous. However, no mind need be confined to a single purpose. If we have talent for something better than we are doing now, or if we wish to awaken some talent that we long to possess, we may proceed now to think that we can do what we long to do. We shall thus give more and more power to that faculty until it becomes sufficiently strong to be applied in actual practice. In the mean time, we should continue to think that we can do better and better what we are doing now. We shall thereby advance steadily in our present work, and at the same time, prepare ourselves for a greater work in the coming days.

When we think that we can, we must enter into the very soul of that thought and be thoroughly in earnest. It is in this manner that we awaken the finer creative energies of mind, those forces that build talent, ability and genius those forces that make man great. We must be determined to do what we think we can do, This determination must be invincible, and must be animated with that depth of feeling that arouses all the powers of being into positive and united action. The power that can do what we think we can do will thus be placed at our command, and accordingly we may proceed successfully to do what we thought we could do.

The fact that you have failed to get the lesser proves conclusively that you deserve the greater. So therefore, dry those tears and go in search of the worthier prize.

Count nothing lost; even the day that sees "no worthy action done" may be a day of preparation and accumulation that will add greatly to the achievements of tomorrow. Many a day was made famous because nothing was done the day before.

Know what you want and continue to want it. You will get it if you combine desire with faith. The power of desire when combined with faith becomes invincible.

Some of the principal reasons why so many fail to get what they want is because they do not definitely know what they want or because they change their wants almost every day.

Chapter 10

How We Secure What We Persistently Desire

The purpose of desire is to inform man what he needs at every particular moment to supply the demands of change and growth in his life; and in promoting that purpose, desire gives expression to its two leading functions. The first of these is to give the forces of the human system something definite to do, and the second is to arouse those forces or faculties that have the natural power to do what is to be done.

In exercising its first function, desire not only promotes concentration of action among the forces in man, but also causes those forces to work for the thing that is wanted. Therefore, it is readily understood why the wish, if strong, positive, determined and continuous, will tend to produce the thing wished for.

If you can cause all the elements and powers in your being to work for the one thing that you want you are almost certain to get it. In fact, you will get it unless it is so large that it is beyond you, or beyond the power of your present capacity to produce; though in that case you have exercised poor judgment; you have permitted yourself to desire what lies outside of your sphere; and what you could neither appreciate nor use were you to get it.

What you can appreciate, enjoy and use in your present sphere of existence, you have the power, in your present state of development, to produce; that is, you can produce it if all your power is applied in your effort to produce it; and when you desire any particular thing with the full force and capacity of your desire you cause all your power to be applied in producing that particular thing.

In exercising its second function, desire proceeds directly into that faculty or group of forces that can, if fully applied, produce the very thing that is desired. In its first function it tends to bring all the forces of the system together, and inspires them with the desire to work for what is wanted. It acts upon the system in general and gives everything in the system something definite to do, that something definite in each case being the one thing desired. In its second function it acts upon certain parts of the system in particular; always upon those parts that can do what is wanted done; and it tends to arouse all the life and power that those particular parts may contain. How desire proceeds, and how it secures results in this respect is easily illustrated.

We will take, for example, a man who is not earning as much as he feels that he needs. Naturally, he will begin to desire more money; and we will suppose that this desire becomes stronger and stronger until it actually stirs every atom of his being. Now what happens? He is not only arousing a great deal of latent and unused energy, but all of his active energy is becoming more and more alive. But what becomes of all this energy? It goes directly into his moneymaking faculties, and tends to increase decidedly the life, the power, the capacity and the efficiency of those faculties. There is in every mind a certain group of faculties that is made by nature for financial purposes. In some minds these faculties are small and sluggish, while in other minds they are large and active. And that the latter kind should be able to make more money and accumulate things in a greater measure is quite natural.

But is it possible to take those faculties that are small and sluggish and make them large and active? If so, those who now have limited means may in the course of time have abundance. To answer this question, we will ask what it is that can arouse any faculty to become larger and more active, and we find that it is more energy, and energy that is more alive. No matter how sluggish a faculty may be, if it is thoroughly charged, so to speak, with highly active energy, it simply must become more active. And no matter how small it may be, if it continues to receive a steady stream of added life, energy and power, day after day, month after month, year after year, it simply must increase in size and capacity. And whenever any faculty becomes greater in capacity and more alive in action it will do better work; that is, it will gradually gain in ability and power until it has sufficient ability and power to produce what you wished for.

Returning to the man in our illustration, we will see how the principle works. His moneymaking faculties are too small and too sluggish to produce as much money as he needs. He begins to desire for more. This desire becomes strong enough to arouse every element and force in his moneymaking faculties; for here be it remembered that the force of any desire goes directly into that faculty that can, by nature, produce the thing desired. This is one of the laws of mind. In addition, the action of his desire tends to arouse all the other forces of his system, and tends to concentrate those forces upon the idea of making more money.

In the beginning, no important change in his financial ability may be noticed, except that he feels more and more confidence in his power to secure the greater amount desired. In a short time, however, possibly within a few months, he begins to get new ideas about the advancement of his work. His mind is beginning to work more actively upon the idea of increased gain. Accordingly, suggestions as to how he might increase the earning capacity of his business are constantly coming up in his mind, and ways and means and plans are taking shape and form more and more completely. The actions of his moneymaking faculties are also beginning to change; that is, they are becoming finer, more penetrating, and more keen so that his insight into financial matters is steadily improving. He is therefore securing the necessary essentials to greater financial gain, and as he applies them all things will naturally begin to take a turn.

To state it briefly, his strong, persistent desire for more money has aroused his moneymaking faculties. They have become stronger, more active, more wide-awake and more efficient. And as a strong, wide-awake faculty can do many times as good work as one that is only partly alive, we understand how his desire for more money has given him the ability to make more money. As he continues this desire, making it stronger and more persistent, his financial ability will increase accordingly, and his financial gains continue to increase in proportion.

Many may doubt the efficiency of the plan just presented, because as is well known, most people desire more money but do not always get it. But do they always wish hard enough? It is not occasional desire, or halfhearted desire that gets the thing desired. It is persistent desire; and persistent desire not only desires continually, but with all the power of life and mind and soul.

The force of a half alive desire, when acting upon a certain faculty, cannot cause that faculty to become fully alive. Nor can such a desire marshal all the unused forces of the system and concentrate them all upon the attainment of the one thing wanted. And it is true that the desires of most people are neither continuous nor very deep. They are shallow, occasional wishes without enough power to stir to action a single atom.

Then we must also remember that results do not necessarily follow the use of a single force. Sometimes the force of persistent desire alone may do wonders, but usually it is necessary to apply in combined action all the forces of the human system. The force of desire, however, is one of the greatest of these, and when fully expressed in connection with the best talents we may possess, the thing desired will certainly be secured.

We may take several other illustrations. Suppose you have a strong desire for more and better friends. The action of that desire, if deep, wholehearted and persistent will tend to impress the qualities of friendship upon every element of your character. In consequence, you will in time become the very incarnation of friendship; that is, you will become a better and a better friend, and he who becomes a better friend will constantly receive more and better friends. In other words, you become like the thing you desire, and when the similarity has become complete you will get what you want through the law of like attracting like.

You may desire to succeed in a certain line of work; we will say, in the literary field. If your desire for success in that field is full and persistent, the power of that desire will constantly increase the life, the activity and the capacity of your literary faculties, and you will naturally do better work in that field. The same is true with regard to any other line of work, because your desire for greater success in your work will arouse to fuller action those faculties that you employ in that work. But, in every case, the desire must be deep, whole-souled, persistent and strong. It is therefore evident that results in all lines of endeavor depend very largely upon the power of desire, and that no one can afford to let their desires lag for a moment.

The law should be: Know what you want, and then want it with all the life and power that is in you. Get your mind and your life fully aroused. Persistent desire will do this. And that it is most important to do this is proven by the fact that in thousands of instances, a partly alive mind is the only reason why the goal in view has not been reached. It is necessary, however, that your desires continue uninterruptedly along the lines you have chosen. You may desire a score or more of different things, but continue each desire without change, unless you should find that certain changes are necessary to secure the greater results you have in mind.

To desire one thing today and another tomorrow means failure. To work for one thing this year and another thing next year is the way to empty handedness at the end of every year. Before you begin to apply the power of desire, know with a certainty what you want because when you get what you have desired, you may have to take it. If you do not know definitely what you really do want, desire a better judgment, a clearer understanding and a more balanced life. Desire to know what is best for you, and the force of that desire will tend to produce normal action in every part of your system. Then you will feel distinctly what the highest welfare of your nature actually demands.

In deciding upon what you want, however, do not be timid, and do not measure the possible with the yardstick of general appearances. Let your aspirations be high, only be sure that you are acting within the sphere of your own inherent capacity; though in this connection it is well to remember that your inherent capacity is many times as great as it has been supposed to be; and also that it can be continuously enlarged.

In choosing what you are to desire, act within reason, but go after the best. If the full power of desire is applied upon all the elements of your mind and character, what is latent within you will be aroused, developed and expressed;

you will become much more than you are and thereby will not only desire the best, but be able to be of service to the best. And this latter fact is important. When we desire the great and the wonderful we must ask what we have to give the great and the wonderful in return. It is not only necessary to get the best to realize our ideal, but it is also necessary to be so good and so great that we can give to the best as much as we are receiving from the best.

Before we begin to wish for an ideal, we must ask what that ideal is going to get when it comes. Coupled with our desire for the ideal, therefore, we must have an equally strong desire for the remaking of ourselves so that we may become equal to that ideal in every respect. If we want an ideal companion, we must not only wish for such a companion, but we must also desire the development of those qualities in ourselves that we know would make us agreeable to that companion.

If we want a different environment we should wish for such an environment with all the life and soul we possess, and should at the same time wish for the increase of those powers in our own talents that can earn such an environment. If we want a better position we should desire such a position every minute and also desire that we may become more competent to fill it when it comes.

The power of desire not only tends to arouse added life and power in these faculties upon which it may act, but it also tends to make the mind as a whole more alert and wide-awake along those lines. This is well illustrated by the fact that when we have a strong, continuous desire for information on a certain subject, we always find someone or something that can give us that information. And the reason is that all the faculties of the mind are prompted by the force of this desire to be constantly on the lookout for that information. That the same law will apply in the desire or search for wisdom, new ideas, better plans, better opportunities, more agreeable environments and more ideal companions, is clearly understood. And when we couple this fact with the fact that the power of desire tends to increase the life, the ability, the working capacity and the efficiency of these faculties or forces that can produce what we desire, we must certainly admit that those who have found the secret of using desire have made a great find indeed.

But, as stated before, and it cannot be repeated too often, the desire must be persistent and strong, as strong as all the life and soul we possess. In other words, we must wish hard enough, and we wish hard enough when our desires are sufficiently full and deep and strong to thoroughly arouse those faculties that have the natural ability to fulfill those desires.

Many desires are only strong enough to arouse their corresponding faculties to a slight degree not enough to increase the activity or working capacity of these faculties, while most desires are too weak to arouse any force or faculty in the least. The act of wishing hard enough, however, does not imply hard mental work. If you make hard work of your wishing, you will use up your energy instead of turning it into those channels where it can be applied to good account. It is depth of desire and fullness of desire combined in an action that is directed continuously upon the one thing desired that constitutes true desire. To wish hard enough is simply to wish for all that you want with all that is in you. But we cannot wish with all that is in us unless our wish is subconscious as well as conscious because the subconscious is a part of us the larger part of us.

To make every desire subconscious, the subconscious mind should always be included in the process of desire; that is, whenever we express a desire we should think of the subconscious, and combine the thought of that desire with our thought of the subconscious mind. Every desire should be deeply felt as all deeply felt mental actions become subconscious actions. It is an excellent practice to let every desire sink into the deeper mental life, so to speak; and also to act in and through that deeper mental life, whenever we give expression to desire; or, in other words, when we turn on the full force and power of that desire.

To become proficient in these methods requires some practice, though all that is necessary to become proficient is to continue to try. No special rule is required. Begin by feeling your desires through and through. Make them as strong and as deep as you can, and always combine the living action of your desire with your thought of those faculties through which you know that desire is to work.

To illustrate: If you desire greater success in your work, think of those faculties that you are using in your work whenever you give full expression to your desire. If you are a business man, think of your business faculties whenever you desire greater business success. If you are a musician, think of your musical faculties whenever you desire greater proficiency in your music. Though in case your desires should be such that you do not know through what kinds of faculties it will naturally be expressed, never mind. Continue to desire what you want; the power of that desire, if persistent and strong, will find a way to make your wish come true.

When we understand how desire works, and know that it works only when it is persistent, we realize that we have found, not only a great secret, but also a simple explanation for many of the failures in life as well as many of its greatest achievements. And from the facts in the case we conclude that no matter what an individual's condition or position may be today, if they will decide upon that something better that they want, they may get it, provided their wish for it is as strong as their own life and as large as their own soul.

The optimist lives under a clear sky; the pessimist lives in a fog. The pessimist hesitates, and loses both time and opportunity; the optimist makes the best use of everything now, and builds themselves up, steadily and surely, until all adversity is overcome and the object in view realized. The pessimist curbs their energies and concentrates their whole attention upon failure; the optimist gives all their thought and power to the attainment of success, and arouses their faculties and forces to the highest point of efficiency. The pessimist waits for better times, and expects to keep on waiting; the optimist goes to work with the best that is at hand now, and proceeds to create better times. The pessimist pours cold water on the fires of their own ability; the optimist adds fuel to those fires. The pessimist links their mind to everything that is losing ground; the optimist lives, thinks and works with everything that is determined to press on. The pessimist places a damper on everything; the optimist gives life, fire and go to everything. The optimist is a building force; the pessimist is always an obstacle in the way of progress. The pessimist lives in a dark, soggy unproductive world, the optimist lives in that mental sunshine that makes all things grow.

Chapter 11

Concentration and the Power Back of Suggestion

The purpose of concentration is to apply all the active forces of mind and personality upon that one thing which is being done now, and it may therefore be called the master key to all attainments and achievement. In its last analysis, the cause of all failure can be traced to the scattering of forces, and the cause of all achievement to the concentration of forces. This does not imply however, that concentration is the only essential, but it does imply that concentration must be perfect, or failure is inevitable no matter how many good methods one may employ. The ruling thought of concentration is, " This one thing I do," and it can be stated as an absolute truth that whenever the mind works completely in the attitude of that thought, concentration is perfect.

The value of concentration is very easily illustrated by taking, for example, a wheel of twenty spokes with every spoke a pipe, and all those pipes connected with another conveying steam. The steam will thereby pass out through twenty channels. Then connect an engine with one of the pipes. That engine will accordingly receive only one-twentieth of the steam conveyed through the wheel, while nineteen twentieths will pass out in waste. But suppose the other nineteen pipes were plugged so that all the steam would pass out through the one pipe connected with the engine. The engine would then have twenty times as much power as before.

The average mind is quite similar to such a wheel. An enormous amount of energy is generated at the hub, so to speak, or at the vital centre of mental life; but as a rule, that power passes out through a score of channels, so that the channel of action receives only a fraction of the power generated in the human system. But here we must remember that you can apply your power effectively only in one direction at a time; therefore, if all your power is to be applied in that one direction, all other channels must be closed up for the time being; or in other words, all the power of mind and thought must be concentrated where you are acting at the time.

In learning how to concentrate, it is necessary in the beginning to remember that the usual methods are of no value. You cannot develop concentration by fixing thought or attention upon some external object. Real concentration is subjective, and subjective thought is deep; that is, it acts through the deeper or interior realms of mind. When you fix your attention, however, upon some external object, like a spot on the wall, as has been suggested by some would be instructors in this field, your thought goes out towards the surface, so that you are actually getting away from the true field of concentration. Any method, or any line of thinking that tends to draw the mind out towards the surface, will produce a superficial attitude, and when the mind is in such an attitude, deep mental action is not possible; but deep mental action is absolutely necessary in all concentration.

There is no use trying to concentrate unless the action of the mind is deep. That is the first essential. In other words, the mind must go into the psychological field; the mind must act, not on the surface of things, but through the deeper life of its thought process. To develop concentration, all that is necessary is to apply consciously those two factors that are invariably found in natural concentration. In the conscious application of these two factors, the following two methods will be found sufficient; in fact, nothing further will be required in the attainment of concentration to any degree desired. The first method is to train the mind to act in the subjective or psychological field; in other words, cause all thinking, all feeling and all actions of thought, will and desire to become deeper and finer; in fact, deepen as far as possible all mental action. Whenever you concentrate or turn your attention upon any subject or object, try to feel deeply, try to think deeply and try to turn thought into deeper realms of feeling. The moment your mental action begins to deepen, you will find your attention directed upon the object in mind with perfect ease and with full force.

Whenever you are thinking about anything, try to feel your thought getting into the vital life of that something, and wherever you turn your attention, try to feel that the force of that attention acts through your whole mind instead of simply on the surface of your mind. To state it briefly, whenever you concentrate, deepen your thought, and the deeper your thought becomes, the more perfectly will the full force of your mind and thought focus upon the point of concentration. Whatever you have to do, deepen your thought while giving that work your attention, You will find that you will thereby give all your energy to that work and this is your purpose.

The second method is to become interested in that upon which you desire to concentrate. If you are not interested in that subject or object, begin at once to look for the most interesting point of view. You will be surprised to find that no matter how uninteresting a subject may seem, the very moment you begin to look for the most interesting viewpoints of that subject, you will almost immediately become interested in that subject itself. And it is a well-known fact that whenever we are thoroughly interested in a subject we concentrate thoroughly and naturally upon that subject. To make concentration perfect, so that you can turn all the power of mind and thought upon any subject or object desired, these two methods should be combined.

Always look for the most interesting points of view, and while you are looking for those viewpoints, deepen the action of your mind by trying to feel the real vital life of those actions. You thereby become interested in the subject on the one hand, and you make every action of the mind subjective on the other hand; and when perfect interest is combined with subjective mental action, you have perfect concentration.

The constant practice of these two methods will develop the power of concentration to such an extent that you can concentrate completely at any time and for any length of time, by simply deciding to do so; and that such an attainment is of enormous value is evident when we understand how much power there is in man, and how concentration can turn all of that power upon the one thing that is being done now.

All modern psychologists agree that there is enough power in any human being to accomplish what they have in view, provided it is all constructively applied in that one direction. And when man can concentrate perfectly, he can use all of his power wherever he may choose to act. Then, if we combine scientific thinking and constructive mental action with concentration, nothing can prevent us from realizing our very highest ambition.

Another important essential in the use of the forces of mind and thought, is that of understanding suggestion and the power back of suggestion; and this becomes especially true when we realize that there is no factor or condition that we may come in contact with anywhere or under any circumstances, that does not suggest something. To define suggestion, it may be stated that anything is a suggestion that brings into mind some thought, idea or feeling that tends to undermine some similar idea, thought or feeling that happens to be in the mind at the time.

When you have certain ideas or feelings, and you meet circumstances that tend to remove those ideas or feelings, the power of suggestion is working in your mind. If your mind is in a wholesome state and an unwholesome picture removes that wholesome state by replacing something that is degrading, your mind is in the power of suggestion. If you feel joyous and some idea given to you makes your mind depressed, you are in the hands of suggestion; in fact, when anything enters your mind in such a manner as to remove certain similar or opposite states already in your mind, it exercises the power of suggestion. It is therefore necessary to understand how this power works, so that we can take advantage of good suggestions and avoid those that are not good.

The great majority are receiving all sorts of suggestions every hour, and they respond to a very large number of them; in fact, we can truthfully say that most people are controlled, most of the time, by suggestions that come to them from their environment.

Those minds, however, who understand the power of thought, and who know the difference between detrimental and beneficial suggestions, can close their minds to the former and open them fully to the latter. And the method to apply is this, that whenever you are in the presence of an adverse suggestion, concentrate your attention upon some idea or mental state which you know will act as a counter suggestion; in other words, when adverse suggestion is trying to produce in your mind what you do not want, persist in suggesting to yourself what you do want.

This practice, if employed frequently, will soon make you so strong in this direction that you will unconsciously, so to speak, be on your guard; in fact, the very moment that an adverse suggestion is given, your mind will spring up of its own accord with a wholesome suggestion to meet the requirements.

To avoid becoming a victim to adverse suggestions and we have such suggestions about us almost constantly fill your mind so full of good, wholesome thoughts and suggestions that there is no room for anything else. Feel right at all times, and nothing from without can tempt you to think wrong. Make every good thought subconscious, and no adverse thought from without can possibly get into your subconscious mind at any time.

A great many suggestions do not produce results, a fact which should be perfectly understood, because every thought that we think does contain some suggestion. When we are trying to impress good thoughts upon our minds, we want the good suggestions conveyed by those thoughts to take effect, but frequently they do not, and the reason is that a suggestion takes effect only when we exercise the power that is back of suggestion. The outward suggestion itself is simply the vehicle through which another power is acting, and that other power is nothing more nor less than the real life of that idea which the suggestion intends to convey.

To simplify this matter, we will suppose that you are suggesting to yourself that you are well. The suggestion itself is simply a vehicle conveying the idea of health, but if your mind is not in touch with the interior or living force of that idea of health at the time you are giving the suggestion, you have not exercised the power back of suggestion, and the idea of health will not be conveyed to your subconscious mind. On the other hand, if you can actually feel the power of this interior idea of health when you are giving the suggestion, you are in mental touch with the power back of that suggestion, and whenever you touch the power back of suggestion you use that power. Results, therefore, will be forthcoming.

To explain further, we might say that you use the power back of suggestion whenever you mentally feel that vital idea which the suggestion aims to convey. When you feel that idea, you respond to the suggestion, but when you do not feel it, you do not respond. This explains why the power of suggestion so frequently fails, not only in everyday life, but also in mental healing.

When you think health, you will produce health in your system if you feel the real or interior life of health at the time. When you think harmony you will produce harmony in your system, if your mind actually goes into the soul of harmony at the time. When you place yourself in the mental world of happiness whenever you are thinking happiness, you will actually produce happiness in your mind, because you are applying the power that is back of the thought that suggests happiness.

Two men may present the same proposition under the same circumstances, and you will accept the proposition from the one, while ignoring the arguments of the other completely. The reason will be that while the one is talking about his proposition, the other is talking through his proposition. The mind of the one goes on the outside of his arguments and his suggestions, while the mind of the other goes through the real inner life of those arguments and suggestions. Therefore, the one is only using suggestion, while the other is also using the power back of suggestion; and it is the power back of suggestion that produces results, whenever results are secured. The same idea is illustrated when a person is speaking on a certain subject. If their description deals simply with the shell of that subject, they do not attract attention, but the moment they touch the vital or inner factors of that subject, everybody is interested. The reason is, they have touched the power back of their theme. But we all have ideas or suggestions to present at frequent intervals. Therefore, if we can use the power back of our suggestion at such times we may receive a hearing, but if we cannot, we attract little or no attention.

Thus we understand the value of knowing how to use the power back of suggestion, and we can learn to use this power by training ourselves to get into the real life of every idea and every thought that we may try to think or convey. When we try to live our ideas and thoughts, we will begin to express that interior power, and we shall succeed in living our ideas when we try to feel consciously and constantly the real life and the real truth that is contained in those ideas.

To secure the best results from the power of thought in its various modes of application, we must understand that there is something back of everything that takes form or action in life, and that it is through this something that the actions of mind should move whenever we use thought or suggestion in any manner whatever.

When we are conscious only of the body of our ideas, those ideas convey no power. It is when we become conscious of the soul of those ideas that we have aroused that something within that alone produces results in the mental world. Any thought or suggestion that conveys simply the external form, invariably falls flat.

There is nothing to it. It is entirely empty, and produces no impression whatever. But our ideas and suggestions become alive with the fullness of life and power when we also convey the real life or the real soul that is contained within the body of those thoughts. We have, at such times, entered the depths of mental life. We are beginning to act through undercurrents, and we are beginning to draw upon the immensity of that power that exists in the vast interior realms of our own mental world.

Say to yourself a hundred times every day, and mean it with all your heart: I will become more than I AM. I will achieve more and more every day because I know that I can. I will recognize only that which is good in myself, only that which is good in others; only that in all things and places that I know should live and grow. When adversity threatens I will be more determined than ever in my life to prove that I can turn all things to good account. And when those whom I have trusted seem to fail me, I will have a thousand times more faith in the honor and nobleness of man. I will think only of that which has virtue and worth. I will wish only for that which can give freedom and truth. I will expect only that which can add to the welfare of the race. I will live to live more. I will speak to give encouragement, inspiration and joy. I will work to be of service to an ever-increasing number. And in every thought, word and action my ruling desire shall be, to enrich, ennoble and beautify existence for all who come my way.

Chapter 12

The Development of the Will

No force in the human system can be properly used unless it is properly directed, and as the will is the only factor in man that has the power to direct or control, a thorough development of the will, as well as a clear understanding of its application under every circumstance, becomes absolutely necessary if we are to use all the forces within us to the very best advantage.

To define the will with absolute exactness is hardly possible, though a clear knowledge as to its general nature and special functions must be secured. In a previous chapter, it was stated that the "I AM" is the ruling principle in man, and it may be added here that when the "I AM" exercises this function of rulership anywhere in the human system, will power is the result; or, it may be stated that the will is that attribute of the "I AM" which is employed whenever there is a definite intention followed by actual action, with a view of initiating, controlling or directing. To state it briefly therefore, will power is the result of the "I AM" either taking initiative action or controlling and directing any action after it has been taken.

Among the many functions of the will, the principal ones are as follows: The will to initiate; the will to direct; the will to control; the will to think; the will to imagine; the will to desire; the will to act; the will to originate ideas; the will to give expression to those ideas; the will to will into action any purpose, the will to carry through that purpose; the will to employ the highest and most perfect action of any force or faculty in mind; and the will to push up, so to speak, any talent in the mind to its highest point of efficiency. This last mentioned function has been ignored, but it is by far the most important in the practical life of attainment and achievement.

To illustrate this idea, we will suppose that you have a group of faculties, all of which are well developed, and contain a great deal of ability and power. But how can those faculties be caused to act? The fact is they will not act in the least until the will wills them into action. The will therefore must first be applied, but the act of initiating action among those faculties is not its only function. To illustrate again, we will suppose that your will is very weak. It therefore stands to reason that the original impulse given those faculties will also be weak.

Then when we understand that it is necessary for the will to continue to prompt or impel the continued action of any faculty we realize how weak, halfhearted and limited such an action will necessarily be when the will is weak. On the other hand, if your will is very strong, the original impulse given to the faculty will be strong and the continued action of that faculty will be much stronger, larger and more efficient.

In brief, when a faculty is backed up, so to speak, with a powerful will, it easily doubles its capacity and efficiency; in other words, it is pushed up to a higher state of action. We understand therefore the great importance of having a strong will, though such a will is not only an advantage in promoting a fuller and larger expression of any faculty we may possess, but also in promoting a larger and more perfect expression of any force that may be applied, either in the personality, in character or in mind. A powerful will, however, is never domineering or forceful. In fact, a domineering will is weak. It may be seemingly strong on the spur of the moment, but it cannot be applied steadily for any length of time. A strong will, however, is deep, continuous, and persistent. It calls into action your entire individuality, and as you exercise such a will you feel as if a tremendous power from within yourself had been calmly, though persistently aroused.

When we analyze the human mind, in the majority we find the will to be weak, and in fact, almost absent in a great many. Such people do not have the power to take a single original step. They have no initiative, and accordingly drift with the stream. Among others, who are a little higher in the mental scale, we find a will somewhat stronger, but not sufficiently strong to exercise with any degree of efficiency a single one of its functions. Among what can be called "the better class," we invariably find the will to be fairly well developed, and among the great leaders in all the different phases of human life and action, we find the will to be very strong in fact, there is not a single mental or spiritual giant in history, who did not have a tremendous will, and this was one their great secrets.

To illustrate further with regard to the last mentioned of the special functions, we will suppose that you have some talent for music. If you should will to exercise that talent to a slight degree only, it is evident that your efficiency along that line would not be marked. On the other hand, if your will was so strong that you could push up, so to speak, your musical faculty to its very highest point of efficiency, you would soon find yourself on the verge of musical genius; in fact, musical genius is absolutely impossible unless you have a strong will, no matter how much musical talent you may possess.

Though it must be remembered in this connection that it is not sufficient simply to have a strong will. The majority do not possess a strong will, and most of those who do have a strong will, have not learned how to apply it so as to secure greater efficiency in anything they may do; and here it is important to state that anyone who will increase the power of their will, and properly train it for the purpose just indicated, may expect to increase their efficiency anywhere from twenty-five to two hundred per cent. The majority have many times as much ability and working capacity as they are using at the present time; in fact, they apply only a small fraction of what is in them, and the principal reason why they do not apply all that is in them, is that they do not have sufficient power of will to act on this larger scale.

In this connection, we find another condition which is very important, and especially with regard to overcoming circumstances. A great many people have good intentions, and they have sufficient will power to originate those intentions, but they have not sufficient will power to carry them out; in other words, they have the will to think, but not the will to act.

And here we can use our own imagination in picturing that state of human affairs that would inevitably come into being if all good intentions became actions. Thousands of people start out right, but they have not the power of will to continue, so that where ten thousand make a good beginning, less than a score finish the race. We find this condition in all walks of life and in all undertakings, and it illustrates most eloquently the necessity of a strong will in every mind.

Realizing the importance of a strong will, and knowing that the will is weak in the minds of the great majority, we may well ask what might be the cause of this weakness; and the answer is that there are several marked causes, all of which we shall proceed to consider. The first among these causes is alcohol. The use of alcohol weakens the will, not only in the individual who partakes of it, but in their children and grandchildren, and many generations following. It has been estimated by those who have studied this subject carefully, that the use of alcohol from generation to generation through the centuries is one of the principal causes for this weakness in the human will that we find to be almost universal. And when we study the psychology of the subject we soon discover the reason why.

Nearly every nation, as far back in history as we can go, has been using alcohol in some form or other, and as its weakening effect upon the will is transmissible from one generation to another, we realize that practically every member of the race has been burdened, more or less, with this adverse inheritance. But in this connection, we must remember that it is not necessary to be disturbed by this dark picture, because no matter what we have inherited, we can overcome it absolutely. However, we do not wish to do anything that will be in our own way, or in the way of generations that are to follow.

It is therefore necessary that we consider this subject thoroughly, and act upon it accordingly. The fact that the human race has transmitted a weak will from generation to generation explains why the human family does not have enough power to produce more than an occasional mental giant. Here and there we find in history, men and women who tower above the rest. Their minds are strong, their wills powerful, and their souls invincible; but how different is the condition among the majority. Most of them constitute mere driftwood, and follow blindly the leadership of these mental giants the race has produced. This, however, is not the intention of nature. Nature intends all men and women to be mental and spiritual giants, and does not intend that anyone should follow the will of another. But the human race has, in this respect, ignored the intentions of nature.

The reason why the use of alcohol weakens the will, is very easily explained. When you take anything into the system that tends to take control over your desires, feelings or intentions, you permit yourself to be controlled by an outside agency, and accordingly the will for the time being is laid aside; and the law is, that whenever the will is laid aside by anything whatever it is weakened; that is, you undermine, so to speak, that element of the will which gives it the power to direct and control. When this practice is continued and repeated a number of times, we can readily understand how the power of the will is gradually decreased more and more, until its very foundation has been practically removed.

When you permit an outside agency to control your feelings and emotions at frequent intervals for a prolonged period, your system will soon get into the habit of submitting to the control of this outside agency, and will not respond any longer to any effort that the will may make to regain its original power of control. This being true, we find an explanation for a number of perplexing questions. We learn why great men and women are not more numerous. We learn why the majority are so easily influenced by temptations. We learn why powerful characters are found only here and there, and we also learn why every great nation of past history has fallen.

When we study history, we find that every great nation, after coming to a certain point of supremacy, began to decline, and there are several reasons for this strange termination of national power. But there is only one reason that stands out as the most vital of them all, and as possibly the cause of them all. We refer to the fact that a decrease of great men and women invariably precedes the decline of a nation. To keep any great nation up to a high standard of civilization there must be enough superior characters to hold the balance of power, but the very moment the balance of power gets into the hands of second grade men and women, a decline of that nation is inevitable.

Therefore, if any great nation in the present age is to continue to grow in real greatness and real power, we must make a special effort to increase the number of great men and women in every generation. The greater a nation becomes, the more great men and women are required to govern and direct the forces of progress and growth that are at work in that nation. We therefore understand what is required of us in this generation if we want present civilization to advance and rise in the scale.

Another cause of this weakness in the will is found in what may be called psychical excess. And it is unfortunate that so many people have permitted themselves to be placed under psychical influences during the last fifty or seventy-five years; though it is a fact that a great many people have permitted their minds to be controlled or influenced by the psychical or the occult in every age. Another tendency therefore towards weakness in the will has been transmitted from generation to generation down through the ages, and we all have the effect of this misuse of mind also to overcome at the present time; but again let us remember that we have the power to overcome anything that we might have inherited.

Whenever you give up your individuality, or any part of your mind or thought, to some unknown force or influence that you know little or nothing about you are permitting an outside agency to usurp the function of the will. You lay the will aside, you undermine its power to some extent, and thereby weaken those elements in its nature that constitute self-mastery and self-control. That psychical excess has this tendency to a most pronounced degree is well illustrated by the fact that every individual, who is fascinated with psychical experience, invariably lacks in self-control. Such people are usually so sensitive that they are swayed in every direction by every suggestion or influence or environment with which they may come in contact.

But here we may well ask what we are living for if we are living to give up to the influence of environment, visible or invisible, or if we are living to attain such full control over the powers and talents that are within us, that we cannot only control, modify, and perfect environment, but also so perfectly control ourselves that we can become all that nature intends that we should become.

If we are to rise in the scale, we must attain greater degrees of self-mastery, but we cannot learn to master ourselves so long as we are constantly permitting ourselves to be mastered by something else; and those who indulge in psychical experiences to any degree whatever, are permitting themselves to be mastered by something else. They are therefore losing ground every day. Their characters are becoming weaker, their standards of morality and rightness becoming more and more lax, as we all have discovered, and their power to apply those faculties and forces in their natures through which they may accomplish more and achieve more, are constantly decreasing both in working capacity and in efficiency.

If man wants to live his own life as it should be lived; if he wants to master circumstances and determine his own destiny, he must have the power to say under all sorts of conditions what he is going to think and what he is going to do; but he cannot exercise this power unless his own will is permitted to have absolute control over every thought, effort and desire in his life. Emotional excess is another cause that weakens the will, and by emotional excess we mean the act of giving way to uncontrolled feelings of any kind. To give way to anger, hatred, passion, excitability, intensity, sensitiveness, grief, discouragement, despair, or any other uncontrolled feeling, is to weaken the will. The reason is that you cannot control yourself through your will when you permit yourself to be controlled by your feelings; and any act that rules out the will, weakens the will. Whenever you permit yourself to become angry, you weaken the will. Whenever you permit yourself to become offended or hurt you weaken your will.

Whenever you permit yourself to become despondent or discouraged, you weaken your will. Whenever you give way to grief, mental intensity or excitability, you weaken your will. You permit some artificial mental state to take possession of your mind, and your will at the time is put aside. We therefore should avoid absolutely all emotional excess. We must not permit any feeling whatever to take possession of us, or permit ourselves to be influenced in any form or manner by anything that may enter the mind uncontrolled through the emotions; but this does not mean that we should ignore emotion. Emotion is one of the most valuable factors in human life, and should be used and enjoyed under every normal circumstance, but should never become a ruling factor in mind, thought or feeling.

You may look at a beautiful picture, and lose yourself, so to speak, in its charms. You may listen to exceptional music, and be carried away, or be thrilled through and through by the joy of its harmony; or you may witness some scene in nature that causes your soul to take wings and soar to empyrean heights. You may permit yourself to enjoy any or all of these ecstasies at anytime, provided you have conscious control over every movement of your emotions at the time. Whenever you feel the touch of some sublime emotion, try to direct the force of that emotion into a finer and a higher state of expression; thus you will not be controlled by it, but will exercise control over it, and accordingly will enjoy the pleasure of that emotion many times as much.

It is a well-known fact that whenever we control any feeling, whether it be physical or mental or spiritual, and try to turn it into a larger sphere of expression, we enjoy far more the pleasure that naturally comes through the exercise of that feeling. To control our emotions therefore is to lose nothing and gain much.

Another cause of weakness in the will is what might be called mental dependence. To depend upon anybody or anything outside of yourself, is to weaken the will, for the simple reason that you let the will of someone else rule your actions, while your own will remains dormant. Nothing, however, that remains dormant can grow or develop. On the other hand, it will continue to become weaker and weaker, like an unused muscle, until it has no strength whatever. We therefore understand why those multitudes of people, who have followed blindly the will and leadership of others, not only in religion but in all other things, have practically no will power at all. And here we wish to state that it is positively wrong for any individual or any group of individuals to follow anyone man or anyone woman or any group of men or women under any circumstances whatever.

We are here in this life to become something. We are here to make the best use of what we possess in mind, character and personality, but we cannot cause any element, faculty or power within us to express itself to any extent so long as we are mere dependent weaklings. In everything, depend upon yourself, but work in harmony with all things. Do not depend even upon the Infinite, but learn to work and live in harmony with the Infinite. The highest teachings of the Christ reveal most clearly the principle that no soul was created to be a mere helpless instrument in the hands of Supreme Power, but that every soul should act and live in perfect oneness with that Power. And the promise is that we all are not only to do the things that Christ did, but even greater things.

Man is no credit to Supreme Creative Power if he remains in the puppet stage, but he is a credit to that Power if he becomes a giant in character, mind and soul. In our religious worship we have given unbounded praise to God for His wonderful power in creating man, and the very next moment we have announced the hymn, "Oh To Be Nothing." The absurdity of it all is too evident to need comment, but when we understand that character and manhood, as well as practical efficiency in life, are the products of strength and not of weakness, we must come to the conclusion that every system of thought in the present age, be it religious, moral, ethical, or philosophical, needs complete reconstruction.

We are here to become great men and women, and with that purpose in view, we must eliminate everything in our religion and philosophy that tends to make the human mind a dependent weakling. If you would serve God and be truly religious, do not kneel before God, but learn to walk with God, and do something tangible every day to increase the happiness of mankind. This is religion that is worthwhile, and it is such religion alone that can please the Infinite.

Another cause which is too large and diversified to outline in detail, is that of intemperance; that is immoderation in anything in life. To indulge excessively any desire or appetite, be it physical or mental, is to weaken the will. Partake only of that which is necessary and good, and observe moderation. Control yourself under all circumstances, and resolve never to go too far in anything, because too much of the good may be more of an evil than not enough of it. The effects of weakness in the will are numerous, but there are two in particular that should receive marked attention. The first is that when the will is weak, the human system becomes incapable of resisting temptations, and therefore moral weakness or a complete moral downfall is inevitable. Character in the largest sense of the term is impossible without a strong will, and it is impossible to accomplish anything that is of permanent value without character.

The second is that weakness in the will inevitably implies weak mental actions; that is, no matter how much ability you may possess, if your will is weak, you will apply only a fraction of that ability; and there are thousands of able men and women who are failures in life simply because they have not the will to apply all their ability. If they would simply increase the power of their will, and properly train that will, they would immediately pass from failure to success, and in many instances, remarkable success. It is the power of the strong will alone that can give full expression to every talent or faculty you may possess, and it is only such a power that can push up the actions of every faculty to a point of high efficiency.

In learning to develop the will and to use the will, realize what the will is for. Understand clearly what its functions actually are, and then use it in all of those functions. Avoid anything and everything that tends to weaken the will, and practice every method known that can strengthen the will. Do not give in to any feeling or desire until you succeed in directing that feeling or desire as you like. Feel only the way you want to feel, and then feel with all the feeling that is in you. Whatever comes up in your system, take hold of it with your will and direct it so as to produce even greater results than were at first indicated. Use the will consciously as frequently as possible in pushing up your faculties to the highest point of efficiency; that is, when you are applying those faculties that you employ in your work, try to will them into stronger and larger actions. This is a most valuable practice, and if applied every day will, in the course of a reasonable time, not only increase the capacity and ability of those faculties, but will also increase decidedly the power of the will.

Whenever you will to do anything, will it with all there is in you. If no other practice than this were taken, the power of the will would be doubled in a month. Depend upon the power that is in you for everything, and determine to secure the results you desire through the larger expression of that power. Never give in to anything that you do not want.

When a certain desire comes up that you do not care to entertain, turn your attention at once upon some favorable desire, and give all the power of your will to that new desire. This is very important, as the average person wastes more than half of their energy entertaining desires that are of no value, and that they do not intend to carry out. Whenever any feeling comes up in the system ask yourself if you want it. If you do not, turn your attention in another direction; but if you do want it, take hold of it with your will and direct it towards the highest states of mind that you can form at the time.

In brief, every action that enters the system, whether it comes through thought, feeling, desire or imagination, should be redirected, by the power of the will and turned into higher and greater actions. Whenever you think, make it a practice to think with your whole mind. Make your thinking wholehearted instead of halfhearted. Whenever you act, act with all there is in you. Make every action firm, strong, positive and determined; in other words, put your whole soul into everything that you feel, think or do. In this way, you turn on, so to speak, the full current of the will, and whenever the will is used to its full capacity, it will grow and develop.

Try to deepen every action of mind and thought; that is, do not think simply on the surface, but also think subconsciously. Think and act with your deeper mental life. You thereby give the power of the will a deeper field of action, and it is established in the larger life of your individuality instead of in the surface thought of your objective mind.

The difference between a superficial will and a deeply established will is readily found in everyday experience. When you will to do anything and your intentions are easily thwarted by the suggestion of someone else, your will is on the surface. But when your intentions are so deeply rooted in the subconsciousness of your mind that nothing can thwart those intentions, your will has gained that great depth which you desire.

The more easily you are disturbed, the weaker your will, while the stronger the will, the more difficult it is for anything to disturb your mind. When the will is strong, you live and exercise self-control in a deeper or interior mental world, and you look out upon the confusions of the outer world without being affected in the least by what takes place in the external.

Whenever you exercise the will, try to place the action of that will as deeply in the world of your interior mental feeling as you possibly can; that is, do not originate will action on the surface, but in the depth of your own supreme individuality. Try to feel that it is the "I AM" that is exercising the power of the will, and then remember that the "I AM" lives constantly upon the supreme heights of absolute self-mastery. With this inspiring thought constantly in mind, you will carry the throne of the will, so to speak, farther and farther back into the interior realms of your greater mental world, higher and higher up into the ruling power of the supreme principle in mind. The result will be that you will steadily increase the power of your will, and appropriate more and more the conscious control of that principle in your greater nature through which all the forces in your possession may be governed and directed.

He who would become great must live a great life.

Happiness adds life, power, and worth to all your talents and powers. It is most important, therefore, that every moment should be full of joy.

However much you may do, always remember you have the ability to do more. No one has as yet applied all the ability in their possession. But all of us should learn to apply a greater measure every year.

While you are waiting for an opportunity to improve your time, improve yourself.

The man who never weakens when things are against him, will grow stronger and stronger until he will have the power to cause all things to be for him.

Chapter 13

The Building of a Great Mind

A great mind does not come from ancestors, but from the life, the thought and the actions of the individual; and such a mind can be constructed by anyone who understands the art of mind building, and who faithfully applies this art.

You may have a small mind today, and your ancestors for many generations back may have been insignificant in mental power; nevertheless, you may become even exceptional in mental capacity and brilliancy if you proceed to build your mind according to the principles of exact science; and those principles anyone can apply.

There are two obstacles, however, that must be removed before this building process can begin, and the first one of these is the current belief in heredity. That we inherit things is true, but the belief that we cannot become any larger or any better than our inheritance is not true. As long as a person believes that greatness is not possible to them because there were no great minds among their ancestors, they are holding themselves down, and cannot become any more than they subconsciously think they can; while on the other hand, the person who expects to become much because they had remarkable grandfathers is liable to be disappointed because they depend too much upon their illustrious forefathers and not enough upon themselves.

Blood will tell when combined with ambition, energy and enterprise, but the very best of blood will prove worthless in the life of one who expects ancestral greatness to carry them through. When we have received good things we must turn them to good account or nothing is gained. Our success will not come from the acts of our forefathers, but can come alone from what we are doing now. Those who have inherited rich blood can use that richness in building greatness in themselves, but those who have not the privilege of such inheritance need not be discouraged. They can create their own rich blood and make it as rich as they like.

Whether your forefathers were great or small matters not. Do not think of that subject, but live in the conviction that you may become what you wish to become by using well the good you have received, and by creating those essentials that you did not receive. If you have inherited undesirable traits, remember that evil is but valuable power misdirected. Learn to properly direct all your forces and your undesirable traits will be transformed into elements of growth, progress and advancement.

We all have met men and women with remarkable talents who persisted in thinking that they would never amount to anything because there was no genius among their ancestors. But if there had been a genius in the family some time during past generations, the question would be where that genius actually received their genius. If we all have to get greatness from ancestors, where did the first great ancestor get their greatness? There must be a beginning somewhere to every individual attainment, and that beginning might just as well be made by us now. What others could originate in their time, we can originate in our time. The belief that we must inherit greatness from someone in order to attain greatness is without any scientific foundation whatever, and yet there are thousands of most promising minds that remain small simply because they entertain this belief.

To believe that heredity is against you and that you therefore will not accomplish anything worthwhile, is to make your work a wearing process instead of a building process. In consequence, you will not advance, and you will constantly remain in the rear; but the moment you realize that it is in your power to become as much as you may desire, your work and study will begin to promote your own growth and advancement. When you live, think and act in the belief that you can become much, whatever you do will cause you to become more.

Thus all your actions will develop power and ability, and living itself will become a building process.

That man may become great regardless of the fact that there were no great minds among his ancestors many thinkers will admit, provided there are indications of exceptional ability in the man himself, but they entertain no hope if they see nothing in the man himself.

And here we have the second obstacle to the building of a great mind. This obstacle, however must be removed in every mind that aims to rise above the ordinary, because the belief that the average person has nothing in them is the cause of fully three-fourths of the mental inferiority we find in the world. But the new psychology has conclusively demonstrated the fact that the man or woman who has nothing in them does not exist. All minds have the same possibilities, though most of those possibilities may be dormant in the minds of the majority.

The difference between a great mind and a small mind is simply this, that in the former the greater possibilities have come forth into objective action, while in the latter those possibilities are still in subjective inaction. When we say that a man has nothing in them we are contradicting the very principle of existence, because to be a man, a man must have just as much in him as any other man. What is in him may not be in action, and his mentality may appear to be small, but the possibilities of greatness are there. There is a genius somewhere in his mind, because there is a genius in every mind, though in most minds that genius may as yet be asleep.

When every child is taught the great truth that it has unlimited possibilities within its own subconscious mind, and that it can, through the scientific development of those possibilities, become practically what it may desire to become, we shall have laid the foundation for the greatest race of people that the ages have known. But we need not wait for future generations to demonstrate the possibilities of this truth.

Every mind that begins to apply the principle of this truth now may begin to enlarge their mind now, and they may continue this process of enlargement indefinitely. When we have removed the two obstacles mentioned and have established ourselves in the conviction that we have unlimited possibilities within us, more than sufficient to become whatever we may desire, we are ready to proceed with the building of a great mind. To promote the building of a great mind, the two prime essentials, scope and brilliancy, must be constantly kept in the foreground of consciousness. The mind that is not brilliant is of little value even though its scope may be very large. Likewise, the mind that is narrow or circumscribed is extremely limited, however brilliant it may be. A great mind is great both in capacity and ability. It can see practically everything and see through practically everything. To see everything is to have remarkable scope. To see through everything is to have exceptional brilliancy.

To give scope to the mind, every action of mind must be trained to move toward that which is greater than all persons or things. Those feelings or desires that cause the mind to become absorbed in someone thing or group of things, will limit the mental scope. Therefore in love, sympathy, and purpose the sphere of action must be universal. When we live only with that love that centers attention upon a limited number of persons, one of the greatest actions of mind will work in a limited world. When our sympathies go only to a chosen few, the same thing occurs, and when our purpose in life has a personified goal, we keep the mind within the limitations of that personification. To give universality to our feelings and actions, may require considerable training of the mental tendencies, but it is absolutely necessary if we will develop a great mind.

It is only those mental forces that move towards the verge of the limitless in every direction that can cause the mind to transcend limitations; therefore, all the forces of the mind should be given this transcending tendency. To develop mental scope, consciousness must move in every direction, and it must move along right lines, so that no obstacle may be met during that continuous expansive process. Such obstacles, however, are always produced by limitations of thought. Therefore, they may be avoided when all the actions of mind are placed upon a universal scale.

In the mental actions of love, we find many forces, all of which are true in their own places, but all of these forces must be exercised universally; that is, they must act upon a scale that is without bounds in the field of your own consciousness. The mind must go in every direction as far as it possibly can go in that direction, and must act in the conviction that wherever it may go it can go farther still. The understanding must know that there is no obstacle where the mind may seem to cease in its onward action, and that the mind is forever growing, thereby going as far each day as that day's development requires. When this idea is applied to a personal love between man and woman, the feeling of love must be based upon the principle that those two souls have the power to love each other more and more indefinitely; that the larger the love becomes the more lovable will the objects of that love become, and that the consciousness of perfect unity in pure affection increases constantly as the two souls become more and more individualized in their own sublime nature. It is possible to make conjugal love universal and continuous between one man and one woman when the love of each is directed toward the sublime nature of the other.

Through this law, each individual develops through the consciousness of the largeness of the real nature of the other, and the more the two love each other in this universal sense, the more they will see in each other to love. In addition, the minds of both will constantly enlarge in scope, because when love acts upon this larger scale, the whole mind will act upon this larger scale, as there is no stronger power in mind than love.

The love between parent and child can, in like manner, be made universal. In this attitude, the parent will love all of the child, not only the visible person, but the undreamed of wonders that are waiting in that child-mind for expression. The child already loves the parent in this larger sense, and this is one reason why the child-mind lives so much nearer to the limitless, the universal, the ideal and the beautiful. And when the parent will do likewise, there will arise between the two a love that sees more and more to love the more love loves in this larger, sublime sense.

The idea is not only to love the tangible, but also that other something that transcends the tangible that something that appears to the soul in visions, and predicts wonders yet to be. That such a love will expand and enlarge the mind anyone can understand, because practically all the elements of the mind will tend to follow the actions of the love nature, when that nature is exceptionally strong. But we must not imagine that we shall, through this method, love the person less. The fact is, we shall love the person infinitely more, because we shall discern more and more clearly that the person is the visible side of that something in human life that we can only describe as the soul beautiful that something that alone can satisfy the secret longings of the heart.

The love of everything can, through the same law, become universal. Even friendship, which is always supposed to be confined to a small world, may become universal and limitless in the same way; and when it does, you will see more to admire in your friend every day. You will both have entered the boundless in your admiration for each other, and having entered the boundless, you will daily manifest new things from the boundless, and thus become delightfully surprised at each other constantly. The same may be employed in making sympathy universal; that is, never sympathize with the lesser, but always sympathize with the greater. The lesser is combined in the greater, and by sympathizing with the greater, the mind becomes greater.

In the fields of motives, objects, aims and purposes, we find that nearly every mental action is occupying a limited scope, and is acting in such a manner that its own limitations are being perpetuated. This tendency, however, must be removed if a greater mind is to be constructed, because every action of the mind must aim to change itself into a larger action.

To cause every aim or purpose to become universal in its action, the mind must transcend shape, form, space and distance in its consciousness of everything that it may undertake to do. When we confine our thought to so far or so much, we place the mind in a state of limitations, but when we promote every object with a desire to go as far as the largest conception of the present may require, and proceed to attain as much as present capacity can possibly appropriate, we are turning all purposes and aims out upon the boundless sea of attainment. And we shall not only accomplish all that is possible in our present state of development, but we will at the same time constantly enlarge the scope of the mind.

It is absolutely necessary to have a fixed goal whatever our purpose in life may be, but we must never give special shape or size to that goal. We must think of our goal as being too large to be measured, even in the imagination. When we have a goal in mind that is only so and so large, all the creative energies of the mind will limit themselves accordingly. They will create only so and so much, regardless of the fact that they may be able to create many times as much. But when we think of our goal as being too large to be measured, the creative energies will expand to full capacity, and will proceed to work for the largest attainment possible. They will act constantly on the verge of the limitless, and will cause the mind to outdo itself every day.

In the field of desire, the same law should be applied, and applied constantly, as there are no actions in the mind that exercise a greater influence over the destiny of man than that of desire. When desire is low or perverted, everything goes down or goes wrong, but when desire changes for the better, practically everything else in the human system changes to correspond. To train desire to become universal in action, every individual desire should be changed so as to set only for the promotion of growth. Those desires which when fulfilled, do not make for the enlargement of life, are detrimental. The power of all such desires therefore must be changed in their course.

Your object is to become more and achieve more, and to constantly promote that object, development and growth must be perpetual throughout your system. For this reason, every action must have growth, for its purpose, and as every action is the result of some desire, no desire must be permitted that is not conducive to growth. It is not necessary, however, to remove a single desire from the human system to bring about this change, because every desire can be trained to promote the building of a greater life. When every desire is caused to move towards the larger and the greater through the mind's irresistible desire for the larger and the greater, all the creative forces of the mind will move towards the same goal, and will constantly build a greater mind.

The principle is this, that when all the actions of mind are trained to move towards the larger, they will perpetually enlarge. The first essential to the building of a great mind will thereby be promoted. To promote the second essential, mental brilliancy, the actions of mind must be made as high and as fine as possible; that is, the vibrations of the mental life must be in the highest scale attainable. To see through everything the mind will require the very finest rays of mental light, and as this mental light is produced by the vibrations of the actions of mind, these actions should be as high in the scale as we can possibly reach at every stage of our mental ability.

The light of intelligence is created by the mind itself, and the more brilliant this light becomes, the greater will become the powers of intelligence, discernment, insight, understanding, ability, talent and genius. And the power of mind to create a more brilliant mind increases as the mind places itself more and more in the consciousness of the absolute light of universal intelligence. To cause the mind to become more brilliant, all the tendencies of mind should fix their attention upon the highest mental conception of mental brilliancy. Every expression of the mind should be animated with a refining tendency. Every force of the mind should rise towards the absoluteness of mental light.

Those states of mind that tend to magnify the inferior must be eliminated, and this is accomplished by thinking only of the superior that is possible in all things. All mental actions that are critical, depressing or depreciative must be replaced by their constructive opposites, as every action of the mind must concentrate its attention upon the largest and the best in all fields of consciousness. The mind must be kept high in every respect, because the higher in the mental scale the mind functions, the more brilliant will become the mental light.

To increase the rapidity of the vibrations in these higher mental states, creative energy must be supplied in abundance, and to comply with this requirement, all that is necessary is to retain in the human system all the energy that is already created. The human system creates and generates an enormous amount of creative energy every day. Therefore, when all this energy is retained and transmuted into finer mental elements, the mind will be abundantly supplied with those finer energies that can increase both the power and the brilliancy of thought and mind. The mind that is animated with a strong desire to constantly refine itself, and that is thoroughly charged with creative energy, will always be brilliant, and will become more and more brilliant as the laws given above are faithfully and thoroughly applied.

Remove the sting; remove the whine; remove the sigh. They are your enemies. They are never conducive to happiness; and we all live to gain happiness, to give happiness. From every word remove the sting. Speak kindly. To speak kindly and gently to everybody is the mark of a great soul. And it is your privilege to be a great soul. From the tone of your voice remove the whine. Speak with joy. Never complain. The more you complain, the smaller you become, and the fewer will be your friends and opportunities. Speak tenderly, speak sweetly, speak with love. From all the outpourings of your heart, remove the sigh. Be happy and contented always. Let your spirit sing, let your heart dance, let your soul declare the glory of existence, for truly life is beautiful. Every sigh is a burden, a self-inflicted burden. Every whine is a maker of trouble, a forerunner of failure. Every sting is a destroyer of happiness, a dispenser of bitterness. To live in the world of sighs is to be blind to everything that is rich and beautiful. The more we sigh, the less we live, for every sigh leads to weakness, defeat, and death. Remove the sting, remove the whine, remove the sigh. They are not your friends. There is better company waiting for you.

Chapter 14

How Character Determines Constructive Action

All the elements of life are good in themselves; and should produce good results when in action; that is, when the action is properly directed; but when any action is misdirected, evil follows, and this is the only cause of the ills of human existence.

Everything that is wrong in the world has been produced by the perversion and the misuse of the good. Therefore, to eliminate wrong, man must learn to make the proper use of those things that exist in his sphere of action.

The misuse of things comes either from ignorance or lack of character, or both. That person who does not understand the elements and the forces of the world in which they live will make many mistakes, and will make the wrong use of nearly everything unless they are guided by instructions of those who understand.

The leadership of greater minds is therefore necessary to the welfare of the race, but this leadership is not sufficient. Guidance from great minds will help to a limited degree so long as the actions of the individual are simple, but when greater development is sought, with its more complex actions, the individual must learn to master the laws of life for themselves. They can no longer depend upon others. Therefore, though the leadership of greater minds be necessary to the welfare of the race, it is also necessary for that leadership to be used, not for keeping the multitude in a state of simplemindedness and dependence, but for promoting the intelligence of each individual until external guidance is needed no more.

The true purpose of the strong is to promote greater strength in the weak, and not to keep the weak in that state where they are at the mercy of the strong. Our united purpose should be to develop more great men and women, and to do everything possible to lead the many from dependence to independence. Every state of individual attainment is preceded by a childhood period, but this period should not be unnecessarily prolonged, nor will it be, when every strong mind seeks to develop strength in the weak instead of using the weakness of the weak for their own gain.

Those who understand the laws of life may inform the ignorant what to do and what not to do, and may thereby prevent most of the mistakes that the ignorant would otherwise make. But this guidance will not prevent all the mistakes, as experiences demonstrate, because it requires a certain amount of understanding to even properly apply the advice of another.

Those who do not have the understanding will therefore misuse the elements of life at every turn, no matter how well they are guided by wiser persons, while those who do have this understanding will invariably begin to do things without consulting their so-called superiors. It is therefore evident that more understanding for everybody is the remedy, as far as this side of the subject is concerned, but there is also another side.

A great many people go wrong because they do not know any better. To them, a better understanding of life is the path to emancipation. They will be made free when they know the truth, but the majority of those who go wrong do know better. Then why do they go wrong? The cause is lack of character. When you fail to do what you want to do, your character is weak. The same is true when you preach one thing and practice another. When you fail to be as perfect, as good or as ideal as you wish to be, or fail to accomplish what you think that you can accomplish, your character is at fault. It is the character that directs the action of the mind. It is the lack of character, or a weak character that produces misdirections; and when you fail to accomplish what you feel you can accomplish, something is being misdirected.

What you feel that you can do that you have the power to do. Therefore, when you fail to do it, some of the powers of your being are being misdirected. To be influenced to do what you would not do if you were normal, means that your character is weak, and to be affected by surroundings, events, circumstances and conditions against your will indicates the same deficiency.

A strong character is never influenced against their will. They are never disturbed by anything, never become upset, offended or depressed. No one can insult them because they are above small states of mind, and stronger than those things that may tend to produce small states of mind.

All mental tendencies that are antagonistic, critical or resisting indicate a deficiency in character. The desire to criticize becomes less and less as the character is developed. It is the mark of a fine character never to be critical and to mention but rarely the faults of others. A strong character does not resist evil, but uses their strength in building the good. They know that when the light is made strong, the darkness will disappear of itself. A strong character has no fear, never worries and never becomes discouraged. If you are in the hands of worry, your character needs development. The same is true if you have a tendency to submit to fate, give in to adversity, give up in the midst of difficulties, or surrender to failure or wrong.

It may be stated, without any exceptions or modifications whatever, that the more temper, the less character. Anger is always misdirection of energy, but it is the function of character to properly direct all energies. Therefore, there can be no anger when the character is thoroughly developed. The mind that changes easily, that is readily carried away by every new attraction that may appear, and that does not retain a well balanced attitude on any subject lacks character.

A strong character changes gradually, orderly, and only as each step is thoroughly analyzed and found to be a real step forward. The more individuality, the more character, and the more one is oneself, the stronger the character.

Practice being yourself, your very best self, and your very largest self, and your character will be developed. The more one is conscious of flaws and defects, the weaker the character, and the reason is because nearly everything is being misdirected when the character is weak. The strong character is conscious only of the right because such a character is right, and is causing everything in its sphere of action to do right.

To the average person, character is not important as far as this life is concerned; and as most theological systems have declared that it was repentance and not character that would insure human welfare in the world to come, the development of character has naturally been neglected. But when we realize that it is character that determines whether our actions in daily life are to go right or wrong and that every mistake is due to a lack of character, we shall feel that the subject requires attention.

It is the power of character that directs everything that is done in the human system or by the human system.

Character is the channel through which all expressions must pass. It is character that gives human life its tone, its color and its quality, and it is character that determines whether our talents and faculties are to be their best or not. The man or woman who has a well developed character is not simply good. They are good for something, because they have the power to turn all their energies to good account.

A strong character not only turns all the elements and energies of life to good account, but has the power to hold the mind in the right attitude during the most trying moments of life, so that they will not make mistakes nor fall a victim to insidious temptation. A strong character will keep all the faculties and forces of life moving in the right direction, no matter what obstacles we may meet in the way. We shall turn neither to the right nor to the left, but will continue to move directly towards the goal we have in view, and will reach that goal without fail.

Thousands of people resolve every year to press on to higher attainments and greater achievements. They begin very well, but before long they are turned off the track. They are misled or switched off by counter attractions. They have not the character to keep right on until they have accomplished what they originally set out to do.

True, it is sometimes wisdom to change one's plans, but it is only lack of character to change one's plans without reason, simply because there is a change of circumstance. To change with every circumstance is to drift with the stream of circumstance and those who drift can only live the life of a log. They will be victim of every external change that they may meet. They will control little or nothing, and will accomplish little or nothing.

We all can develop the power to control circumstances or rather to cause all circumstances to work with us and for us in the promotion of the purpose we have in view; and this power is character. Never permit circumstances to change your plans, but give so much character to your plans that they will change circumstances. Give so much character to the current of your work that all things will be drawn into that current, and that which at first was but a tiny rivulet, will thus be swelled into a mighty, majestic stream.

When the various forces of the system are properly directed and properly employed, the development of the entire mentality will be promoted; and this means greatness. The power that directs the forces of the system is character, and it is character that causes the mind to use those forces in the best and most instructive manner.

There must be character before there can be true greatness, because any deficiency in character causes energy to be wasted and misdirected. It is therefore evident that the almost universal neglect in the development of character is one of the chief reasons why great men and women are not as numerous as we should wish them to be.

Many may argue, however, that great minds do not always have good characters, and also that some of our best characters fail to manifest exceptional ability. But we must remember that there is a vast difference between that phase of character that simply tries to follow the moral law, and real character the character that actually is justice, virtue and truth. Then we must also remember that character does not mean simply obedience to a certain group of laws, but the power to use properly all the laws of life. That person who uses mental laws properly, but fails to comply with moral laws does not possess a complete character. Nevertheless, the character of this person is just as good as that of the person who follows moral laws while constantly violating mental laws.

In the study of character, it is very important to know that the violation of mental laws is just as detrimental as the violation of moral laws, though we have been in the habit of condemning the latter and excusing the former. That person who uses properly the mental laws, will to a degree promote the development of the mind even though they may neglect the moral laws; and this accounts for the fact that a number of minds have attained a fair degree of greatness in spite of their moral weakness. But it is a fact of extreme importance, that those minds who attain greatness in spite of their moral weakness could become two or three times as great if they had also developed moral strength.

That person who complies with the mental laws but who violates the moral laws, wastes fully one-half of the energies of their mind, and sometimes more. Their attainment and achievement will, therefore, be less than one-half of what they might be if they had moral character as well as mental character. The same is true, however, of that person who complies with the moral laws, but who violates the mental laws; fully one-half of their energy is wasted and misdirected. This explains why the so-called good characters are not any more brilliant than the rest, for though they may be morally good, they are not always mentally good; that is, they do not use their minds according to the laws of mind, and therefore cannot rise above the level of the ordinary.

The true character tries to turn all the energies of the system into the best and most constructive channels, and it is the mark of a real character when all the various parts of the being of man are working together harmoniously for the building of greatness in mind and soul. When the character is weak, there is more or less conflict among the mental actions. Certain actions have a tendency to work for one thing, while other actions are tending to produce the very opposite. The same is true of the desires. A character that lacks development will desire one thing today, and something else tomorrow.

Plans will change constantly, and little or nothing will be accomplished. In the strong character, however, all actions work in harmony and all actions are constructive. And this is natural because it is the one supreme function of character to make all actions in the human system constructive to make every force in the human life a building force.

Be good and kind to everybody and the world will be kind to you. There may be occasional exceptions to this rule, but when they come pass them by and they will not come again.

Ideals need the best of care. Weeds can grow without attention, but not so with the roses.

Not all minds are pure that think they are. Many of them are simply dwarfed.

It does not pay to lose faith in anybody. It is better to have faith in everybody and be deceived occasionally than to mistrust everybody and be deceived almost constantly.

When you meet a person who does not look well, call their attention to the sunny side of things, and aim to say something that will give them new interest and new life. You will thereby nip in the bud many a threatening evil, and carry healing with you wherever you go.

Chapter 15

The Art of Building Character

Character is developed by training all the forces and elements of life to act constructively in those spheres for which they were created, and to express themselves in those actions only that promote the original purpose of the being of man. Every part of the human system has a purpose of its own a purpose that it was created to fulfill.

When those elements that belong to each part express themselves in such a way that the purpose of that part is constantly promoted, all actions are right; and it is character that causes those actions to be right. Character is therefore indispensable, no matter what one's object in life may be. Character is the proper direction of all things, and the proper use of all things in the human system. And the proper use of anything is that use that promotes the purpose for which that particular thing was created.

To develop character it is therefore necessary to know what life is for, to know what actions promote the purpose of that life, and to know what actions retard that purpose. When the secret of right action is discovered, and every part of man is steadily trained in the expression of right action, character may be developed.

But whatever is done, character must be applied in its fullest capacity. It is only through this full use, right use and constant use that anything may be perpetuated or developed. Character develops through a constant effort to cause every action in the human system to be a right action; that is, a constructive action, or an action that promotes the purpose of that part of the system in which the action takes place. This is natural because since character is the power of right action, every effort to extend the scope of right action will increase the power of character.

To have character is to have the power to promote what you know to be the purpose of life, and to be able to do the right when you know the right. To have character is to know the right, and to be so well established in the doing of the right that nothing in the world can turn you into the wrong. The first essential is therefore to know the right; to be able to select the right; to have that understanding that can instinctively choose the proper course of action, and that knows how each force and element of life is to be directed so that the original purpose of human life will be fulfilled.

The understanding of the laws of life will give this first essential in an intellectual sense, and this is necessary in the beginning; but when character develops, one inwardly knows what is right without stopping to reason about it. The development of character enables one to feel what is right and what course to pursue regardless of exterior conditions or intellectual evidence. The intellect discerns that the right is that which promotes growth and development; character inwardly feels that the right leads to greater things and to better things, and that the wrong leads invariably to the inferior and the lesser.

The presence of character produces a consciousness of growth throughout the system; and the stronger the character, the more keenly one can feel that everything is being reconstructed, refined, perfected and developed into something superior, This is but natural because when the character is strong, everything in the system is expressed in right action, and the right action of anything causes the steady development of that particular thing. To distinguish between the right and the wrong becomes simplicity itself when one knows that the right promotes growth, while the wrong retards growth. Continuous advancement is the purpose of life; therefore, to live the right life is to live that life that promotes progress and growth, development and advancement in everything that pertains to life. For this reason, that action that promotes growth is in harmony with life itself, and must consequently be right. But that action that retards growth is at variance with life; therefore it is wrong; and wrong for that reason alone.

Everything that promotes human advancement is right. Everything that interferes with human advancement is wrong.

Here we have the basis of a system of ethics that is thoroughly complete, and so simple to live that nobody need err in the least. An intellectual understanding of the laws of life will enable anyone to know what action promotes growth and what action retards growth, but as character develops, one can feel the difference between right and wrong action in one's own system, because the consciousness of right becomes so keen that anything that is not right is discerned at once. It is therefore evident that the power to distinguish the right from the wrong in every instance will come only through the development of character.

No matter how brilliant one may be intellectually, they cannot truly know the right until they have a strong character. The external understanding of the right can be misled, but the consciousness of the right is never mistaken; and this consciousness develops only as character develops.

The second essential is to create a subconscious desire for the right a desire so deep and so strong that nothing can tempt the mind to enter into the wrong. When this desire is developed, one feels a natural preference for the right; to prefer the right, under all circumstances becomes second nature, while every desire for the wrong will disappear completely. When every atom in one's being begins to desire the right, the entire system will establish itself in the right attitude, and right action will become the normal action in every force, function and faculty. In addition, this same desire will produce mental tendencies that contain the power of right action, which always means constructive action.

It is a well known fact that all the forces and energies of the system, and all the movements of mind follow mental tendencies; therefore, when the mental tendencies are right actions, everything that takes place in the system will produce right action; and everything will be properly directed. The desire for the right may be developed by constantly thinking about the right with deep feeling. Every thought that has depth, therefore, will impress itself upon the subconscious, and when that thought is inspired with a strong desire for the right, the conscious impression will convey the right to the subconscious.

Every impression that enters the subconscious will cause the subconscious to bring forth a harvest of that which the impression conveyed; therefore, when the right is constantly held in mind with deep feeling, the right thought will soon become the strongest in the mind; and our desires are the results of our strongest thoughts. You always desire that which is indicated in your strongest thought. You can therefore change those desires completely by thinking with deep feeling about that which you want to desire. No desire should be destroyed. All desires should be transmuted into the desire for the right, and when you subconsciously desire the right, every action in your being will be a right action.

The two fundamental essentials, therefore, to the development of character are to know the right and to desire the right, but the term "right" as employed here must not be confounded with that conception of right which includes only a few of the moral laws. To be right according to the viewpoint of completeness, is to be in harmony with all the principles of life, and all the laws of the present sphere of human existence.

To know the right, it is necessary not simply to memorize rules that other minds have formulated, but to inwardly discern what life is for, and what mode of thought and action is conducive to the realization of that which is in life. To desire the right, according to this view of the right, the mind must actually feel the very soul of right action, and must be in such perfect touch with the universal movement of right action, that all lesser and imperfect desires are completely swallowed up in the one desire the desire that desires all that is in life, and all that is in perfect harmony with that which is in life.

It is the truth, that when we come into perfect touch with the greater, we cease to desire the lesser, and the closer we get to the one real desire, the less we care for our mistaken desires. Therefore, to remove an undesirable desire, the course is not to resist that desire, but to cultivate a greater and a better desire, along the same line. In this connection, we must remember that the adoption of a greater desire does not compel us to sacrifice those things that we gain from the lesser desires. He who adopts the greater loses nothing, but is on the way to the gaining of everything.

To know the right and to desire the right, according to the complete significance of the right we must interiorly discern the very right itself.

We cannot depend upon another's definition of the right, but must know fully the spirit of the right with our own faculties. That faculty that knows and feels the right, and that naturally knows and desires the right is character. Therefore, it is through the development of character that each individual will know for themselves how to live, think and act in perfect harmony with the laws of all life. When the consciousness of right action has been attained, a clear mental picture should be deeply impressed upon mind and every desire should be focused upon that picture. This concentration should be made as strong as possible, so that all the energies of the system are not only aroused, but caused to move towards the ideal of right action. And by right action, we mean that action that is thoroughly constructive, that builds for greater things and greater things only. Everything is right that builds for greater things. If it were not right, it could not produce the greater.

To clearly picture upon the mind the image of right action, and to concentrate with strong desire the whole attention upon that mental image, will cause all the tendencies of mind to move in the same direction. There will therefore be perfect harmony of mental action, and that action will be right action, because everything that moves towards the right must be right.

This mental picture of right action should always be complete; that is, one's mental conception of the right should not be confined to certain parts of the system only, but should include every action conceivable in the being of man. That person who pictures themselves as virtuous, but forgets to picture themselves above anger, fear and worry, is not forming a complete picture or ideal of the right. They are not giving the creative energies of the system a perfect pattern; the character that those energies are to build will therefore be one-sided and weak.

First ask yourself what you would have all the energies, powers, functions and faculties in your system do. Answer that question in the best manner possible, and upon that answer, base your picture of right action. Whenever a new line of action is undertaken, the mind should continue in that original line of action until the object in view has been reached. To do this in all things, even in trivial matters, will not only cause every action to produce the intended results, but real character will steadily be made stronger thereby. The habit of giving up when the present task is half finished and try something else is one of the chief causes of failure. The development of a strong character, however, will remove this habit completely.

To constantly think of the highest and the greatest results that could possibly follow the promotion of any undertaking or line of action will aid remarkably in causing the mind to keep on. To expect much from what we are doing now is to create a strong desire to press on towards the goal in view. To press on towards the goal in view is to reach the goal, and to reach the goal is to get what we expected.

An essential of great importance in the building of character is the proper conception of the ideal. No mind can rise higher than its ideals, but every mind can realize its ideals no matter how high they may be. Our ideals therefore cannot be too high. The ideal should not only be a little better than the present real, but should be perfection itself. Have nothing but absolute perfection in all things as the standard and the goal, and never think of your goal as anything less.

Do not simply aim to improve yourself in just one more degree. Aim to reach absolute perfection in all your attainments and all your achievements, and make that desire so strong that every atom in your being thrills with its power. To form all one's ideals in accordance with one's mental conception of absolute perfection, will cause the mind to live above the world of the ordinary, and this is extremely important in the building of character. A great character cannot be developed so long as the mind continues to dwell on the ordinary, the trivial or the superficial. Neither can true quality and true worth find expression so long as thought continues on the common plane; and the life that does not continue to grow into higher quality and greater worth has not begun to live.

When character is highly developed, both the personality and the mentality will feel the stamp of quality and worth. High mental color will be given to every characteristic, and the nature of man will cease to be simply human. It will actually be more. In building character, special attention must be given to hereditary tendencies or those traits of character that are born in us.

But as all such traits are subconscious, they can be changed or removed by directing the subconscious to produce the opposite characteristics or tendencies. It matters not in the least what we may have inherited from our ancestors. If we want to change those things, we can do so. The subconscious will not only respond to any direction that we may make, but is fully capable of doing anything in the world of mind or character that we may desire to have done.

Examine the tendencies of your mind and character, and fix clearly in consciousness which ones you wish to remove and which ones you wish to retain. Those that you wish to retain should be made strong by daily directing the subconscious to give those tendencies more life, more power and more stability. To remove those tendencies that you do not wish to retain, forget them. Do not resist them nor try to force them out of the mind. Simply forget them and direct the subconscious to create and establish new tendencies that are directly opposite to the nature of the ones that you wish to remove. Build up those qualities that constitute real character, and every bad trait that you have inherited from your ancestors will disappear.

To build up those qualities, picture in your mind the highest conceptions of those qualities that you can possibly form; then impress those conceptions and ideas upon tile subconscious. Such impressions should be formed daily and especially before going to sleep as the building process in the subconscious is more perfect during sleep.

By impressing the idea of spotless virtue upon the subconscious every day for a few months, your moral tendencies will become so strong that nothing can tempt you to do what you know to be wrong. Not that physical desire will disappear; we do not want any natural desire to disappear, but your control of those desires will be so complete that you can follow them or refuse to follow them just as you choose. And your desire to remain absolutely free from all wrong will become so strong that nothing can induce you to do what your finer nature does not wish to have done.

There are millions of people who are morally weak in spite of the fact that they do not wish to be, but if these people would employ this simple method, their weakness would soon disappear, because by impressing the idea of spotless virtue upon the subconscious, the subconscious will produce and express in the personality the power of virtue; and if this process is continued for some time, the power of virtue in the person will become so strong that it can overcome and annihilate instantly every temptation that may appear.

Impress upon the subconscious the idea of absolute justice, and your consciousness of justice will steadily develop until you can discriminate perfectly between the right and the wrong in every imaginable transaction. Whatever quality you wish to develop in your character, you can increase its worth and its power steadily by applying this subconscious law; that is, what is impressed upon the subconscious will be expressed through the personality, and since the seed can bring forth ten, thirty, sixty and a hundred fold, one tiny impression, therefore, may have the power to bring forth a great and powerful expression.

Everything multiplies in the subconscious, whether it be good or otherwise. Therefore, by taking advantage of this law and giving to the subconscious only those ideas and desires that have quality and worth, we place ourselves in the path of perpetual increase of everything good that the heart may desire.

The two predominating factors in character are justice and virtue. The former gives each element in life its proper place. The latter turns each element to proper use. The consciousness of justice is developed through the realization of the fact that nothing can use what is not its own. To try to use what is not one's own will result in misuse. When the consciousness of justice is thoroughly developed, everything in the human system will be properly placed. That very power of the mind that feels justice the true placing of things will cause all things within man to be properly placed. And when justice rules among all things in the interior life of man, that man will naturally be just to all things in the exterior life.

It is not possible for any person to deal justly with people and matters in the external world until they have attained the consciousness of justice within themselves. They may think they are just, or may try to be just, but their dealings will not be absolutely just until they can feel justice in their own life. To feel justice within oneself is to keep the entire system in a state of equilibrium. The mentality will be balanced and no force or element will be misplaced. It is therefore something for which we may work with great profit.

To be virtuous in the complete sense of the term, is to use all things properly, and the proper use of things is that use that works for greater things. Virtue is therefore applicable to every force, function and faculty in the being of man, but in its application there must be no desire or effort to suppress or destroy. Virtue means use right use never suppression. When things cannot be used in their usual channels, the energies in action within those things should be turned in their courses and used elsewhere. When creative energy cannot be properly applied physically, it should be employed metaphysically; and all energy can be drawn into mind for the purpose of building up states, faculties, talents or powers. (Practical methods through which this may be accomplished will be given in the next chapter.)

When a certain desire cannot be expressed with good results in its present purpose, the power of that desire should be changed and caused to desire something else something of value that can be carried out now. The power of that desire therefore is not lost, neither is enjoyment sacrificed, because all constructive forces, give joy to the mind. "And the greatest of joys shall be the joy of going on."

The desire for complete virtue is developed through the realization of the fact that the greatest good comes only when each part fulfils, physically and metaphysically, what nature intended. In the application of virtue, the purpose of nature may be fulfilled metaphysically when the physical channel does not permit of true expression at the time; though when physical expression may be secured, the metaphysical action should always be in evidence, because the greatest results always follow when physical and metaphysical actions are perfectly combined.

In the building of character, the two principal objects in view should be the strong and the beautiful. The character that is strong but not beautiful may have force, but cannot use that force in the building of the superior. The character that is beautiful but not strong will not have sufficient power to carry out its lofty ideals. It is the strong and the beautiful combined that builds mind and character, and that brings into being the superior man.

When the creative energies are daily transmuted, and turned into muscle, brain and mind, a virtuous life can be lived without inconvenience. Besides, the body will be healthier, the personality stronger and the mind more brilliant.

Hold yourself constantly in a positive, masterful attitude, and fill that attitude with kindness. The result will be that remarkable something that people call personal magnetism.

Creative energy when retained in the system will give vigor to the body, sparkle to the eye, and genius to the brain.

There is enough power in any man to enable him to realize all his desires and reach the highest good he has in view. It is only necessary that all of this power be constructively applied.

Chapter 16

The Creative Forces in Man

The human system may well be termed a living dynamo, as the amount of energy, especially creative energy, generated in the mind and personality of man is simply enormous. If we should try to measure the amount produced in the average healthy person, we should become overwhelmed with surprise; though we should naturally become even more surprised after learning how much power nature gives to man, and then finding that he applies only a fraction of it. We shall soon see the reason for this, however, and learn exactly why all of this vast amount of energy is not turned to practical use.

What is called creative energy in its broadest, largest sense, is that power in man that creates, forms or reproduces anywhere in the human system, and it divides itself into a number of groups, each one having its special function. One group creates thought, another brain cells, another nerve tissues, another muscular tissues, another manufactures the various juices of the system, another produces ideas, another creates talent and ability, another reproduces the species, and a number of other groups produce the various chemical formations in the system. We therefore have all kinds of creative processes going on in the human system, and corresponding energies with which these processes are continued.

One of the most interesting facts in connection with this study is that Nature generates more energy for each group than is required for normal functioning through its particular channel. In consequence, we find a great deal of surplus energy throughout the system. Each function supplies a certain percentage, and as it is not used by the function itself, the larger part of it naturally goes to waste. And here is where our subject becomes decidedly important. All kinds of creative energy are so closely related that they can be transformed and transmuted into each other. What is wasted in one function can therefore be turned to actual use in another function.

An extra supply can thereby be secured for the creation of thoughts and ideas if such should be necessary, or an extra supply can be secured for the manufacture of the different juices of the system, or for the increase of muscular activity or functional activity in anyone of the vital organs. Each group will readily change and combine with any other group, thus producing additional power in any part of the system at any time.

More than half of the energy generated in the human system is surplus energy, and is not needed for normal functioning, either in mind or body, though there are many personalities that generate so much energy that fully three-fourths of the amount generated is surplus. The question is therefore what shall be done with this surplus energy, and how any amount of it can be applied through any special function or faculty desired? If a person can accomplish a great deal, sometimes remarkable things by only using a fraction of his energy, it is evident that he could accomplish a great deal more if some means could be found through which he might apply all of his energy. In fact, if such means were found, his working capacity, as well as his ability, might be doubled or trebled, and his achievements increased in proportion.

If a certain amount of energy produces a certain degree of working capacity, twice as much energy would naturally double that working capacity, and this has been demonstrated a number of times. A great many people, who have tried to transmute their creative energies, and direct those energies into some special faculty, have found that the working capacity of that faculty has been increased for the time being to a remarkable degree, but this is not the only result secured. The same process will also increase the brilliancy of the mind, and here let us remember that genius, in most instances, is accounted for by the fact that practically all of the surplus energy of the personality flows naturally into that faculty where genius is in evidence.

To illustrate the idea further, take two men of equal personal power. Let one of them permit his surplus energy to flow into the different functions as usual, giving over a part to normal requirements, and the other to mere waste. We shall not find this man doing anything extraordinary.

But let the other man give over to normal functions only what is actually required, and then turn the remainder into his mind, or those parts of his mind that are being applied in his work. We shall find in this second case that ability will rapidly increase, and that in the course of time actual genius be developed. That genius could be developed by this process in every case, has not been demonstrated, though it is quite probable that it could be demonstrated without a single exception. However, no individual can turn surplus energy into any faculty without becoming more able, more efficient and more competent in that faculty.

To learn how this process can be carried out successfully under any circumstances is therefore thoroughly worthwhile. To proceed, we must first learn how these different groups of creative energy naturally act; and we find that each group goes, either naturally or through some habit, into its own part of mind or body; in other words, we find in the human system, a number of streams of energy flowing in different directions, performing certain functions on their way, using up a fraction of their power in that manner, the rest flowing off into waste. Knowing this, the problem before us is to learn how to redirect those streams of energy so as to turn them to practical use where they can be used now, and thus not only prevent waste, but increase the result of our efforts in proportion.

In brief, we want to know how we can take up all surplus energy, that is, all energy that remains after normal functioning has been provided for, and use that surplus in promoting more successfully the work in which we are engaged. And to learn how to do this, we must study the art of transmutation.

What we call transmutation is not some mysterious something that only a few have the power to understand and apply, but one of the simplest things in Nature, as well as one of the most constant of her processes. Nature is continually transmuting her energies, and it is in this manner that extraordinary results are found anywhere in the realms of Nature, or anywhere in human nature where unconscious actions along greater lines have been the cause.

Whenever any individual has accomplished more than usual, it is the law of transmutation through which the unusual has been secured. The use of the law may have been unconscious, though everything that is applied in past and unconsciously, can be applied fully and thoroughly through conscious action. When anyone is using his mind continually along a certain line, and is so thoroughly absorbed in that line of action that it takes up his whole attention, we invariably find that the mind while in that condition, draws an extra amount of energy from the body. Sometimes it draws too much, so that every desire of the body is, for the time being, suspended and the vitality of the different physical organs decreased below normal.

A man while in this condition frequently loses desire for food, and we all know of inventors who have been so absorbed in their experiments that they have neither taken nor desired food for days. We have also found the same condition in many others, especially among authors, composers and artists, where the mind was given over completely to the subject at hand. And what is the cause but transmutation? When the mind takes up for its own use a great deal of the energy naturally employed in the body, the power of normal functioning will have so decreased that the desire for normal functioning will have practically disappeared for the time being.

Another illustration with which we are all familiar, is where every natural desire of the body disappears completely, for a time, when the mind is completely absorbed in some entirely different desire; and here we find the law that underlies the cure of all habits. If you would turn your mind upon some desire that was directly opposite to the desire that feeds your habit, and if you would give over your whole attention to that opposite desire, you would soon draw all the energy away from that desire which perpetuates the habit.

The habit in question therefore would soon die of starvation. In the same way, people who are inclined to be materialistic could overcome that tendency entirely by concentrating attention constantly and thoroughly upon the idealistic side of life. In this case, those forces of the system that are perpetuating materialistic conditions would be transmuted into finer energies, and would thereby proceed to build up idealistic or more refined conditions of body, mind and personality.

Both Nature and human experience are full of illustrations of transmutation, so that we are not dealing in this study with something that lies outside of usual human activity. We are dealing with something that is taking place in our systems every minute, and we want to learn how to take better control of this something, so that we can apply the underlying law to the best advantage. In learning to apply the law of transmutation, our first purpose should be to employ all surplus energy either in promoting our work or in developing faculties and talents.

This process alone would practically double the working capacity of any mind, and would steadily increase ability and talent; and also to turn energy to good account that cannot be used in its own channel now. To illustrate, suppose you have a desire for a certain physical or mental action, and you know that it would not be possible to carry out that desire at the time. Instead of permitting the energy that is active in that desire to go to waste, you would turn that energy into some other channel where it could be used to advantage now.

Our second purpose should be to direct all surplus energy into the brain and the mind in case we had more energy in our body than we could use, or that was required for physical functioning, and thereby become stronger and more efficient in all mental activities. Our third purpose should be to transmute all reproductive energy into talent and genius when there was no need of that energy in its own particular sphere. And in this connection, it is well to mention the fact that a man who is morally clean, other things being equal, has in every instance, greater agility, greater capacity, and greater endurance by far than the man who is not. While the latter is wasting his creative energies in useless pleasures, as well as in disease producing habits, the former is turning all of his creative energy into ability and genius, and the result is evident.

In carrying out these three purposes we can prevent all waste of mental and personal power. We can control our desires completely; we can eliminate impurity, and we can turn life and power into channels that will invariably result in greater mental power and brilliancy, if not marked ability and rare genius. To experiment, turn your whole attention upon your mind for a few minutes, and desire gently to draw all your surplus energy into the field of mental action.

Then permit yourself to think along those lines where the mind is inclined to be most active. In a few moments you will discover the coming of new ideas and in many instances, you will for several hours receive ideas that are brighter and more valuable than what you have received for some time. Repeat the process later, and again and again for many days in succession, and it will be strange indeed, if you do not finally secure a group of ideas that will be worth a great deal in your special line of thought or work.

Whenever you feel a great deal of energy in your system, and try to direct it into the mind, you will have the same result. Ideas will come quick and rapidly, and among them all you will surely find a few that have exceptional merit.

In learning the art of transmutation, the first essential is to train your mind to think that all surplus energy is being turned into the channel you have decided upon; that is, if you are a business man, you naturally will want all your surplus energy to accumulate in your business faculties. To secure this result, think constantly of your surplus energy as flowing into those faculties. This mode of thinking will soon give your energies the habit of doing what you desire to have done. It is a well-known law, that if we continue to think deeply and persistently along a certain line, Nature will gradually take up that thought and carry it out. Another law of importance in this connection is that if we concentrate attention upon a certain faculty or upon a certain part of the system, we create a tendency among our energies to flow towards that faculty or part. We understand therefore the value of constantly hearing in mind the idea that we wish to realize. What we constantly impress upon the mind through our thoughts and desires, finally becomes a subconscious habit, and when any line of action becomes a subconscious habit, it acts automatically; that is it works of itself.

Before taking up this practice, however, it is necessary to determine positively what you actually desire your surplus energy to do. You must know what you want. Then continue to want what you want with all the power of desire that you can arouse. Most minds fail in this respect. They do not know with a certainty what they wish to accomplish or perfect. Their energies therefore are drawn into one channel today and another tomorrow, and nothing is finished. If you are an inventor, train your mind to think that all your surplus energy is constantly flowing into your faculties of invention. If you are a writer, train your mind to think that all your surplus energy is flowing into your literary talents; or whatever it is that you may be doing or want to do, direct your energy accordingly. You will soon find that you will increase in power, ability, and capacity along the lines of your choice, and if you continue this process all through life, your ability will continue to increase, no matter how long you may live.

The second essential is to desire deeply and persistently that all your surplus energy shall flow into those functions or faculties that you have selected for greater work. Wherever your desire is directed, there the force of your system will also tend to go, and herein we find another reason why persistent desire has such extreme value. The use of desire in this connection, however, must always be deep and calm, and never excited or over wrought.

The third essential is to place your mind in what may be termed the psychological field, and while acting in that field, to concentrate upon that part or faculty where you want your surplus energy to accumulate. This essential or process constitutes the real art of transmutation, though it is by no means the easiest to acquire. To master this method a great deal of practice will be required, but whenever you can place your mind in the psychological field and concentrate subjectively upon any part of your system where you want surplus energy to accumulate, all your surplus energy positively will accumulate in that part within a few moments' time.

Through the same process, you can annihilate any desire instantaneously, and change all the energy of that desire into some other force. You can also, in the same way, reach your latent or dormant energies, and draw all of those energies into any channel where high order of activity is desired; in fact, through this method, you can practically take full possession of all the power, active or latent, in your system, and use it in any way that you may wish.

That you should, after you learn to apply this method successfully, become highly efficient in your work, is therefore evident, though this is not all. Extraordinary capacity, mental brilliancy and genius can positively be developed through the constant use of this method, provided, however, that nothing is done, either in thought, life or conduct, to interfere with the underlying law of the process.

To place your mind in the psychological field, try to turn your conscious actions into what may be termed the finer depths of the personality; that is, try to become conscious of your deeper life; try to feel the undercurrents of mind and thought and consciousness, and try to act in perfect mental contact with those deep, underlying forces of personality and mentality that lie at the foundation of your conscious activity.

An illustration in this connection will be found valuable. When you listen to music that seems to touch your soul, so that you can feel the vibrations of its harmony thrill every atom of your being, you are in the psychological field. You are alive in another and a finer mental world, a mental world that permeates your entire personal existence. You are also in the psychological field when you are stirred by some emotion to the very depth of your innermost life. A deepening of thought, feeling, life and desire will take the mind, more or less, into the psychological field; and whenever the mind begins to act in that field, you should concentrate your attention upon that faculty or part of your system where you wish extra energy to accumulate.

Make your concentration alive, so to speak, with interest, and make every action of that concentration as deep as possible, and all your surplus energy will positively flow towards the point of concentration. The power of this process can be demonstrated in a very simple manner. Place your mind in the psychological field, and then concentrate subjectively upon your hand, arousing at the time a deep desire for the increase of circulation in your hand. In a few moments, the veins on the back of your hand will be filled to capacity, and your hand, even though it might have been cold in the beginning, will become comfortably warm. Another experiment that is not only interesting in this connection, but may prove very valuable, is to concentrate in this same manner upon your digestive organs, in case the digestive process is retarded. You will soon feel more energy accumulating throughout the abdominal region, and any unpleasant sensation that you might have felt on account of indigestion will disappear entirely; in fact, even chronic indigestion can be cured in this way if the method is applied for a few minutes immediately before and after each meal.

The idea is simply this, that when you give extra energy to an organ, it will be able to perform its function properly, and whenever any function is performed properly, any ailment that might have existed in the organ of that function, will disappear. A number of similar experiments may be tried, all of which will prove equally interesting, and besides, will train the mind to apply this great law of transmutation.

The following effects may be secured through transmutation: Working capacity in any part of the personality or mentality may be constantly increased; all the energy generated in the system may be employed practically and successfully; the mind may be made more brilliant, as it is an extraordinary amount of creative energy going into the mind that invariably causes mental brilliancy. Any faculty selected can be given so much of this surplus energy of the system, that it will almost from the beginning, manifest an increase in ability, and will, in the course of time, manifest rare talent and even genius.

Moral purity may become second nature, as all that energy that was previously squandered in impure thought, impure desire or impure action can be transmuted readily, and applied in the building of a more vigorous personality and a more brilliant mind. A better control of all the forces of the personality may be obtained, and that mysterious something called personal magnetism may be acquired to a remarkable degree. The attainment or accumulation of personal magnetism is something that we all desire, and the reason why is evident. What is called personal magnetism is the result of an extra amount of creative energy stored up in the personality and caused to circulate harmoniously throughout the personality. And the effect of this power is very marked. People who possess it are invariably more attractive, regardless of shape and form, and they are invariably more successful, no matter what their work may be.

Hundreds of illustrations could be mentioned proving conclusively the extreme value of personal magnetism, though we are all so familiar with the fact that we do not require proof in the matter. What we want to know is what this power really is, how it may be produced, and why those who possess it have such a great advantage over those who do not possess it. To illustrate, we may take two women who look alike in every respect; who have the same character and the same mentality, and who are equals in every respect but one, and that is that the one has personal magnetism while the other has not. But we need not be told of the fact. The woman who does not possess this power cannot be compared in any way with the woman who does possess it. The woman who does possess this power is far more attractive, far more brilliant, and seems to possess qualities of far greater worth; and the reason is that personal magnetism tends to heighten the effect of everything that you are, or that you may do.

If we should compare two business men of equal ability and power, the one having personal magnetism and the other one not, we should find similar results. The one having this power would be far more successful, regardless of the fact that his ability and power in other respects were the same as his associate. Even men of ordinary ability succeed remarkably when they have personal magnetism; and we all know of women who are as plain as nature could make them, and yet being in possession of personal magnetism, are counted among the most attractive to be found anywhere.

The most ordinary human form becomes a thing of beauty if made alive with this mysterious power, and a personality that had no attraction whatever, will fascinate everybody to a marked degree if charged with this power. We all know this to be true; we are therefore deeply interested to know how this power might be secured. In the first place, we must remember that personal magnetism does not exercise its power by controlling or influencing other minds as many have supposed. The fact is if you try to influence others, you will lose this power, and lose it completely no matter how strong it may be at the present time.

The secret of personal magnetism simply lies in the fact that it tends to bring out into expression the best that is in you, and tends to heighten the effect of every expression; or, in other words, it causes every expression to act to the best advantage; though we find this power exercising its peculiar effect not only in the personality and in the mentality of the individual, but also in his work.

When a musician has this power, his music charms to a far greater degree than if he does not possess it. There is something not only in the singing voice, but also in the speaking voice that indicates the absence or presence of this power. What it is no one can exactly describe, but we know it is there, and it adds immeasurably to the quality of what is expressed through the voice.

In the field of literature we find the action of this power to be very marked. A writer who does not possess this mysterious force may write well, but there is something lacking in what he has written. On the other hand, if he has this power, he gives not only added charm to what he has written, but his ideas invariably appear to be more brilliant. In fact, there seems to be a power in everything he writes that is not ordinarily found on the printed page.

On the stage this power is one of the principal factors, and we frequently find that the only difference between the good actor and a poor one, is the possession of a high degree of personal magnetism. No matter how well an actor may act, if he lacks in this power, he cannot succeed on the stage. When we go into the social world, we find the same fact.

Those who possess this power are invariably the favorites, even though they may be lacking in many other qualities. In the business world we find in every case that a man who is lacking in personal magnetism is at a disadvantage, while the one who has an abundance of this power will have no difficulty, other things being equal, in working himself to the fore.

In a deeper study of this force, we find that it affects every movement of the body, every action of the mind, and every feeling or expression that mind and personality may produce; that is, it seems to give something additional to every action or movement, and makes everything about the individual more attractive. We might say that this force sets off everything about the person to a greater advantage. This power therefore does not act directly upon others, but acts directly upon the one who has it, and thereby makes the individual more striking, as well as more attractive, both in appearance and in conduct.

What is good in you is made better if charged with this force, and every desirable effort that you may make produces a better effect in proportion. Added charm, added attractiveness and added efficiency these invariably follow where the individual is in possession of a marked degree of this power. That which is beautiful is many times as beautiful where personal magnetism is in action, and that which is brilliant, becomes far more brilliant when combined with this mysterious force.

Many people are born with it and apply it unconsciously, though the majority who have it, have acquired it through various forms of training. Any system of, exercise that tends to harmonize the movements of the body, will tend to increase to some extent the power of this force; though when such exercises are combined with the transmutation of creative energy, the results will be far greater. The reason for this is found in the fact that what is called personal magnetism is the result of a great deal of creative energy held in the system, or transmuted into harmonious muscular or mental activity.

The development of this power depends upon the proper training of the body in rhythmic movements, and the training of the surplus energy in the system to act harmoniously along the lines of constructive action in mind and body. A very important essential is to cultivate poise, which means peace and power combined. Try to feel deeply calm throughout your entire system, and at the same time, try to give full and positive action to every power in your system. Try to hold in your system all the energy generated, and the mere desire to do this will tend to bring about what may be called accumulation of energy.

To experiment, try for several minutes to hold all your energy in your personality, and at the same time, try to give all of that energy harmonious action within your personality. In a few moments, you will actually feel alive with power, and if you have succeeded very well with your experiment, you will really feel like a storage battery for the time being. You will have so much energy that you will feel as if you could do almost anything. Experiment in this way at frequent intervals until you get your system into the habit of carrying out this process unconsciously. You will thereby cause your surplus energy to accumulate more and more in your system, and you will produce what may be called a highly charged condition of your personality, a condition that invariably means the attainment of personal magnetism.

To secure this result, however, it is necessary to keep the mind in an undisturbed attitude, to avoid all bad habits, physical or mental, to be in harmony with everything and everybody, and to exercise full self-control under every circumstance.

In cultivating this power realize that it is the result of surplus energy held in the system, and caused to circulate harmoniously through every part of the system; remember that it is a power that does not act intentionally upon persons or circumstances; that its aim is not to control or influence anybody, but simply to act within the individual self, and heighten the effect of everything that he may be or do.

Never think or speak of that which you do not wish to happen.

The whine, the sting, and the sigh these three must never appear in a single thought or a single word.

You can win ten times as many friends by talking happiness as you can by talking trouble. And the more real friends you have the less trouble you will have.

Speak well of everything good you find and mean it. When you find what you do not like keep quiet. The less you think or speak of what you do not like the more you have of what you do like.

Magnify the good; emphasize that which has worth; and talk only of those things that should live and grow.

When you have something good to say, say it. When you have something ill to say, say something else.

Chapter 17

The Building Power of Constructive Speech

There is a science of speech, and whoever wishes to promote his welfare and advancement must understand this science thoroughly and regulate his speech accordingly. Every word that is spoken exercises a power in personal life, and that power will work either for or against the person, depending upon the nature of the word. You can talk yourself into trouble, poverty or disease, and you can talk yourself into harmony, health and prosperity. In brief, you can talk yourself into almost any condition, desirable or undesirable.

Every word is an expression and every expression produces a tendency in some part of the system. This tendency may appear in the mind, in the body, in the chemical life of the body, in the world of desire, in character, among the various faculties, or anywhere in the personality, and will work itself out wherever it appears. Our expressions determine largely where we are to go, what we are to accomplish, and how we are to meet those conditions through which we may pass.

When our expressions produce tendencies towards sickness and failure, we will begin to move towards those conditions, and if the tendency is very strong, all the creative energies in the system will move in the same direction, focusing their efforts upon sickness and failure, or taking those conditions as their models, and thereby producing such conditions in the system. On the other hand, when our expressions produce tendencies towards health, happiness, power and success, we will begin to move towards those things, and in like manner create them in a measure.

Every word has an inner life force, sometimes called the hidden power of words, and it is the nature of this power that determines whether the expression is to be favorable or not. This power may be constructive or destructive. It may move towards the superior or the inferior. It may promote your purpose in life or it may retard that purpose, and it is the strongest when it is deeply felt. Therefore the words which we inwardly feel are the words that act as turning points in life.

When you feel that trouble is coming, and express that feeling in your speech, you are actually turning in your path and are beginning to move towards that trouble. In addition you are creating troubled conditions in your system. We all know that the more trouble we feel in the midst of trouble, the more troublesome that trouble will become. And we also know that that person who retains poise and self-control in the midst of trouble, will pass through it all without being seriously affected; and when it is over, is much wiser and stronger for the experience.

When you feel that better days are coming, and express that feeling in your speech, you turn all the power of your being towards the ideal of better days, and those powers will begin to create the better in your life. Whenever you talk about success, advancement, or any desirable condition, try to express the feeling of those things in your words. This inner feeling determines the tendencies of your creative powers; therefore, when you feel success in your speech, you cause the creative powers to create qualities in yourself that can produce success, while if you express the feeling of doubt, failure or loss in your words, those creative powers will produce inferiority, disturbance, discord, and a tendency to mistakes. It is in this way that the thing we fear comes upon us. Fear is a feeling that feels the coming of ills or other things we do not want; and as we always express through our words the feelings that we fear, we form tendencies toward those things, and the creative powers within us will produce them.

Whether the inner life force of a word will be constructive or destructive depends upon several factors, the most important of which are the tone, the motive and the idea. The tone of every word should be harmonious, wholesome, pleasing, and should convey a deep and serene expression. Words that express whines, discontent, sarcasm, aggressiveness and the like are destructive; so much so, that no one can afford to employ them under any circumstance whatever. Nothing is ever gained by complaints that are complaining, nor by criticisms that criticize. When things are not right, state so in a tone of voice that is firm and strong, but kind. A wronged customer who employs sweetness of tone as well as firmness of expression is one who will receive the first attention and the best attention, and nothing will be left unturned until the matter is set right. The words that wound others do far more injury to the person who gives them expression.

No one therefore can afford to give expression to a single word that may tend to wound. Words of constructive power are always deeply felt. They are never loud or confusing, but always quiet and serene, filled with the very spirit of conviction. Never give expression to what you do not wish to encourage. The more you talk about a thing the more you help it along. The "walls have ears " and the world is full of minds that will act upon your suggestion. Never mention the dark side of anything. It will interfere with your welfare. To tell your troubles may give you temporary relief, but it is scattering sited broadcast that will produce another crop of more trouble. If you have troubles, turn your back upon them and proceed to talk about harmony, freedom, attainment and success, and feel deeply the spirit of these new and better conditions. Thus you will begin to create for yourself a new life, new opportunities, new environment and a new world. Never speak unless you have something to say that gives cheer, encouragement, information or wholesome entertainment. To talk for the mere sake of talking is to throw precious energy away, and no human chatterbox will ever acquire greatness.

The motive back of every word should be constructive, and the life expressed in every word should convey the larger, the better, and the superior. Such words have building power, and are additions to life of extreme value. Every word should express, as far as possible, the absolute truth, and should never convey ideas that are simply indicated by appearances. What is meant by speaking the absolute truth, however, is a matter that the majority do not understand, and as it is a very large subject, it would require pages to give even a brief scientific definition. But for practical purposes, the subject can be made sufficiently clear through the use of a few illustrations taken from the world's daily speech.

People who think they have to say something and have nothing in particular to say, always take refuge in a brief description of the weather. In their descriptions they usually employ such expressions as "It is terribly hot," " it is an awful day," " This is terrible weather," "This is a miserably cold day," and so on. But such expressions do not change the weather, and there is no use of talking if your words are not to be of value in some way. You may say all sorts of disagreeable things about the weather without changing the weather in the least, but will such expressions leave you unchanged? Positively not! Whenever you declare that something is horrible, you cause horrible thoughts to send their actions all through your nervous system. These actions may be weak, but many drops, no matter how small, will finally wear away a rock.

When people talk about themselves, they seldom fail to give expression to a score of detrimental statements. Here are a few: "I can't stand this," "I feel so tired," "I cannot bear to think of it," "I AM thoroughly disgusted," "I AM so susceptible to climatic changes," "I AM so sensitive and so easily disturbed," "I AM getting weak and nervous," "My memory is failing," "I AM getting old," " I cannot work the way I used to," " My strength is gradually leaving me," "There is no chance for me anymore," "Everything in life is uphill work," "I have passed a miserable night," " This has been a hard day," "I have nothing but trouble and bad luck," "You know I AM human and so very weak," " There is always something wrong no matter how hard you try," "You know I have to be so very careful about what I eat as nearly everything disagrees with me."

A thousand other statements, all of them destructive, might be mentioned, but anyone who understands the power of thought will realize at once that such statements can never be otherwise but injurious and should therefore be avoided absolutely. But these statements are not only injurious they are also untrue absolutely untrue in every sense of the term.

The fact is you can stand almost anything if you forget your human weakness and array yourself in spiritual strength. You do not have to get tired. Work does not make anyone tired so long as he gets eight hours of sleep every night. It is wrong thinking that makes people tired. These are scientific facts. That person who permits himself to become disgusted at anything whatever is talking himself down to the plane of inferiority. When you feel disgusted you think disgusting thoughts, and such thoughts clog the mind. You cannot afford to think disgusting thoughts simply because something else is disgusting, because we daily become like the thoughts we think. We cannot improve disagreeable things by making ourselves disagreeable. Two wrongs never made a right. The proper course is to forgive the wrongdoer, forget the wrong and then do something substantial to right the whole matter. When we think kindly of the weather, place ourselves in harmony with Nature, think properly and dress properly, we shall not be susceptible to changes in the atmosphere; but so long as we say that we are affected by changing atmospheres, we not only make ourselves negative and susceptible, but we also produce detrimental effects in our systems through our own unwholesome beliefs.

The man who constantly thinks he is easily disturbed disturbs himself. When we are in harmony with everything including ourselves and refuse to be otherwise, nothing will ever disturb us. That person who is nervous can make the matter worse by saying that he is nervous, because such a statement is a nervous statement and is full of discord. When we begin to feel nervous, we can remedy the matter absolutely by resolving to remain calm, and by employing only quiet, wholesome and constructive speech. Your words will cause you to move in the direction indicated by the nature of those words, and it is just as easy to use words that bring calmness and poise, as those that bring inharmony and confusion.

Modern science has demonstrated conclusively that there is nothing about a person that gets old. Therefore, to say that you are getting old is to persist in speaking the untruth, and it is but natural that you should reap as you sow. We must remember that a false appearance comes from the practice of judging from appearances. To state that your strength is failing is likewise to speak the untruth. There is but one strength in the universe the strength of the Supreme and that strength can never fail. You may have as much of that strength as you desire. All that is necessary for you to do is to live in perfect touch with the Supreme, and never think, do or say anything that will interfere with that sublime oneness. The strength of the Supreme is just as able to fill your system with life and power now as it was at any time in the past. Therefore, there is no real reason whatever why your power should diminish. Be true to the truth and your power will perpetually increase.

The belief that there are no opportunities for you is caused by the fact that you have hidden yourself in a cave of inferiority. Go out into the life of worth, ability and competence, and you will find more opportunities than you can use. The world is ever in search of competent minds, and modern knowledge has made it possible for man to develop his ability. No one therefore has any legitimate reason for speaking of hard luck or hard times unless he prefers to live in want. The more you complain about hard times, the harder times will become for you, while if you resolve to forget that there is such a thing as failure and proceed to make your own life as you wish it to be, the turn in the lane will surely come.

The idea that the pathway of life is all uphill work is also a false one, and if we give that idea expression we are simply placing obstacles in our way. Nothing is uphill work when we approach it properly, and there is nothing that helps more to place us in true relationship with things than true expression.

If the night has been unpleasant, never mention the fact for a moment. To talk about it will only produce more unpleasantness in your system. There is nothing wrong about the night. The unpleasantness was most likely produced by your own perverse appetite, or by some reckless inexcusable act. Forgive yourself and declare that you will never abuse nature any more. Such powerful words if repeated often, will turn the tendency of your habits, and your life will become natural and wholesome. No day would be hard if we met all things with the conviction that we are equal to every occasion. Live properly, think properly, work properly and talk properly, and trouble and ill luck will not trouble you seriously anymore. That person who declares that there is always something wrong is always doing something to make things wrong. When we have wrong on the brain we will make many mistakes, so there will always be something wrong brewing for us. When wrong things come, set them right and look upon the experience as an opportunity for you to develop greater mastership.

When you agree with yourself, all wholesome and properly prepared food will agree with you. But you cannot expect food to agree with you so long as you are disagreeable; and to declare that this or that always disagrees with you, is to fill your system with disagreeable thoughts, disturbed actions and conditions of discord. That nature can digest food under such circumstances no one can justly expect. There is nothing that injures digestion more than the habit of finding fault with the food. If you do not think that you can eat this or that, leave it alone, but leave it alone mentally as well as physically. it is not enough to drop a disagreeable thing from your hands; you must also drop it from your mind.

Remember, you are mentally living with everything that you talk about, and there is nothing that affects us more than that which we take into our mental life. It is therefore not only necessary to speak the truth about all things, but also to avoid speaking about those things that are unwholesome. To speak about that which is wrong or inferior is never wholesome, no matter how closely we think we stand by the facts. Seeming facts, or what is called relative truth, should never receive expression unless they deal with that which is conducive to higher worth; and when circumstances compel us to make exceptions to this rule, we should avoid giving any feeling to what we say.

The greatest essential, however, is to make all speech constructive. Search for the real truth that is at the foundation of all life, and then give expression to such words as convey the full significance to that truth. The results, to say the least, will be extraordinary. In daily conversation, the law of constructive speech should be most conscientiously applied. What we say to others will determine to a considerable degree what they are to think, and what tendencies their mental actions are to follow; and since man is the product of his thought, conversation becomes a most important factor in man.

We steadily grow into the likeness bf that which we think of the most, and what we are to think about depends largely upon the mode, the nature and the subject matter of our conversation. When conversation originates or intensifies the tendency to think about the wrong, the ordinary or the inferior, it becomes destructive, and likewise it tends to keep before mind the faults and defects that may exist in human nature. To be constructive, conversation should tend to turn attention upon the better side, the stronger side, the superior side of all things, and should give the ideal the most prominent place in thought, speech or expression.

All conversation should be so formed that it may tend to move the mind towards the higher domains of thought, and should make everybody more keenly conscious of the greater possibilities that exist within them. No word should ever be spoken that will, in any way, bring the person's faults or shortcomings before his mind, nor should any form of speech be permitted that may cause sadness, offence, depression or pain. Every word should convey hope, encouragement and sunshine.

To constantly remind a person of his faults is to cause him to become more keenly conscious of those faults. He will think more and more about his faults, and will thereby cause his faults to become more prominent and more troublesome than they ever were before. The more we think about our weakness, the weaker we become; and the more we talk about weakness, the more we think about weakness. Conversation therefore should never touch upon those things that we do not wish to retain or develop. The only way to remove weakness is to develop strength, and to develop strength we must keep attention constantly upon the quality of strength. We develop what we think about provided all thinking has depth, quality and continuity.

Conversation has exceptional value in the training of young minds, and in many instances may completely change the destinies of these minds. To properly train a child, his attention should be directed as much as possible upon those qualities that have worth and that are desired in his development; and the way he is spoken to will largely determine where he is to give the greater part of his attention. To scold a child is to remind him of his faults. Every time he is reminded of his faults he gives more attention, more thought, and more strength to those faults.

His good qualities are thereby made weaker while his bad qualities are made worse. It is not possible to improve the mind and the character of the child by constantly telling him not to do " this " or " that." As a rule, it will increase his desire to do this other thing, and he will cease only through fear, or after having wasted a great deal of time in experiences that have become both disgusting and bitter. It is the tendency of every mind to desire to do what it is told not to do, the reason being that negative commands are nearly always associated with fear; and when mind is in the attitude of fear, or dread or curiosity, it is very easily impressed by whatever it may be thinking about.

When we are warned we either enter a state of fear or one of curiosity, and while in those states, our minds are so deeply and so easily impressed by that from which we are warned, that we give it our whole attention. The result is we think so much about it that we become almost completely absorbed in it; and we are carried away, so to speak, not away from the danger, but into it. When anyone is going wrong, it is a mistake to warn him not to go further. It is also a mistake to leave him alone. The proper course is to call his attention to something better, and frame our conversation in such a way that he becomes wholly absorbed in the better. He will then forget his old mistakes, his old faults and his old desires, and will give all his life and power to the building of that better which has engaged his new interest.

The same law may be employed to prevent sickness and failure. When the mind becomes so completely absorbed in perfect health that all sickness is forgotten, all the powers of mind will proceed to create health, and every trace of sickness will soon disappear. When the mind becomes so completely absorbed in higher attainments and in greater achievements that all thought of failure is forgotten, all the forces of mind will begin to work for the promotion of those attainments and achievements. The person will be gaining ground every day, and greater success will positively follow.

To cause the mind to forget the wrong, the lesser and the inferior, constructive conversation may be employed with unfailing results; in fact, such conversation must be employed if the mind is to advance and develop. Our conversation must be in perfect accord with our ambitions, our desires, and our ideals, and all our expressions must aim to promote the real purpose we have in view.

It is the tendency of nearly every mind to try to make his friends perfect according to his own idea of perfection, and he usually proceeds by constantly talking to his friends about their faults, and what they should not do in order to become as perfect as his ideal. Parents, as a rule, do the same with their children, not knowing that through this method many are made worse; and it is only those who are very strong in mind and character that are not adversely affected by this method.

To help our friends or our children to become ideal, we should never mention their faults. Our conversation should deal with the strong points of character and the greater possibilities of mind. We should so frame our conversation that we tend to make everybody feel there is something in them. Our conversation should have an optimistic tendency and an ascending tone. It should deal with those things in life that are worthwhile, and it should always give the ideal the greatest prominence. Weaknesses of human nature should be recognized as little as possible, and should seldom, if ever, be mentioned.

When people engage in destructive conversation in our midst we should try to change the subject, by calling their attention to the better side. There always is another and a better side; and when examined closely will be found to be far greater and infinitely more important than the ordinary side. Admirable qualities exist everywhere, and it will prove profitable to give these our undivided attention.

The first mark of a master mind is that he is able to promote his own perpetual improvement. The second is that he is able to be strong, joyous and serene under every circumstance.

The imagining faculty is the creative faculty of the mind, the faculty that creates plans, methods and ideas. Our imagination therefore must always be clear, lofty, wholesome, and constructive if we would create superior ideas and build for greater things.

Before you can have greater success you must become a greater man. Before you can become a greater man you must reach out toward the new and the greater along all lines; and this is possible only through the constructive use of imagination.

You get your best ideas when your mind acts in the upper story. And in all fields of action it is the best ideas that win.

Chapter 18

Imagination and the Master Mind

The forces of the human system must have something definite to work for; that is, they must have an ideal upon which to concentrate their attention, or some model or pattern to follow as they proceed with their constructive actions.

To form this model, it is the power of imagination that must be employed, and that power must, in each case, be applied constructively. What we imagine becomes a pattern for the creative energies of mind and personality, and as the creations of these energies determine what we are to become and attain, we realize that the imaging faculty is one of the most important of all our faculties. We therefore cannot afford to lose a moment in learning how to apply it according to the laws of mental construction and growth.

To proceed, imagine yourself becoming and attaining what you wish to become and attain. This will give your energies a model, both of your greater future self and your greater future achievements. When you think of your future, always imagine success and greater things, and have no fear as to results. If you fear, you give your creative energies a model of failure, and they will accordingly proceed to create failure. Then we must also remember if we wish to succeed, our faculties must work successfully, but no faculty can work successfully when filled with fear. It is only when constantly inspired by the idea of success that any faculty or power in the human system can do its best.

To inspire our faculties with this idea, we should always imagine ourselves obtaining success. The picture of success should be placed upon all the walls of the mind, so that the powers within us will see success, and success only as their goal. Hang up pictures in your mind that will inspire you to do your best; hang up pictures in your mind that will cause you to think constantly of that which you desire to accomplish, and this you may do by imagining yourself being that greater something that you want to be and doing that greater something that you want to do.

An excellent practice is to use your spare moments in creating such pictures in your imagination and placing them in the most conspicuous position of your mind, so that all your faculties and powers can see them at all times. We are always imagining something. It is practically impossible to be awake without imagining something. Then why not imagine something at all times that will inspire the powers within us to do greater and greater things?

To aid the imagination in picturing the greater, the higher and better, we should "hitch our wagon to a star." The star may be something quite out of reach as far as present circumstances indicate, but if we hitch our wagon to something in such a lofty position, our mind will begin to take wings. It will no longer be like a worm crawling in the dust. We shall begin to rise and continue to rise. The only thing that can cause the mind to rise is imagination. The only thing that can make the mind larger than it is, is imagination. The only thing that can make the mind act along new lines is imagination. This being true, it is unwise to use the imagination for any other purpose than for the best that we can think or do.

In this connection, there are a few suggestions that will be found of special value. First, make up your mind as to what you really want in every respect. Determine what surroundings or environment you want. Decide upon the kind of friends you want and what kind of work you would prefer. Make all those ideals so good and so perfect that you will have no occasion to change them. Then fix those ideals so clearly in mind that you can see them at all times, and proceed to desire their realization with all the power of mind and soul. Make that your first step.

Your second step should be to imagine yourself living in those surroundings that you have selected as your ideal; then make it a point to live in that imagination every moment of every day. Instead of imagining a number of useless things during spare moments, as people usually do, imagine yourself living in those surroundings and those ideals. Imagine yourself in the presence of friends that are exactly what you wish your ideal friends to be, and permit your fancy to run as far as it may wish along all of those idealistic lines. If you have not found your work, proceed to imagine yourself doing what you wish to do. If you have already found your work, imagine yourself doing that work as well as you would wish, and imagine the coming of results as large as your greatest desires could expect. Devote every moment of your spare time to the placing of those ideals before your attention, and you will give your power and forces something strong and definite to work for.

Every mental force is an artist, and it paints according to the model. What you imagine is the model, and there is not a single mental action that is not inspired or called forth into action by some picture or model which the imagination has produced.

The imagination can call forth the ordinary or the extraordinary. It can give the powers of your being an inferior model or an extraordinary model, and if the imagination is not directed to produce the extraordinary and the superior, it is quite likely to produce the ordinary and the inferior. Your second step, therefore, should be to imagine yourself actually living in those surroundings that you have selected as your ideal, and in actually becoming and doing what you are determined to become and do.

This practice would, in the first place, give you a great deal of pleasure, because if you have definite ideals and imagine yourself attaining those ideals, you will certainly enjoy yourself to a marked degree for the time being. But in addition to that enjoyment, you will gradually and steadily be training your mind to work for those greater things. The mind will work for that which is upper most in thought and imagination. Therefore, we should invariably place our highest ideals uppermost, so that the whole of our attention may be concentrated upon those ideals, and all the powers of our mind and personality directed to work for those ideals.

Your third step should be to proceed to apply the power of desire, the power of will, the power of scientific thought, and in brief, all your powers, in trying to realize those beautiful ideals that you continue to imagine as your own. Do as the ancient Hebrews did. First make your prediction. Then go to work and make it come true. What you imagine concerning your greater future is your prediction, and you can cause that prediction to come true if you apply all the power in your possession in working for its realization every day.

The constructive use of imagination therefore will enable you to place a definite model or pattern before the forces of your system, so that those forces may have something better and greater to work for. In brief, instead of permitting most of your energies to go to waste and the remainder to follow any pattern or idea that may be suggested by your environment, or your own helter-skelter thinking, you will cause all your energy to work for the greatest and the best that you may desire. This is the first use of imagination, and it easily places this remarkable faculty among the greatest in the human mind. Another use of the imagination is found in its power to give the mind something definite to think about at all times, so that the mind may be trained to always think of that which you really want to think; that is, through this use of the imagination, you can select your own thought and think your own thought at all times; and he who can do this is gradually becoming a master mind.

The master mind is the mind that thinks what it wants to think, regardless of what circumstances, environment or associations may suggest. The mind that masters itself creates its own ideas, thoughts and desires through the original use of imagination, or its own imaging faculty. The mind that does not master itself forms its thoughts and desires after the likeness of the impressions received through the senses, and is therefore controlled by those conditions from which, such impressions come; because as we think, so we act and live. The average mind usually desires what the world desires without any definite thought as to his own highest welfare or greatest need, the reason being that a strong tendency to do likewise is always produced in the mind when the desires are formed in the likeness of such impressions as are suggested by external conditions. It is therefore evident that the person who permits himself to be affected by suggestions will invariably form artificial desires; and to follow such desires is to be misled.

The master mind desires only that which is conducive to real life and in the selection of its desires is never influenced in the least by the desires of the world. Desire is one of the greatest powers in human life. It is therefore highly important that every desire be normal and created for the welfare of the individual himself. But no desire can be wholly normal that is formed through the influence of suggestion. Such desires are always abnormal to some degree, and easily cause the individual to be misplaced. A great many people are misplaced. They do not occupy those places wherein they may be their best and accomplish the most. They are working at a disadvantage, and are living a life that is far inferior to what they are intended to live. The cause is frequently found in abnormal or artificial desires. They have imitated the desires of others without consulting their present needs. They have formed the desire to do what others are doing by permitting their minds to be influenced by suggestions and impressions from the world, forgetting what their present state of development makes them capable of doing now. By imitating the lives, habits, actions and desires of others, they are led into a life not their own; that is, they are misplaced.

The master mind is never misplaced because he does not live to do what others are doing, but what he himself wants to do now. He wants to do only that which is conducive to real life, a life worthwhile, a life that steadily works up to the very highest goal in view.

The average mind requires a change of environment before he can change his thought. He has to go somewhere or bring into his presence something that will suggest a new line of thinking and feeling. The master mind, however, can change his thought whenever he so desires. A change of scene is not necessary, because such a mind is not controlled from without. A change of scene will not produce a change of thought in the master mind unless he so elects. The master mind changes his thoughts, ideals or desires by imaging upon the mind the exact likeness of the new ideas, the new thoughts, and the new desires that have been selected.

The secret of the master mind is found wholly in the intelligent use of imagination. Man is as he thinks, and his thoughts are patterned after the predominating mental images, whether those images are impressions suggested from without, or impressions formed by the ego acting from within. When man permits his thoughts and desires to be formed in the likeness of impressions received from without, he will be more or less controlled by environment and he will be in the hands of fate, but when he transforms every impression received from without into an original idea and incorporates that idea into a new mental image, he uses environment as a servant, thereby placing fate in his own hands.

Every object that is seen will produce an impression upon the mind according to the degree of susceptibility. This impression will contain the nature of the object of which it is a representation. The nature of this object will be reproduced in the mind, and what has entered the mind will be expressed more or less throughout the entire system. Therefore, the mind that is susceptible to suggestions will reproduce in his own mind and system conditions that are similar in nature to almost everything that he may see, hear or feel. He will consequently be a reflection of the world in which he lives. He will think, speak and act as that world may suggest; he will float with the stream of that world wherever that stream may flow; he will not be an original character, but an automaton.

Every person that permits himself to be affected by suggestion is more or less an automaton, and is more or less in the hands of fate. To place fate in his own hands, he must use suggestions intelligently instead of blindly following those desires and thoughts that his surroundings may suggest. We are surrounded constantly by suggestions of all kinds, because everything has the power to suggest something to that mind that is susceptible, and we are all more or less susceptible in this respect. But there is a vast difference between permitting oneself to be susceptible to suggestion and training oneself to intelligently use those impressions that suggestions may convey. The average writer on suggestion not only ignores this difference, but encourages susceptibility to suggestion by impressing the reader with the remark that suggestion does control the world. If it is true that suggestion controls the world, more or less, we want to learn how to so use suggestion that its control of the human mind will decrease steadily; and this we can accomplish, not by teaching people how to use suggestion for the influencing of other minds, but in using those impressions conveyed by suggestion in the reconstruction of their own minds.

Suggestion is a part of life, because everything has the power to suggest, and all minds are open to impressions. Nothing therefore can be said against suggestion by itself. Suggestion is a factor in our midst; it is a necessary factor. The problem is to train ourselves to make intelligent use of the impressions received, instead of blindly following the desires produced by those impressions as the majority do.

To proceed in the solution of this problem, never permit objects discerned by the senses to reproduce themselves in your mind against your will. Form your own ideas about what you see, hear or feel, and try to make those ideas superior to what was suggested by the objects discerned. When you see evil do not form ideas that are in the likeness of that evil; do not think of the evil as bad, but try to understand the forces that are back of that evil forces that are good in themselves, though misdirected in their present state. By trying to understand the nature of the power that is back of evil or adversity, you will not form bad ideas, and therefore will feel no bad effects from experiences that may seem undesirable. At the same time, you will think your own thought about the experiences, thereby developing the power of the master mind.

Surround yourself as far as possible with those things that suggest the superior, but do not permit such suggestions to determine your thought about the superior. Those superior impressions that are suggested by superior environment should be used in forming still more superior thoughts. If you wish to be a master mind, your thought must always be higher than the thought your environment may suggest, no matter how ideal that environment may be.

Every impression that enters the mind through the senses should be worked out and should be made to serve the mind in its fullest capacity. In this way the original impression will not reproduce itself in the mind, but will become instrumental in giving the mind a number of new and superior ideas. To work out an impression, try to see through its whole nature. Look at it from every conceivable point of view, and try to discern its actions, tendencies, possibilities and probable defects. Use your imagination in determining what you want to think or do, what you are to desire and what your tendencies are to be. Know what you want, and then image those things upon the mind constantly. This will develop the power to think what you want to think, and he who can think what he wants to think is on the way to becoming what he wants to become.

The principal reason why the average person does not realize his ideals is because he has not learned to think what he wants to think. He is too much affected by the suggestions that are about him. He imitates the world too much, following desires that are not his own. He is therefore misled and misplaced. Whenever you permit yourself to think what persons, things, conditions or circumstances may suggest, you are not following what you yourself want to think. You are not following your own desires but borrowed desires. You will therefore drift into strange thinking, and thinking that is entirely different from what you originally planned. To obey the call of every suggestion and permit your mind to be carried away by this, that or the other, will develop the tendency to drift until your mind will wander. Concentration will be almost absent and you will become wholly incapable of actually thinking what you want to think. One line of constructive thinking will scarcely be begun when another line will be suggested, and you will leave the unfinished task to begin something else, which in turn will be left incomplete. Nothing, therefore, will be accomplished.

To become a master mind, think what you want to think, no matter what your surroundings may suggest; and continue to think what you want to think until that particular line of thought or action has been completed. Desire what you want to desire and impress that desire so deeply upon consciousness that it cannot possibly be disturbed by those foreign desires that environment may suggest; and continue to express that desire with all the life and power that is in you until you get what you want. When you know that you are in the right desire, do not permit anything to influence your mind to change. Take such suggestions and convert them into the desire you have already decided upon, thereby giving that desire additional life and power. Never close your mind to impressions from without. Keep the mind open to the actions of all those worlds that may exist in your sphere and try to gain valuable impressions from every source, but do not blindly follow those impressions. Use them constructively in building up your own system of original thought. Think what you want to think, and so use every impression you receive that you gain greater power to think what you want to think. Thus you will gradually become a master mind.

Follow the vision of the soul. Be true to your ideals no matter what may happen now. Then things will take a turn and the very things you wanted to happen will happen.

The ideal has a positive drawing power towards the higher, the greater, and the superior. Whoever gives his attention constantly to the ideal, therefore, will steadily rise in the scale.

Take things as they are today and proceed at once to make them better.

Expect every change to lead you to something better and it will. As your faith is so shall it be.

To be human as not to be weak. To be human is to be all that there is in man, and the greatness that as contained in the whole of man is marvelous indeed.

Chapter 19

The Higher Forces in Man

It is the most powerful among the forces of the human system that we least understand, and though this may seem unfortunate, it is not unnatural. All advancement is in the ascending scale. We learn the simplest things first and the least valuable in the beginning. Later on, we learn that which is more important. We find therefore the greatest forces among those that are almost entirely hidden, and for that reason they are sometimes called the hidden forces, the finer forces, or the higher forces.

As it is in man, so it is also in nature. We find the most powerful among natural forces to be practically beyond comprehension. Electricity is an illustration. There is no greater force known in nature, and yet no one has thus far been able to determine what this force actually is. The same is true with regard to other natural forces; the greater they are and the more powerful they are, the more difficult it is to understand them. In the human system, there are a number of forces of exceptional value that we know nothing about; that is, we do not understand their real nature, but we can learn enough about the action, the purpose and the possibilities of those forces to apply them to practical life; and it is practical application with which we are most concerned.

The field of the finer forces in mind may be termed the unconscious mental field, and the vastness of this field, as well as the possibilities of its functions, is realized when we learn that the greater part of our mental world is unconscious. Only a fraction of the mental world of man is on the surface or up in consciousness; the larger part is submerged in the depths of what might be called a mental sea of subconsciousness. All modern psychologists have come to this conclusion, and it is a fact that anyone can demonstrate in his own experience if he will take the time.

In the conscious field of the human mind, we find those actions of which we are aware during what may be called our wide-awake state; and they are seemingly insignificant in comparison with the actions of the vast unconscious world, though our conscious actions are found to be highly important when we learn that it is the conscious actions that originate unconscious actions. And here let us remember that it is our unconscious actions that determine our own natures, our own capabilities, as well as our own destiny. In our awakened state we continue to think and act in a small mental field, but all of those actions are constantly having their effect upon this vast unconscious field that is found beneath the mental surface.

To realize the existence of this unconscious mental world, and to realize our power to determine the actions of that world, is to awaken within us a feeling that we are many times as great and as capable as we thought we were, and the more we think of this important fact, the larger becomes our conscious view of life and its possibilities.

To illustrate the importance of the unconscious field and your finer forces, we will take the force of love. No one understands the nature of this force, nor has anyone been able to discover its real origin or its actual possibilities; nevertheless, it is a force that is tremendously important in human life. Its actions are practically hidden, and we do not know what constitutes the inner nature of those actions, but we do know how to control those actions in a measure for our own good; and we have discovered that when we do control and properly direct the actions of love, its value to everybody concerned is multiplied many times. It is the same with a number of other forces with which we are familiar. They act along higher or finer lines of human consciousness, and they are so far beyond ordinary comprehension that we cannot positively know what they are, but we do know enough about them to control them and direct them for our best and greatest good.

In like manner, the unconscious mental field, though beyond scientific analysis, is sufficiently understood as to its modes of action, so that we can control and direct those actions as we may choose. When we analyze what comes forth from the unconscious field at any time, we find that it is invariably the result of something that we caused to be placed in that field during some past time. This leads up to the discovery of unconscious mental processes, and it is not difficult to prove the existence of such processes.

Many a time ideas, desires, feelings or aspirations come to the surface of thought that we are not aware of having created at any time. We come to the conclusion, therefore, that they were produced by some unconscious process, but when we examine those ideas or desires carefully, we find that they are simply effects corresponding exactly with certain causes that we previously placed in action in our conscious world. When we experiment along this line we find that we can produce a conscious process at any time, and through deep feeling cause it to enter the unconscious mental world. In that deeper world, it goes to work and produces according to its nature, the results coming back to the surface of our conscious mentality days, weeks or months later.

The correspondence between conscious and unconscious mental processes may be illustrated by a simple movement in physical action. If a physical movement began at a certain point, and was caused to act with a circular tendency, it would finally come back to its starting point. It is the same with every conscious action that is deeply felt. It goes out into the vastness of the unconscious mental field, and having a circular tendency, as all mental actions have, it finally comes back to the point where it began; and in coming back, brings with it the result of every unconscious experience through which it passed on its circular journey.

To go into this subject deeply, and analyze every phase of it would be extremely interesting; in fact, it would be more interesting than fiction. It would require, however, a large book to do it justice. For this reason, we can simply touch upon the practical side of it, but will aim to make this brief outline sufficiently clear to enable anyone to direct his unconscious process in such a way as to secure the best results.

Every mental process, or every mental action, that takes place in our wide-awake consciousness will, if it has depth of feeling or intensity, enter the unconscious field, and after it has developed itself according to the line of its original nature, will return to the conscious side of the mind. Here we find the secret of character building, and also the secret of building faculties and talents. Everything that is done in the conscious field to improve the mind, character, conduct or thought will, if it has sincerity and depth of feeling, enter the unconscious field; and later will come back with fully developed qualities, which when in expression, constitutes character.

Many a man, however, after trying for some time to improve himself and seeing no results, becomes discouraged. He forgets that some time always intervenes between the period of sowing and the period of reaping. What he does in the conscious field to improve himself, constitutes the sowing, when those actions enter the conscious field to be developed: and when they come back, it may be weeks or months later, the reaping time has arrived. Many a time, after an individual has given up self-improvement, he discovers, after a considerable period, that good qualities are beginning to come to the surface in his nature, thereby proving conclusively that what he did months ago along that line was not in vain.

The results of past efforts are beginning to appear. We have all had similar experiences, and if we would carefully analyze such experiences, we would find that not a single conscious process that is sufficiently deep or intense to become an unconscious process will fail to come back finally with its natural results.

Many a time ideas come into our minds that we wanted weeks ago, and could not get them at that time; but we did place in action certain deep, strong desires for those ideas, at that particular time, and though our minds were not prepared to develop those ideas at once, they finally were developed and came to the surface. The fact that this process never fails indicates the value of giving the mind something to work out for future need. If we have something that we want to do months ahead, we should give the mind definite instruction now and make those instructions so deep, that they will become unconscious processes.

Those unconscious processes will, according to directions, work out the ideas and plans that we want for that future work, and in the course of time, will bring results to the surface. To go into detail along the line of this part of our study would also be more interesting than fiction, but again, a large book would be required to do it justice. However, if we make it a practice to place in action our best thoughts, our best ideas and our best desires now and every moment of the eternal now, we will be giving the unconscious mental field something good to work for at all times; and as soon as each product is finished, or ready to be delivered from the unconscious world, it will come to the surface, and will enter the conscious mind ready for use.

Some of the best books that have been written have been worked out during months of unconscious mental processes; the same is true with regard to inventions, dramas, musical compositions, business plans, and in fact, anything and everything of importance that could be mentioned. Every idea, every thought, every feeling, every desire, every mental action, may, under certain circumstances, produce an unconscious process corresponding with itself, and this process will in every instance bring back to consciousness the result of its work.

When we realize this, and realize the vast possibilities of the unconscious field, we will see the advantage of placing in action as many good unconscious processes as possible. Give your unconscious mental world something important to do every hour. Place a new seed in that field every minute. It may take weeks or months before that seed brings forth its fruit, but it will bring forth, after its kind, in due time without fail.

We understand therefore, how we can build character by sowing seeds of character in this field, and how we can, in the same way, build desirable conduct, a different disposition, different mental tendencies, stronger and greater mental faculties, and more perfect talents along any line. To direct these unconscious processes, it is necessary to apply the finer forces of the system, as it is those forces that invariably determine how those processes are to act. Those forces, however, are very easily applied, as all that is necessary in the beginning is to give attention to the way we feel. The way we feel determines largely what our finer forces are to be and how they are to act, and there is not an hour when we do not feel certain energies at work in our system. All the finer forces are controlled by feeling. Try to feel what you want done either in the conscious or the unconscious mental fields, and you will place in action forces that correspond to what you want done. Those forces will enter the unconscious mental world and produce processes through which the desired results will be created.

Whenever you want to redirect any force that is highly refined, you must feel the way you want that force to act. To illustrate, we will suppose you have certain emotions in your mental world that are not agreeable. To give the energies of those emotions a new and more desirable force of action, change your emotions by giving your whole attention in trying to feel such emotions as you may desire.

And here let us remember that every emotion that comes up in the system is teeming with energy; but as most emotions continue to act without any definite control, we realize how much energy is wasted through uncurbed emotions. We know from experience, that whenever we give way to our feelings, we become weak. The reason is that uncontrolled feeling wastes energy. A great many people who are very intense in their feelings, actually become sick whenever they give way to strong or deep emotions. On the other hand, emotions that are controlled and properly directed, not only prevent waste, but will actually increase the strength of mind and body.

Here is a good practice. Whenever you feel the way you do not wish to feel, begin to think deeply and in the most interesting manner possible, of those things that you wish to accomplish. If you can throw your whole soul, so to speak, into those new directions, you will soon find your undesired feelings disappearing completely. Every individual should train himself to feel the way he wants to feel, and this is possible if he will always direct his attention to something desirable whenever undesired feelings come up. Through this practice he will soon get such full control over his feelings that he can always feel the way he wants to feel, no matter what the circumstances may be. He will thus gain the power not only of controlling his emotions and using constructively all those energies that invariably appear in his emotions, but he will also have found the secret of continued happiness. Whenever mental energy moves in a certain direction, it tends to build up power for good along that line. We realize therefore the value of directing all our attention upon those things in mind, character and life that we wish to build and develop.

In building character we find the results to be accumulative; that is, we make an effort to improve our life or conduct, and thereby produce an unconscious process, which will later on, give us more strength of character to be and live the way we wish to be and live. This in turn will enable us to produce more and stronger unconscious processes along the line of character building, which will finally return with a greater number of good qualities. The result of this action will be to give us more power to build for a still greater character, and so this process may be continued indefinitely.

The same is true with regard to building the mind. The more you build the mind, the greater becomes your mental power to build a still greater mind: but in each case, it is the unconscious process that must be produced in order that the greater character or greater mind may be developed from within. In this connection, it is well to remember that the principal reason why so many people fail to improve along any line is because their desires or efforts for improvement are not sufficiently deep and strong to become unconscious processes. To illustrate, it is like placing seed on stony ground. If the seed is not placed in good, deep soil it will not grow. You may desire self-improvement for days, but if those desires are weak or superficial, they will not enter the unconscious field; and any action, however good it may be, if it fails to enter the unconscious field, will also fail to produce results along the line of self-improvement. With regard to the building of character, we must also remember that character determines in a large measure the line of action of all the other forces in the human system. If your character is strong and well developed, every force that you place in action will be constructive; while if your character is weak, practically all your forces will go astray.

This is not true in the moral field alone, but also in the field of mental achievement. If the character is weak, your ability will be mostly misdirected no matter how hard you may work, or how sincere you may be in your effort to do your best. This explains why a great many people do not realize their ideals. They have paid no attention to character building, and therefore, nearly every effort that they may have made in trying to work up towards their ideals, has been misdirected and sent astray. Whatever our ideals may be therefore, or how great our desires may be to realize those ideals, we must first have character; and even though we may be able to place in action the most powerful forces in the human system, we will not get results until we have character. It is character alone that can give the powers of man constructive direction, and it is a well known fact that those people who have a strong, firm, well-developed character easily move from the good to the better, no matter what the circumstances.

What may be called the higher forces in man act invariably through our most sublime states of consciousness, and as it is these higher forces that enable man to become or accomplish more than the average, it is highly important that we attain the power to enter sublime consciousness at frequent intervals. No man or woman of any worth was ever known, who did not have experience in these sublime states; in fact, it is impossible to rise above the ordinary in life or achievement without drawing, more or less, upon the higher realms of consciousness.

People are sometimes criticized for not being on the earth all the time, but it is necessary to get above the earth occasionally in order to find something worthwhile to live for and work for while upon earth. The most powerful forces in human life can be drawn down to earth for practical use, but to get them we must go to the heights frequently. No one can write music unless his consciousness touches the sublime. No one can write real poetry unless he has the same experience. No one can evolve ideas worthwhile unless his mind transcends the so-called practical sphere of action, and no individual can rise in the world of attainment and achievement unless his mind dwells almost constantly on the verge of the sublime.

Examine the minds of people of real worth, people who have something in them, people who are beyond the average, people who are rising in the scale, people whom we truly admire, people that we look up to, people who occupy high positions, positions that they have actually won through merit and we find in every instance, that their minds touch frequently the sublime state of consciousness. When we touch that state, our minds are drawn up above the ordinary, and mental actions are developed and worked out that are superior to ordinary or average mental actions. It is therefore simply understood that experience in sublime consciousness if properly employed, will invariably make man greater and better.

When we look upon a man that we can truthfully say is a real man, we find that something unusual has been or is being expressed in his personality; and that something unusual is hidden in every personality. It is a hidden power, a hidden force, which, when placed in action, gives man superior worth, both as to character, ability and life. Real men and real women, people who are real in the true sense of the term, are always born from the sublime state of consciousness; that is, they have, through coming in contact with higher regions of thought, evolved greater worth in their own minds and personalities; and as this possibility is within reach of every man or woman, we see the importance of dealing thoroughly with these higher powers in human nature.

Whenever we touch those finer states in the upper regions of the mind, we invariably feel that we have gained something superior, something that we did not possess before; and the gaining of that something invariably makes life stronger as well as finer. The ordinary has been, in a measure, overcome, and that which is beyond the ordinary is being gradually evolved. If we would rise in the scale in the fullest and best sense of the term, we must pay close attention to those higher forces and make it a practice to enter frequently into close touch with higher states of consciousness; in fact, we simply must do it, because if we do not we will continue to move along a very ordinary level. Then we must also bear in mind that it is our purpose to use all the forces we possess, not simply those that we can discern on the outside or that we are aware of in external consciousness, but also those finer and more powerful forces which we can control and direct only when we ascend to the heights.

In dealing with these greater powers in man, it will be worth our while to reconsider briefly the psychological field.

As long as the mind acts on the surface of consciousness, we have very little control of those finer elements in human life, but when the mind goes into the depths of feeling, into the depths of realization, or into what is called the psychological field, then it is that it touches everything that has real worth or that has the power to evolve, produce or develop still greater worth. It is the active forces of the psychological field that determine everything that is to take place in the life of man, both within himself and in his external destiny. We must therefore learn to act through the psychological field if we would master ourselves and create our own future. The psychological field can be defined as that field of subconscious action that permeates the entire personality, or that fills, so to speak, every atom of the physical man on a finer plane.

The psychological field is a finer field, permeating the ordinary tangible physical elements of life, and we enter this field whenever our feelings are deep and sincere. The fact that the psychological field determines real worth, as well as the attainment of greater worth, is easily demonstrated in everyday experience. When a man has anything in him, his nature is always deep. The same is true of people of refinement or culture: there is depth to their natures, and the man of character invariably lives in that greater world of life and power that is back of, or beneath, the surface of consciousness. If there is something in you, you both live and act through the deeper realms of your life, and those realms constitute the psychological field.

Among the many important forces coming directly through emotion or feeling, one of the most valuable is that of enthusiasm. In the average mind, enthusiasm runs wild, but we have found that when this force is properly directed it becomes a great constructive power. When you are enthusiastic about something, it is always about something new or something better something that holds possibilities that you did not realize before. Your enthusiasm, if properly directed, will naturally cause your mind to move towards those possibilities, and enthusiasm is readily directed when you concentrate attention exclusively upon that something new that inspires enthusiasm. By turning your attention upon the thing that produces enthusiasm, the mind will move forward toward those greater possibilities that are discerned.

This forward movement of the mind will tend to renew and enlarge the mind so that it will gain a still greater conception of those possibilities. This will increase your enthusiasm, which will in turn impel your mind to move forward still further in the same direction. Thus a still larger conception of those possibilities will be secured, which in turn will increase your enthusiasm and the power of your mind to take a third step in advance.

We thus realize that if enthusiasm is directed upon the possibilities that originally inspired that enthusiasm, we will not only continue to be enthused, but we will in that very manner, cause the mind to move forward steadily and develop steadily, so that in time it will gain sufficient power to actually work out those possibilities upon which attention has been directed. In this connection, we must also remember that we can grow and advance only as we pass into the new. It is new life, new thought, new states of consciousness that are demanded if we are to take any steps at all in advance, and as enthusiasm tends directly to inspire the mind to move towards the new, we see how important it is to continue, not only to live in the spirit of enthusiasm, but to direct that spirit upon the goal in view. It is invariably the enthusiastic mind that moves forward, that does things, and that secures results. Two other forces of great value, belonging to this group, are appreciation and gratitude.

Whenever you appreciate a certain thing you become conscious of its real quality, and whenever you become conscious of the quality of anything, you begin to develop that quality in yourself. When we appreciate the worth of a person, we tend to impress the idea of that worth in our own minds, and thereby cause the same effect to be produced, in a measure, in ourselves. The same is true if we appreciate our own worth, in a sensible and constructive manner. If we appreciate what we already are, and are ambitious to become still more, we focus our minds upon the greater, and employ what we already possess as steppingstones towards the greater attainment; but when we do not appreciate ourselves, there are no stepping stones that we can use in attaining greater things.

We thus realize why people that do not appreciate themselves never accomplish much, and why they finally go downgrade in nearly every instance. When we appreciate the beautiful in anything, we awaken our minds to a higher and better understanding of the beautiful. Our minds thus become, in a measure, more beautiful. The same is true with regard to any quality. Whatever we appreciate, we tend to develop in ourselves, and here we find a remarkable aid to the power of concentration, because we always concentrate attention perfectly, naturally and thoroughly upon those things that we fully appreciate. Thus we understand why it is that we tend to develop in ourselves the things that we admire in others.

Whenever you feel grateful for anything, you always feel nearer to the real quality of that particular thing. A person who is ungrateful, however, always feels that there is a wall between himself and the good things in life. Usually there is such a wall, though he has produced it himself through his ingratitude. But the man who is grateful for everything, places himself in that attitude where he may come in closer contact with the best thing; everywhere; and we know very well that the most grateful people always receive the best attention everywhere. We all may meet disappointment at some time and not get exactly what we wanted, but we shall find that the more grateful we are, the less numerous will those disappointments become. It has been well said that no one feels inclined to give his best attention to the man who is always "knocking," and it is literally true.

On the other hand, if you are really grateful and mean it, it is very seldom that you do not receive the best attention from everybody wherever you may go. The most important side of this law, however, is found in the fact that the more grateful you are for everything good that comes into your life, the more closely you place your mind in contact with that power in life that can produce greater good.

Another among the finer forces is that of aspiration. No person should fail to aspire constantly and aspire to the very highest that he can possibly awaken in his life. Aspiration always tends to elevate the mind and tends to lift the mind into larger and greater fields of action. And when the mind finds itself in this larger field of action, it will naturally gain power to do greater things. We all realize that so long as we live down in the lower story, we cannot accomplish very much; it is when we lift our minds to the higher stories of the human structure that we begin to gain possession of ideas and powers through which greater things may be achieved.

The same is true of ambition. Ambition not only tends to draw the mind up into higher and larger fields, but also tends to build up those faculties through which we are to work. If you are tremendously ambitious to do a certain thing, the force of that ambition will tend to increase the power and ability of that faculty through which your ambition may be realized. To illustrate, if you are ambitious to succeed in the business world, the force of that ambition if very strong, will constantly make your business faculties stronger and more able, so that finally your business ability will have become sufficiently great to carry your ambition through. You cannot be too ambitious, provided you are ambitious for something definite and continue to give your whole life and soul to that which you expect or desire to accomplish through that ambition.

When we know the power of ambition, and know that anybody can be ambitious, we realize that anyone can move forward. No matter what his position may be, or where he may be, he can, through the power of ambition begin to gain ground, and continue to gain ground indefinitely. The average mind, however, has very little ambition, and makes no effort to arouse this tremendous force; but we may depend upon the fact that when this force is fully aroused in any mind, a change for the better must positively come before long.

The force of an ideal is another among the finer forces that should receive constant and thorough attention. When you have an ideal and live for it every second of your existence, you place yourself in the hands of a drawing power that is immense, and that power will tend to draw out into action every force, power and faculty that you may possess, especially those forces and qualities that will have to be developed in order that you may realize that ideal.

Have an ideal, and the highest that you can picture. Then worship it every hour with your whole soul. Never come down, and do not neglect it for a moment. We all know very well that it is the people who actually worship their high ideals with mind and heart and soul that finally realize those ideals. It is such people who reach the high places and the reason why is easily explained. Give your attention, or rather, your whole life to some lofty ideal, and you will tend to draw into action all the finer and higher forces of your system those forces that can create greater ability, greater talent, greater genius those forces that can increase your capacity, bring into action all your finer elements and give you superior power and superior worth in every sense of the term those forces which, when aroused, cannot positively fail to do the work you wish to have done.

A fact well known in this connection is that when the mind is turned persistently upon a certain ideal, every power that is in you begins to flow in that direction, and this is the very thing you want. When we can get all that is in us to work for our ideals and to work towards our ideals, then we shall positively reach whatever goal we have in view.

Closely connected with our ideals, we find our visions and dreams. The man without a vision will never be anything but an ordinary man, and the people who never dream of greater things, will never get beyond ordinary things. It is our visions and dreams that lift our minds to lofty realms, that make us feel that there is something greater and better to work for; and when we become inspired with a desire to work for greater and better things, we will not only proceed to carry out those desires, but will finally secure sufficient power to fulfill those desires.

"The nation that has no vision shall perish." This is a great truth that we have heard a thousand times, and we know the reason why; but the same truth is applicable to man. If he has no vision, he will go down; but if he has visions, the highest and most perfect visions he can possibly imagine, and lives constantly for their realization, he will positively ascend in the scale. He will become a greater and a greater man, and those things that were at one time simply dreams, will, in the course of time, become actual realities.

The power of love is another force in this higher group that is extremely valuable, and the reason is that it is the tendency of love to turn attention upon the ideal, the beautiful and the more perfect. When you love somebody, you do not look for their faults; in fact, you do not see their faults. Your whole attention is turned upon their good qualities, and here, let us remember that whatever we continue to see in others, we develop in ourselves. The power of real love always tends to draw out into expression the finer elements of mind, character and life. For that reason, we should always love, love much, and love the most ideal and the most perfect that we can discover in everybody and in everything that we may meet in life.

We have all discovered that when a man really loves an ideal woman, or the woman that constitutes his ideal, he invariably becomes stronger in character, more powerful in personality, and more able in mind. When a woman loves an ideal man, or her ideal, she invariably becomes more attractive. The beautiful in her nature comes forth into full expression and many times the change is so great that we can hardly believe that she is the same woman. The power of love, if genuine, constant and strong, tends to improve everything in human life; and as this power is one of the higher forces in human nature, we readily understand the reason why. We can therefore without further comment, draw our own conclusions as to how we will use this power in the future.

The last of these finer forces that we shall mention, and possibly the strongest, is that of faith; but we must remember if we wish to use this force, that faith does not constitute a belief or any system of beliefs; it is a mental action an action that goes into the very spirit of those things which we may think of or apply at the time we exercise faith. When you have faith in yourself you place in action a force that goes into the very depth of your being and tends to arouse all the greater powers and finer elements that you may possess. The same is true when you have faith in a certain faculty or in a certain line of action. The power of faith goes into the spirit of things and makes alive, so to speak, the all that is in you. The power of faith also produces perfect concentration. Whenever you have faith along a certain line, you concentrate perfectly along that line, and you cause all the power that is in your mind or system to work for the one thing you are trying to do. It has been discovered that the amount of energy latent in the human system is nothing less than enormous, and as faith tends to arouse all this energy, we realize how important and how powerful is faith.

The effect of faith upon yourself therefore is beneficial in the highest and largest sense, but this is not its only effect. The more faith you have in yourself, the more faith people will have in you. If you have no confidence in yourself you will never inspire confidence in anybody; but if you thoroughly believe in yourself, people will believe in you and in your work. And when people believe in you, you can accomplish ten times as much as when they have no confidence in you whatever.

When a man has tremendous faith in himself, he becomes a live wire, so to speak. It is such a man that becomes a real and vital power wherever he may live or go. It is such a man who leads the race on and on. It is such a man who really does things, and it is people of such a type that we love the best. They invariably inspire others to love the nobler life and to attempt greater things in life, and for this reason their presence is of exceptional value to the progress of the race. To go into details, however, is not necessary. We all know and appreciate the value of faith. We all know that it is one of the highest and one of the greatest forces that man can exercise; we therefore realize how important it becomes to train ourselves to have unbounded faith in everything and in everybody at all times, and under all circumstances.

With All Thy Faults I Love Thee Still

Thus sings the poet, and we call him sentimental; that is, at first thought we do. But upon second thought we change our minds. We then find that faults and defects are always in the minority, and that the larger part of human nature is so wonderful and so beautiful that it needs must inspire admiration and love in everybody. With all their defects there is nothing more interesting than human beings; and the reason is that for every shortcoming in man there are a thousand admirable qualities. The poet, being inspired by the sublime vision of truth, can see this; therefore, what can he do but love? Whenever his eyes are lifted and whenever his thoughts take wings, his soul declares with greater eloquence than ever before, " What a piece of work is man!" Thus every moment renews his admiration, and every thought rekindles the fire of his love.

Chapter 20

The Greatest Power in Man

It is the conclusion of modern psychology that the powers and the possibilities inherent in man are practically unbounded. And this conclusion is based upon two great facts. First, that no limit has been found to anything in human nature; and second, that everything in human nature contains a latent capacity for perpetual development.

The discovery of these two facts and no discovery of greater importance has appeared in any age gives man a new conception of himself, a conception, which, when applied, will naturally revolutionize the entire field of human activity.

To be able to discern the real significance of this new conception becomes, therefore, the greatest power in man, and should, in consequence, be given the first thought in all efforts that have advancement attainment or achievement in view.

The purpose of each individual should be, not simply to cultivate and apply those possibilities that are now in evidence, but also to develop the power to discern and fathom what really exists within him. This power is the greatest power, because it prepares the way for the attainment and expression of all other powers. It is the power that unlocks the door to all power, and must be understood and applied before anything of greater value can be accomplished through human thought or action. The principal reason why the average person remains weak and incompetent is found in the fact that he makes no effort to fathom and understand the depths of his real being. He may try to use what is in action on the surface, but he is almost entirely unconscious of the fact that enormous powers are in existence in the greater depths of his life. These powers are dormant simply because they have not been called into action, and they will continue to lie dormant until man develops his greatest power the power to discern what really exists within him.

The fundamental cause of failure is found in the belief that what exists on the surface is all there is of man, and the reason why greatness is a rare exception instead of a universal rule can be traced to the same cause. When the mind discovers that its powers are inexhaustible and that its faculties and talents can be developed to any degree imaginable, the fear of failure will entirely disappear. In its stead will come the conviction that man may attain anything or achieve anything.

Whatever circumstances may be today, such a mind will know that all can be changed, that the limitations of the person can be made to pass away, and that the greater desires of the heart can be realized. That mind that can discern what exists in the depths of the real life of man does not simply change its views as to what man may attain and achieve, but actually begins to draw, in a measure, upon those inexhaustible powers within; and begins accordingly to develop and apply those greater possibilities that this deeper discernment has revealed.

When man can see through and understand what exists beneath the surface of his life, the expression of his deeper life will begin, because whatever we become conscious of, that we tend to bring forth into tangible expressions, and since the deeper life contains innumerable possibilities as well as enormous power, it is evident that when this deeper life is clearly discerned and completely taken possession of in the consciousness, practically anything may be attained or achieved.

The idea that there is more of man than what appears on the surface should be so constantly and so deeply impressed upon the mind that it becomes a positive conviction, and no thoughts should be placed in action unless it is based upon this conviction. To live, think and act in the realization that " there is more of me " should be the constant aim of every individual, and this more will constantly develop, coming forth in greater and greater measure, giving added power and capacity in life to everything that is in action in the human system.

When the average individual fails, he either blames circumstances or comes to the conclusion that he was not equal to the occasion. He therefore easily gives up and tries to be content with the lesser. But if he knew that there was more in him than what he had applied in his undertaking he would not give up. He would know by developing and applying this more, he positively would succeed where he had previously failed. It is therefore evident that when man gives attention to his greater power the power to discern the more that is in him he will never give up until he does succeed, and in consequence he invariably will succeed.

That individual who knows his power does not judge according to appearances. He never permits himself to believe that this or that cannot be done. He knows that those things can be done, because he has discovered what really exists within him. He works in the conviction that he must, can and will succeed, because he has the power; and it is the truth he does have the power we all have the power.

To live, think and work in the conviction that there is more of you within the real depths of your being, and to know that this more is so immense that no limit to its power can be found, will cause the mind to come into closer and closer touch with this greater power within, and you will consequently get possession of more and more of this power. The mind that lives in this attitude opens the door of consciousness, so to speak, to everything in human life that has real quality and worth. It places itself in that position where it can respond to the best that exists within itself, and modern psychology has discovered that this best is extraordinary in quality, limitless in power, and contains possibilities that cannot be numbered.

It is the truth that man is a marvelous being nothing less than marvelous; and the greatest power in man is the power to discern the marvelousness that really does exist within him. It is the law that we steadily develop and bring forth whatever we think of the most. It is therefore profitable to think constantly of our deeper nature and to try to fathom the limitlessness and the inexhaustibleness of these great and marvelous depths.

In practical life this mode of thinking will have the same effect upon the personal mind as that which is secured in a wire that is not charged when it touches a wire that is charged. The great within is a live wire; when the mind touches the great within, it becomes charged more and more with those same immense powers; and the mind will constantly be in touch with the great within when it lives, thinks and works in the firm conviction that "there is more of me," so much more that it cannot be measured.

We can receive from this deeper life only that which we constantly recognize and constantly realize, because consciousness is the door between the outer life and the great within, and we open the door to those things only of which we become conscious.

The principal reason therefore why the average person does not possess greater powers and talents, is because he is not conscious of more; and he is not conscious of more because he has not vitally recognized the great depths of his real life, and has not tried to consciously fathom the possibilities that are latent within him. The average person lives on the surface. He thinks that the surface is all there is of him, and consequently does not place himself in touch with the live wire of his interior and inexhaustible nature. He does not exercise his greatest power the power to discern what his whole nature actually contains; therefore, he does not unlock the door to any of his other powers.

This being true, we can readily understand why mortals are weak they are weak simply because they have chosen weakness; but when they begin to choose power and greatness, they will positively become what they have chosen to become.

We all must admit that there is more in man than what is usually expressed in the average person. We may differ as to how much more, but we must agree that the more should be developed, expressed and applied in everybody. It is wrong, both to the individual and to the race, for anyone to remain in the lesser when it is possible to attain the greater. It is right that we all should ascend to the higher, the greater and the better now. And we all can.

Your Forces and How to Use Them

The Optimist Creed (The Original)

Promise Yourself

To be so strong that nothing can disturb your peace of mind.

To talk health, happiness and prosperity to every person you meet.

To make all your friends feel that there is something in them.

To look at the sunny side of everything and make your optimism come true.

To think only of the best, to work only for the best, and to expect only the best.

To be just as enthusiastic about the success of others as you are about your own.

To forget the mistakes of the past and press on to the greater achievements of the future.

To wear a cheerful countenance at all times and give every living creature you meet a smile.

To give so much time to the improvement of yourself that you have no time to criticize others.

To be too large for worry, too noble for anger, too strong for fear, and too happy to permit the presence of trouble.

To think well of yourself and to proclaim this fact to the world, not in loud words but in great deeds.

To live in the faith that the whole world is on your side so long as you are true to the best that is in you.

www.ingramcontent.com/pod-product-compliance
Lightning Source LLC
Chambersburg PA
CBHW031359290426
44110CB00011B/208